ENVIRONMENTAL POLITICS
IN LATIN AMERICA AND THE CARIBBEAN

Liverpool Latin American Textbooks

Series Editor: Professor Catherine Davies
(University of Nottingham)

Written in an engaging and accessible style, the books in this series facilitate teaching and learning on topics broadly relating to Latin American history, culture and society. As well as including original research, they offer a critical synthesis of research and scholarship to date on relevant themes as well as critical perspectives to encourage further discussion and debate.

Environmental Politics in Latin America and the Caribbean

Volume 2: Institutions, Policy and Actors

Gavin O'Toole

LIVERPOOL UNIVERSITY PRESS

First published 2014 by
Liverpool University Press
4 Cambridge Street
Liverpool
L69 7ZU

British Library Cataloguing-in-Publication data
A British Library CIP record is available

ISBN 978-1-78138-023-9 (hb)
ISBN 978-1-78138-024-6 (pb)

Typeset by Carnegie Book Production, Lancaster
Printed and bound by Booksfactory.co.uk

Contents

Boxes

Figures

Tables

Abbreviations

ACOANA	Asociación Venezolana para la Conservación de Áreas Naturales (Venezuelan Association for the Conservation of Natural Areas)
ADC	Andean Development Corporation
Alba	Alianza Bolivariana para los Pueblos de Nuestra América (Bolivarian Alliance for the Peoples of Latin America)
AMERB	Áreas de Manejo y Explotación de Recursos Bentónicos (Management and Exploitation Areas for Benthic Resources)
ANAM	Autoridad Nacional del Ambiente (National Environment Authority)
ANAMMA	Associação Nacional de Órgãos Municipais de Meio Ambiente (National Association of Municipal Environment Departments)
ANPED	Northern Alliance for Sustainability
CABEI	Central American Bank for Economic Integration
CABS	Center for Applied Biodiversity Science
CAF	Corporación Andina de Fomento (Andean Development Corporation)
CAM	Comisión Ambiental Metropolitana (Metropolitan Environmental Commission)
CAMBio	Central American Markets for Biodiversity
CAOI	Co-ordenadora Andina de Organizaciones Indígenas (Andean Co-ordinator of Indigenous Organizations)
CARs	Corporaciones Autónomas Regionales (Autonomous Regional Corporations)
CBD	Convention on Biological Diversity

CCAD	Comisión Centroamericana de Ambiente y Desarrollo (Central American Commission for Environment and Development)
CDB	Caribbean Development Bank
CDM	clean development mechanism
CEBDS	Conselho Empresarial Brasileiro para o Desenvolvimento Sustentável (Brazilian Business Centre for Sustainable Development)
CEC	Commission for Environmental Co-operation [of North America]
CEDHA	Fundación Centro de Derechos Humanos y Ambiente (Centre for Human Rights and Environment)
CEDLA	Centro de Estudios y Documentación Latinoamer-icanos/Centro de Estudos e Documentaçaõ Latino-Americanos (Centre for Latin American Research and Documentation)
CEGESTI	Centro de Gestión Tecnológica (Centre for Techno-logical Management)
CELAC	Comunidad de Estados Latinoamericanos y Caribeños (Community of Latin American and Caribbean States)
CELDF	Community Environment Legal Defense Fund
CERIS	Centro de Estatísticas Religiosas e Investigação Social (Centre for Religious Statistics and Social Research)
CGPCS	Comitê Gestor Nacional de Produção e Consumo Sustentável (Committee for Sustainable Consumption and Production)
CITMA	Ministerio de Ciencia, Tecnología y Medio Ambiente (Ministry of Science, Technology and the Environment)
CODEFF	Comité Nacional Pro Defensa de la Flora y Fauna (Committee for the Defence of Flora and Fauna)
COMARENA	Comisión del Ambiente y Recursos Naturales (Natural Resource and Environment Committee)
CONACAMI	Confederación Nacional de Comunidades del Perú Afectadas por la Minería (National Confederation of Communities Affected by Mining)

CONAIE	Confederacion de nacionalidades indígenas del Ecuador (Confederation of Indigenous Nationalities of Ecuador)
CSD	Commission on Sustainable Development
CSIS	Center for Strategic and International Studies
CSO	civil society organization
DPLyCS	Dirección de Producción Limpia y Consumo Sustentable (Clean Production and Sustainable Consumption Department)
ECE	environmental compliance and enforcement
ECLAC	Economic Commission for Latin America and the Caribbean
ENGO	environmental non-governmental organization
EPI	Environmental Performance Index
EPIN	environmental protection issue network
EREC	European Renewable Energy Council
EU-LAC	European Union–Latin America and Caribbean Foundation
FAO	Food and Agriculture Organization
FARN	Fundación Ambiente y Recursos Naturales (Environment and Natural Resources Foundation)
FBOMS	Fórum Brasileiro de ONGs e Movimentos Sociais para o Meio Ambiente e o Desenvolvimento (Brazilian Forum of NGOs and Social Movements for the Environment and Development)
FDI	foreign direct investment
FEPP	Fondo Ecuatoriano Popularum Progressio (Ecuadorian Fund for Popular Progress)
FIDA	Foro Interamericano de Derecho Ambiental (Inter-American Forum on Environmental Law)
FONAES	Fondo Ambiental de El Salvador (El Salvador Environment Fund)
FPVA	Federación de Partidos Verdes de las Américas (Federation of Green Parties of the Americas)
GATT	General Agreement on Tariffs and Trade
GEF	Global Environment Facility

GEMA	Grupo Ecológico Mujer y Ambiente (Woman and Environment Ecology Group)
GHG	greenhouse gas
GIC	Global Industry Coalition
GMO	genetically modified organism
GTZ	German Technical Co-operation Agency
GWEC	Global Wind Energy Council
HDI	Human Development Index
IABIN	Inter-American Biodiversity Information Network
IACHR	Inter-American Human Rights Court
IBAMA	Instituto Brasileiro do Meio Ambiente e dos Recursos Naturais Renováveis (Institute of Environment and Renewable Natural Resources)
IBDF	Instituto Brasileiro do Desenvolvimento Florestal (Brazilian Institute of Forest Conservation)
IBWC	International Boundary and Water Commission
ICEAC	International Court of Environmental Arbitration and Conciliation
ICHRP	International Council on Human Rights Policy
ICJ	International Court of Justice
IDB	Inter-American Development Bank
IFAD	International Fund for Agricultural Development
IICA	Inter-American Institute for Co-operation on Agriculture
IIED	International Institute for Environment and Development
IIRSA	Initiative for the Integration of the Regional Infrastructure of South America
IISD	International Institute for Sustainable Development
IKAP	Indigenous Knowledge and Peoples
ILAC	Iniciativa Latinoamericana y Caribeña para el Desarrollo Sostenible (Latin American and Caribbean Initiative for Sustainable Development)
INBio	National Biodiversity Institute
INCE	International Network for Environmental Compliance and Enforcement

INDERENA   Instituto Nacional de los Recursos Naturales Renovables y del Ambiente (National Institute of Renewable Resources and the Environment)

International IDEA   International Institute for Democracy and Electoral Assistance

IPCC   Intergovernmental Panel on Climate Change

ISAAA   International Service for the Acquisition of Agri-Biotech Applications

ITAM   Instituto Tecnológico Autónomo de México

IUCN   International Union for Conservation of Nature and Natural Resources

IWGIA   International Work Group for Indigenous Affairs

JSWG   Joint Summit Working Group

KEPRU   Keele European Parties Research Unit

LACEEP   Latin American and Caribbean Environmental Economics Program

MAB   Man and the Biosphere

MARN   Ministerio de Ambiente y Recursos Naturales (Ministry of the Environment and Natural Resources)

MAS   Movimiento al Socialismo

MBI   market-based instrument

MDB   multilateral development bank

MDSMA   Ministerio de Desarrollo Sostenible y Medio Ambiente (Ministry of Sustainable Development and the Environment)

MEA   multilateral environmental agreement

MEV   Movimiento Ecológico de Venezuela

MIF   Multilateral Investment Fund

MINAET   Ministerio del Ambiente, Energía y Telecomunicaciones (Ministry of the Environment, Energy and Telecommunications)

MIRENEM   Ministerio de Recursos Naturales, Energía y Minas (Ministry of Natural Resources, Energy and Mines)

MMA   Ministério do Meio Ambiente (Ministry of the Environment)

MOVEV	Movimiento Ecológico de Venezuela
MST	Movimento dos Trabalhadores Sem Terra (Landless Workers' Movement)
NACLA	North American Congress on Latin America
NAFTA	North American Free Trade Agreement
NEF	New Economics Foundation
NEP	Política Nacional do Meio Ambiente (National Environmental Policy)
NGO	non-governmental organization
NWF	National Wildlife Federation
OAS	Organization of American States
ODA	official development assistance
ODCA	Organización Demócrata Cristiana de América (Christian Democrat Organization of America)
OECD	Organization for Economic Co-operation and Development
OHCHR	Office of the United Nations High Commissioner for Human Rights
OLADE	Organización Latinoamericana de Energía (Latin American Energy Organization)
OSU	Oregon State University
PAHO	Pan-American Health Organization
PAN	Partido Acción Nacional
PECSA	Proyecto Especial Camélidos Sudamericanos (South American Camelids Special Project)
PEER	Public Environmental Expenditure Review
PES	payment for ecosystem services
PEV	Partido Ecologista Verde
PLAC+e	Programa Latinoamericano del Carbono, Energías Limpias y Alternativas (Latin American Carbon and Clean Alternative Energy Programme)
PPA	Participatory Poverty Assessment
PROCONVE	Programa de Controle das Emissões Veiculares (Vehicular Emission Control Programme)

PRODERS	Programa de Desarrollo Regional Sustentable (Regional Sustainable Development Programme)
PROFEPA	Procuraduría Federal de Protección al Ambiente (Federal Environmental Protection Agency)
PSDB	Partido da Social Democracia Brasileira (Brazilian Social Democracy Party)
PSIA	Poverty and Social Impact Analysis
PT	Partido dos Trabalhadores (Workers' Party)
PV	Partido Verde (Green Party)
PVE	Partido Verde Ecologista
PVEM	Partido Verde Ecologista de México
RADA	Red Argentina de Abogados para la Defensa del Ambiente (Argentine Network of Environmental Defence Lawyers)
REDD	Reducing Emissions from Deforestation and Forest Degradation
RMALC	Red Mexicana de Acción frente al Libre Comercio (Mexican Action Network on Free Trade)
SAyDS	Secretaria de Ambiente y Desarrollo Sustentable (Secretariat for the Environment and Sustainable Development)
SCP	sustainable consumption and production
SEIA	Sistema de Evaluación de Impacto Ambiental
SEMA	Secretaria Especial do Meio Ambiente (Special Department of the Environment)
SEMARNAT	Secretaría de Medio Ambiente y Recursos Naturales
SENER	Secretaría de Energía
SGP	small grants programme
SIA	Sustainability Impact Assessment
SINA	Sistema Nacional Ambiental (National Environmental System)
SISNAMA	Sistema Nacional do Meio Ambiente (National Environment System)
TEK	traditional ecological knowledge

THOA	Taller de Historia Oral Andina (Andean Oral History Workshop)
TIPNIS	Territorio Indígena y Parque Nacional Isiboro Sécure (Isiboro Secure Indigenous Territory and National Park)
UGAM	Unión de Grupos Ambientalistas (Union of Environmentalist Groups)
UNA	Universidad Nacional de Costa Rica
UNASUR	Union of South American Nations
UNCSD	United Nations Conference on Sustainable Development
UNDESA	United Nations Department of Economic and Social Affairs
UNDP	United Nations Development Programme
UNEP	United Nations Environment Programme
UNFCCC	United Nations Framework Convention on Climate Change
UNHRC	United Nations Human Rights Council
UN-NGLS	United Nations Non-Governmental Liaison Service
WCED	World Commission on Environment and Development
WCPA	World Commission on Protected Areas
WRI	World Resources Institute
WSSD	World Summit on Sustainable Development
WTO	World Trade Organization
WWF	World Wildlife Fund
WZB	Wissenschaftszentrum Berlin für Sozialforschung (Berlin Social Science Centre)

Acknowledgements

We are grateful to the following for permission to reproduce their material.

Figure 2.1: "Environmental news stories in Costa Rica and Bolivia", in Paul F Steinberg, "Understanding Policy Change in Developing Countries: The Spheres of Influence Framework", *Global Environmental Politics*, 3:1 (February 2003), pp. 11–32. © 2003 by the Massachusetts Institute of Technology, to Nick Yeaton, Permissions Assistant, The MIT Press, Cambridge, MA; Table 2.1: "Latin America's primary energy demands", from World Energy Outlook, 2009 © OECD/IEA 2009, table 1.2, p. 76 (available online at www.worldenergyoutlook.org/media/weowebsite/2009/WEO2009.pdf), to Eleonor Grammatikas, Office of the Chief Legal Counsel, International Energy Agency, Paris; Table 3.1: "Hydropolitical vulerability in South America's international basins", from UNEP/OSA/UNA 2007, *Hydropolitical Vulnerability and Resilience along International Waters: Latin America and the Caribbean*. Nairobi: United Nations Environment Programme (UNEP) / Oregon State University (OSU) / Universidad Nacional de Costa Rica (UNA), p. 72 (available online at www.unep.org/pdf/hydropolitical_LA.pdf), to Monika G MacDevette, Division of Early Warning & Assessment, United Nations Environment Programme.

Introduction

THE TWO VOLUMES of *Environmental Politics in Latin America and the Caribbean* provide a comprehensive introduction to the historical, political, economic and cultural dimensions of the relationship between human society and environmental change in the region. The first volume introduces students to the essential context in which green politics in the region are developing and should be of value wherever the environment is being studied. It offers students from a broad range of disciplines who may not be familiar with comparative politics, or indeed with the study of Latin America and the Caribbean, a way of coming to this theme for the first time. It provides a broad overview of the region's environmental history, the political legacies and challenges that confront green parties and movements, the current state of its natural environment, and the key issues of political economy that explain how patterns of development in Latin America and the Caribbean have shaped its natural environment and their implications for sustainable development.

This second volume is more specifically aimed at students of politics per se, taking and developing in greater detail and with more theoretical insight themes that are touched on in the first volume, such as institutions, public policies, international relations, political actors and environmental ideologies. For the scholar who wants a comprehensive overview of green politics in Latin America and the

Caribbean, it is aimed to be a complement to the first volume and to be read in conjunction with it.

There are good reasons to focus on Latin America and the Caribbean when studying environmental politics. The environment as a political issue has been giving Latin America and the Caribbean a global profile since the Earth Summit in Rio de Janeiro, Brazil, in 1992. Latin America and the Caribbean is also at the sharp end of global environmental change as one of the most ecologically diverse regions of the planet. Climate change is already having a significant effect on ecosystem goods and services in the region and has risen up the agenda of public policymaking. As a region that has long struggled with high levels of poverty and inequality – yet today enjoys robust growth and is the target of unprecedented flows of foreign investment – Latin America and the Caribbean also exemplifies a dilemma at the heart of all environmental politics: the difficulty of reconciling development with environmental protection.

As a region mostly still consolidating democracy after decades of authoritarian rule from the 1960s to the 1990s, political development in Latin America and the Caribbean provides important lessons in the study of environmental politics. Democratization has placed parties, institutions and values at the heart of comparative politics, providing institutional opportunities and new spaces for green political actors. The region's green parties and indigenous movements are finding it easier than ever before to spearhead an environmental agenda. The rise of centrist politics in its consumer societies is challenging traditional political postures on both left and right and forcing them to respond to a diverse postmodern agenda driven by unremitting growth in the spread of new communication technology. Globalization and the institutional reforms it demands, meanwhile, is testing the concept of the nation state, providing new insights into the transboundary nature of environmental issues, and providing citizens with new, multilateral tools for protecting the natural world. Latin America and the Caribbean is of great importance to the study of politics, development, international relations and other disciplines and can provide us with theoretical tools for the analysis of key themes anywhere in the world such as democratization, institutionalization or US foreign policy. It provides rich comparative examples of processes of development as a region built through European colonialism upon the encounter between different races and cultures and then shaped by neocolonial relationships under capitalism. It can help us to understand our own nation states, which in some cases are in fact younger than the Latin American and Caribbean republics.

An examination of environmental politics also offers the opportunity to present a series of rare success stories from Latin America and the Caribbean that challenge our contemporary understanding of the region – from reforestation in Costa Rica to the concrete progress made by Brazil in slowing Amazon destruction to the protection of endangered marine species by Chile. Indeed, Brazil's government – so often demonized for environmental destruction – has made concrete progress in transforming thinking about environmental governance. The region is turning history on its head by offering models of institutional and political practice – and values that challenge mass consumption – which the developed world would do well to take note of. Just one illustration of this can be found in the humble example set by Uruguay's president José Mujica, who upon taking power in 2010, eschewing the pomp and privilege of office, continued to live in a ramshackle farm off a dirt road outside Montevideo and to give away 90 per cent of his salary to charity. The leftwing vegetarian president has accused other world leaders of having a "blind obsession to achieve growth with consumption, as if the contrary would mean the end of the world" (see Hernández 2012).

These volumes concentrate on Hispanic and Lusophone Latin America and the Caribbean – taking a geopolitical, as opposed to an ecological, focus – while also making some references to Anglophone Caribbean and South American states and to those that often fall outside the formal ambit of area studies by virtue of their peculiarities, such as Francophone Haiti and Spanish-speaking Puerto Rico, a protectorate whose people in 2012 voted in support of US statehood. As a discernible region, Latin American and Caribbean politics have distinctive features deriving from history and culture that make it both viable and necessary to take such a regional view. Nonetheless, this parameter of study is not intended to be a rigid constraint to understanding, and the region is characterized as much by its cultural diversity as by the essentially linguistic terms of reference by which it is defined. This diversity is driving political and institutional development in the region.

Together, these books aim to provide the skeleton of a 10- to 11-unit course on the environmental politics of Latin America and the Caribbean that will appeal to newcomers to the region and to the study of politics itself as well as to those more familiar with these subjects.

Volume 1 examines the environmental history of Latin America and the Caribbean and its impact on political development. It explores the idea of nature in history as well as attitudes towards production and consumption. It provides an overview of key themes in the study of environmental politics, then identifies the principal environmental challenges the region now faces, from land, air and water pollution to biodiversity loss to climate change. Those challenges are intimately related to the legacies of different patterns of development in the region, and the final chapters of the first volume look at the political economy of the environment.

Volume 2 examines the institutional and policymaking dimensions of the environment, and how environmental issues influence international relations in Latin America and the Caribbean. It looks at how states have created modern infrastructures for environmental governance, key variables in the processes by which environmental policy is formulated, and the international and multilateral influences that are shaping the green agenda. This volume then introduces the student to the key political actors in struggles over the environment in Latin America and the Caribbean such as green parties, social movements and NGOs. It explores how both the indigenous movement and businesses are playing an increasingly prominent role in this arena, and sketches out the main ideas that inform green ideology such as environmental justice, eco-socialism and environmental scepticism.

CHAPTER ONE

Institutions

THE STUDY OF DEMOCRATIC POLITICS in Latin America and the Caribbean has shifted its focus from the transition from authoritarian rule to the nature of the institutions in which legitimate power is vested – the state – as well as institutional structures formally outside government within "civil society", such as educational bodies, businesses and the media. Scholars agree that strong, stable, representative institutions are essential for a healthy democracy and that civil society plays an equally important role shaping the behaviour that ensures democratic continuity. Institutions provide stability in policymaking, and if they are weak this can foster uncertainty and scepticism about politics, leading to immobilism, lack of government authority and conflict. Institutions are also crucial for managing the relationship between national and international bodies working towards environmental sustainability. The role of governments is critical to protecting the environment by setting out policy and regulatory frameworks and providing the planning and monitoring of compliance with standards and norms. This chapter examines the role institutions play in politics and factors that can weaken them, which often derive from the nature of the state itself. It looks at the emergence of environmental institutions in the region and how these can be discussed within the notion of governance. Environmental management in Latin America and the Caribbean has developed rapidly, and as this has been codified through the public policy that shapes laws and regulations it has undergone a process of institutionalization as ministries and agencies have been created. Other, political institutions alongside the formal realm of the state – the executive, legislature and judiciary – have played a key role in environmentalism. This chapter examines the evolution of environmental laws in Latin America and the Caribbean and how rights concerning the natural world and access to it are being enshrined in constitutions. Finally, it examines problems that environmental institutions in the region confront and efforts at reform.

The state and environmental governance

It is necessary to understand the context in which the institutions that manage resource use and environmental policy in Latin America and the Caribbean have emerged and this requires us to look at the notion of the state. States in the region have often been too strong or weak, dominated by a small number of interests or detached from society. Migdal (1988) drew attention to the radically different ways states in the developing world have been assessed by scholars and advanced his own influential theory of state–society relations. In the developed world, the state's apparent dominance over society, whereby it shapes all the rules of economic and political life, is often taken for granted. In developing countries, however, the state has a more complex relationship with society and their interactions are different. A strong state, argued Migdal, is one with high capabilities in its capacity to penetrate society, regulate social relationships, extract resources and appropriate and use resources in determined ways. In the developing world, there are many instances where, despite possessing considerable military potential, states have had only limited authority and have been constrained in their capability to perform basic tasks such as collecting taxes or providing public services. These states have often been unable to govern the rural hinterland and border regions adequately and have been constrained by powerful sectors of society. Migdal used the example of Mexico among other countries in an effort to explain why states in the developing world often suffer from weak institutions, and attributed this, in part, to politics – the way ruling individuals and powerful sectors deliberately weaken states in order to undermine rival sources of power. In practice, this means that states are continually being moulded by the societies in which they are embedded, sometimes resulting in conflict outside the formal realms of state power.

In Latin America and the Caribbean, there are many examples of states that give the illusion of strength yet are incapable of carrying out basic tasks. This can be attributed to shortcomings within the formal institutions of public administration controlled by the state itself – the ministries and agencies that we associate with government – as well as to the political institutions that determine how a state functions, and to what end, such as the executive, legislature and judiciary. Governing institutions in the region have often been shaped by factors that have hampered their effectiveness and obstructed the development of democracy such as personalism, authoritarianism, revolution, illegality, populism, corporatism and dependency. Until recently, institutions such as congresses have served merely as window-dressing for dictatorships or oligarchic rule. Although constitutions have formally vested power in executives, legislatures and judiciaries, real power has often been held by groups outside the institutional structures of the state.

The state has been the main axis of competition between rival interests in Latin America and the Caribbean since the achievement of independence in the early nineteenth century and understanding its role in governing the use of natural resources is complex because this touches upon almost every area of policymaking. Institutions help to shape the norms and attitudes that characterize the prevailing culture in a country, and so in the recent era have played a formative role in the development of consumerism (see Volume 1), the culture that determines the main aspects of all resource use today. At the same time, environmental institutions have also been at the forefront of raising awareness about environmental issues in Latin America and the Caribbean. Effective environmental institutions should play three key roles (see World Bank 2003):

- *Information management*. Decision-makers need to know about ecosystems and the services they offer in order to make informed decisions. Environmental institutions should be able to gather and share information about trends. However, there is much evidence of a persistent lack of relevant and up-to-date information and knowledge about the environment in Latin America and the Caribbean (see UNEP 2010; Baud, de Castro and Hogenboom 2011).

- *Balancing interests*. Effective institutions should balance interests fairly and efficiently as policies are formulated. They need mechanisms to ensure that the perspectives and incentives of different stakeholders are taken into account and to co-ordinate different views across social sectors and tiers of government.

- *Implementing laws and ensuring accountability*. Effective institutions must be able to implement policy in an accountable, transparent way.

There are considerable gaps between what is known about environmental issues and the design of institutions. One way of approaching such a broad theme is to employ the concept of environmental governance, which is now being given considerable attention by multilateral bodies (see Box 1.1; Lemos and Agrawal 2006; UNEP 2012a). This phrase has been used to refer to the general approach taken by public institutions to managing environmental issues and as a normative concept to promote best practice. Environmental governance refers to both the *formal* and *informal* practices by which natural resources are managed and contested at local, national and global levels.

In Latin America the notion of environmental governance emerged during the 1980s as a neoliberal concept emphasizing a way of managing natural resources that limited the role of state institutions and encouraged the participation of private enterprise. The resulting policies often included the privatization of natural resources such as water, forests and land, which had a significant environmental impact (Liverman and Villas 2006). For example, agrarian reforms were carried out throughout the region in the 1990s aiming to liberalize the rural economy by weakening existing institutions (see Deere and León 2001). Since the 1990s, however, deepening democratization has generally given state institutions a leading role in environmental governance.

The region has since made significant progress in developing environmental legal and institutional frameworks, although poor design and a limited capacity to implement and enforce rules often hamper their effectiveness. The conditions needed for good environmental governance include adequate budgets, effective scientific research, reliable information, good environmental education and improved environmental awareness as well as the values required for good governance in general: transparency, accountability, equity, sustainability and inclusive participation.

Box 1.1 Environmental governance

Environmental governance refers to diverse areas of policymaking and delivery within both the formal structures of government but also civil society and business to manage the natural environment and public goods such as the atmosphere, climate and biodiversity sustainably. The concept refers to the rules, practices, processes and institutions – formal and informal – by which the environment is managed in many ways, from conservation to the exploitation of natural resources. As a large variety of stakeholders may be involved in dealing with complex issues, environmental governance may imply the need for decision-making and implementation mechanisms that do not conform to traditional political structures and forces such as nation states or existing classes. It departs from a conceptualization of economic and political life as *products* of the environment and so envisages a relationship between societies and the ecosystems in which they live. It implies a need to move away from strategies that divorce a human activity (such as waste disposal) from sustainability (recycling) and towards more circular strategies based upon sustainability. The concept has been the subject of much debate and critics say global environmental governance has been unable to solve problems because of fragmented institutional structures, obstacles to co-ordination, conflicts with economic priorities and divisions among countries. Yet environmental governance has made clear inroads in some areas: in enabling civil society to participate in decision-making; in fostering co-operation between states; and in scrutinizing bodies unrestrained by states, such as multinational corporations.

The relationship between the concept of environmental governance and the concept of sustainability has implications for our understanding of democracy. Sustainable development means that democratic institutions such as governments, political parties and the media will need to change their traditional focus on economic growth (see Volume 1). Some environmental organizations argue that sustainable development implies the need to replace the notion often found in modern democracy of citizens as consumers who vote on the basis of personal economic security with a notion of the common good that is less individualistic and more participatory. Institutional change will be required because governance for sustainable development involves a wide range of agencies, networks and bodies within and outside government that play a role in policymaking and implementation (see UNDESA/UNCSD 2011). Given this, environmental discourses often play an important role in discussions about improving institutions. For example, Latin American leaders have taken an active position within the Earth System Governance agenda, an international social science project dedicated to assessing the best institutional framework for sustainable development (see Biermann et al. 2011).

The development of environmental governance in Latin America and the Caribbean has also challenged a simple understanding of politics as a top-down or bottom-up process. This is because initiatives to confront ecological problems derive both from international pressures external to national states and from civil society below them (see Chapter 5). Civil society organizations, NGOs and academic institutions have often shaped an alternative perspective on governance characterized by use of the term "glocalization" by which local and global actors link up to develop new approaches to environmental management. Governance has also been influenced by developments at regional and sub-regional levels as growing economies have pushed forward regional integration initiatives, some of which have established their own environmental institutions (see Chapter 3).

In recent years an emphasis on environmental governance in Latin America and the Caribbean has also given rise to pioneering initiatives that aim to ensure resources are used sustainably, including co-management initiatives that are based upon participation. Participatory budgeting, for example, in which communities have a direct input into decisions about local spending priorities, has been pioneered with significant success in Brazil.

Institutional development

Environmental management in Latin America and the Caribbean has developed considerably over the last 20 years and governments have incorporated green concerns into public administration through a dynamic process of institution-building. Two main approaches were evident: one that treated the environment as a sector in its own right in which an environmental body eventually gained ministerial status; and another that treated it as a cross-cutting issue, by which a collegiate body brought together the areas of public administration whose decisions impinged upon the environment. In most cases these strategies were consecutive, the former giving way through reform to the latter. Environmental regulatory frameworks and ministerial departments or agencies to establish and implement policy were created throughout much of the region during the mid-1970s (Acuña 1999). However, some of these institutions have their roots in the late nineteenth century when Latin America's young republics had begun to build the infrastructure of modern statehood. In Costa Rica, for example, the Ministerio del Ambiente, Energía y Telecomunicaciones (MINAET, Ministry of the Environment, Energy and Telecommunications) traces its origins back to the foundation in 1888 of the Servicio Meteorológico Nacional (National Meteorological Service). In Mexico, the origins of the environmental ministry can be traced to the revolutionary constitution of 1917 (see Box 1.2).

The evolution of environmental ministries has often been tied to that of agricultural, fisheries, mining and energy ministries safeguarding the economic contribution of natural resources and addressing public health issues. Colombia, for example, began creating an institutional infrastructure responding to environmental issues in 1968 with the formation of the Instituto Nacional de los Recursos Naturales Renovables y del Ambiente (INDERENA, National Institute of Renewable Resources and the Environment) to co-ordinate the management of renewable resources. Given this focus on resource management, during the 1970s and 1980s, environmental responsibilities were often delegated to sectoral agencies at the under-secretary or deputy minister level and without representation in cabinet. Environmental management was often addressed solely from a planning perspective by advisers in councils or commissions linked to planning ministries or presidential secretariats (see Barcena et al. 2002). Environmental agencies themselves often evolved out of the creation of protected areas established to conserve forestry resources. El Salvador's environment ministry, for example, traces its origins to the 1981 creation within the agriculture ministry of the Servicio de Parques Nacionales y Vida Silvestre (National Parks and Rural Affairs Service).

Scientific institutions have also played a key role in environmental institution-building in Latin America and the Caribbean, influencing economic policies and providing an early source of environmental

Box 1.2 Mexico slowly turns green

The concept of environmental protection in Mexico was first addressed in law in Article 27 of the constitution of 1917 stating that the exploitation of natural resources must take the public interest into consideration. However, until the 1930s, this idea was more theoretical than practical and was not enforced or regulated. By the 1970s, the combination of a high population, industry and automobiles was creating serious pollution and the government began to establish mechanisms designed to protect the environment. In 1971, it enacted its first consolidated environmental law, the Ley Federal para Prevenir y Controlar la Contaminación Ambiental (Federal Law for the Prevention and Control of Environmental Pollution). In 1973, just a year after the Stockholm UN Conference on the Human Environment, Mexico's congress imposed on federal bodies a duty to control pollution. The limitations of this legislation led in 1982 to a much broader Ley Federal de Protección del Ambiente (Federal Law for the Protection of the Environment) that aimed to link environmental principles with mechanisms for economic development. This coincided with a process of economic liberalization under President Miguel de la Madrid (1982–88) who issued decrees on reforestation, regulation of air pollution, water purification, relocation of industries and environmental awareness and created Mexico's first federal environmental agency, the Secretaría de Desarrollo Urbano y Ecología (SEDUE, Secretary of Urban Development and Ecology) to oversee legislation and undertake environmental impact assessments. Nonetheless, Mexico was often criticized for failing to enforce its laws and for opting for largely symbolic reform. In 1987, the constitution was amended to give congress authority to promote the further participation of federal, state and local environmental authorities and this led in 1988 to enactment of the Ley General del Equilibrio Ecológico y Protección al Ambiente (LGEEPA, General Law on Ecological Balance and Environmental Protection), which remains in force. LGEEPA decentralized regulation and by 1991 had spawned 23 environmental laws at the state level (see Muñoz 1997). The administration of President Carlos Salinas de Gortari (1988–94) was influenced by the US and the Organization for Economic Co-operation and Development (OECD). Mexico signed the Convention on International Trade in Endangered Species of Flora and Fauna (CITES), became the first country to ratify the Vienna Convention and the Montreal Protocol on Protection of the Ozone Layer, and was active in efforts to establish sanctuaries for the grey whale and prohibit trade in sea turtles. In 1992, in the context of NAFTA negotiations, environmental regulation was transformed to ensure the enforcement of national standards (see Box 5.6). A Procuraduría Federal de Protección al Ambiente (PROFEPA, Attorney General's Office for the Protection of the Environment) was established within the Secretaría de Desarrollo Social (SEDESOL, Secretariat of Social Development), which took over the environmental duties previously assigned to SEDUE. In 1994, President Ernesto Zedillo (1994–2000) transferred SEDESOL's environmental responsibilities to a single federal agency responsible for environmental regulation, the Secretaría de Medio Ambiente, Recursos Naturales y Pesca (SEMARNAP, Ministry of the Environment, Natural Resources and Fisheries). Amendments to the LGEEPA in 1996 significantly expanded the reach of environmental law and incorporated within it a responsibility for sustainable development. In 2000, President Vicente Fox (2000–06) pulled fisheries out of the environmental agency which was duly renamed the Secretaría de Medio Ambiente y Recursos Naturales (SEMARNAT, Ministry of the Environment and Natural Resources) (see Haight, Brown & Bonesteel et al. 1999; Simonian 1995; National Law Center for Inter-American Free Trade: websites below).

activism. Agricultural and public health agencies were established in the late nineteenth century and played a role in identifying environmental concerns. Later environmental activism can often trace its origins to previous generations of scientists raising concerns about the impact of contamination and excessive resource use (see Houck 2000; Carruthers 2001).

Authoritarian rule with a singular focus on economic growth had a significant impact on the environment in Latin America and the Caribbean and fostered growing consciousness about it. Authoritarian regimes often associated conservation issues with national security and sovereignty. In Brazil in 1967, during the first period of military rule, for example, the Instituto Brasileiro do Desenvolvimento Florestal (IBDF, Brazilian Institute of Forest Conservation) was created within the agriculture ministry to develop the Amazon. In 1973, under the more rightwing military regime of General Emílio Garrastazu Médici (1969–74), the Secretaria Especial do Meio Ambiente (SEMA, Special Department of the Environment) was created within the interior ministry and began to consolidate institutional responsibilities. In Cuba and Nicaragua, the institutional development of environmental management had a revolutionary heritage, and both are distinct for the socialist character of subsequent environmental policy stressing collective management (see Houck 2000).

Political instability has often delayed the establishment of environmental policymaking institutions, some of which remain in their infancy. Guatemala, for example, took an active role in the 1972 Stockholm Conference, where it put forward a number of initiatives and officials were discussing the country's environmental problems as early as 1975 through a Comisión Ministerial para la protección del Medio Ambiente (Ministerial Commission for the Protection of the Environment). However, it was not until a level of political stability had been achieved following a long civil war that policymakers were able to turn their attention to issues such as climate change. In 2000, the government brought together scientists and officials in a Comisión Nacional del Medio Ambiente (CONAMA, National Environmental Commission) under the auspices of the UN Framework Convention on Climate Change to examine the impact of global warming on the country and this, in turn, made possible the establishment of the Ministerio de Ambiente y Recursos Naturales (MARN, Ministry of the Environment and Natural Resources) in 2001 (see MARN 2001).

The evolution of environmental governance at an international level has influenced institution-building in Latin America and the Caribbean. States responded to the trend of institutional reform led by Europe and the US in the 1980s and 1990s by creating their own environmental departments. The Rio Declaration at the 1992 Earth Summit, establishing the concept of sustainable development at the heart of the multilateral agenda, gave significant impetus to this process, especially where agencies had not yet achieved ministerial representation in cabinet.

The creation of environmental institutions was often an incremental process that built upon experience gained elsewhere. In El Salvador, for example, the Fondo Ambiental de El Salvador (FONAES, El Salvador Environment Fund) was established in 1994, and thereafter a Secretaría Ejecutiva del Medio Ambiente (SEMA, Department of the Environment) was created within the planning and economic development ministry. Then, in 1997, a cabinet-level environmental ministerial position was established overseeing a new Ministerio de

Medio Ambiente y Recursos Naturales (Ministry of the Environment and Natural Resources) that brought together the responsibilities of the pre-existing bodies.

Multilateral bodies such as the UN, World Bank, Inter-American Development Bank (IDB) and OECD played a formative role in either the creation or reinforcement of national institutions (see Eltz et al. 2010). Cuba's national environmental strategy, for example, was developed with UN assistance from the early 1990s onwards and articulated both environmental goals and the responsibilities of a new Ministerio de Ciencia, Tecnología y Medio Ambiente (CITMA, Ministry of Science, Technology and the Environment) created in 1990. In many cases, multilateral loans have been granted specifically to strengthen environmental institutions and laws (see Chapter 3). Changing geopolitical conditions have also influenced this development. Panama, for example, was a latecomer to environmental legislation largely because of its unique relationship with the US. In 1998, as it prepared to take over control of the Panama Canal, its government created the Autoridad Nacional del Ambiente (ANAM, National Environment Authority) to bring it in line with international norms.

The ways in which international pressure and the emulation of neighbours encouraged the development of ministerial infrastructures for managing environmental policy has similarities with the process of democratization in Latin America and the Caribbean. Countries have been receptive to the proposals generated within international bodies as well as neighbouring states, importing and adapting norms, instruments and institutional forms for domestic use. They have either incorporated principles established by international bodies voluntarily, or through treaty law (see Chapter 3). The 1972 Stockholm Conference propelled federal environmental legislation and in other cases bilateral co-operation was an important driver of change. In Nicaragua, for example, by the mid-1980s, MARENA was receiving aid and advice from Sweden, Norway, Denmark, the Soviet Union, France, the Netherlands, Cuba, Mexico, the Organization of American States (OAS) and the UN Environment Programme (UNEP). In Chile, reforms to environmental governance in 2010, for example, responded to recommendations made by the OECD to enable the country to join it as South America's first member (see Olivares Gallardo 2010). In 1971, Mexico passed its first consolidated environmental law

Table 1.1   Environmental ministries and general laws

	Current name of environmental ministry/agency	General environmental law
Argentina	Secretaria de Ambiente y Desarrollo Sustentable (Ministry of Environment and Sustainable Development)	Ley General del Ambiente (2002)
Bolivia	Ministerio de Medio Ambiente y Agua (Ministry of Environment and Water)	Ley General del Medio Ambiente (1992)
Brazil	Ministério do Meio Ambiente (MMA, Ministry of the Environment)	Política Nacional do Meio Ambiente (1981)
Chile	Ministerio del Medio Ambiente (Ministry of the Environment)	Ley sobre Bases Generales del Medio Ambiente (1994)
Colombia	Ministerio del Ambiente y Desarrollo Sostenible (Ministry of the Environment and Sustainable Development)	Código Nacional de Recursos Naturales Renovables y de Protección al Medio Ambiente (1974), Ley General Ambiental de Colombia (1993)
Costa Rica	Ministerio de Ambiente, Energía y Telecomunicaciones (Ministry of the Environment, Energy and Telecommunications)	Ley Orgánica del Ambiente (1995)
Cuba	Ministerio de Ciencia, Tecnología y Medio Ambiente (Ministry of Science, Technology and the Environment)	Ley de protección del medio ambiente y del uso racional de los recursos naturales (1981), Ley del Medio Ambiente (1997)
Dominican Republic	Secretaría de Estado de Medio Ambiente y Recursos Naturales (Ministry of the Environment and Natural Resources)	Ley General sobre Medio Ambiente y Recursos Naturales (2000)
Ecuador	Ministerio del Ambiente (Ministry of the Environment)	Ley para la Prevención y Control de la Contaminación Ambiental (1976)
El Salvador	Ministerio de Medio Ambiente y Recursos Naturales (Ministry of the Environment and Natural Resources)	Ley de Medio Ambiente (1998)
Guatemala	Ministerio de Ambiente y Recursos Naturales (Ministry of the Environment and Natural Resources)	Ley de Protección y Mejoramiento del Medio Ambiente (1986)
Haiti	Ministre de l'Environnement (Ministry of the Environment)	Constitution of 1987, Section IX
Honduras	Secretaria de Recursos Naturales y Ambiente (Ministry of Natural Resources and the Environment)	Ley General del Ambiente (1993)
Mexico	Secretaría de Medio Ambiente y Recursos Naturales (SEMARNAT, Ministry of the Environment and Natural Resources)	Ley General del Equilibrio Ecológico y la Protección al Ambiente (1988)
Nicaragua	Ministerio del Ambiente y los Recursos Naturales (MARENA, Ministry of the Environment and Natural Resources)	Ley General del Medio Ambiente y los Recursos Naturales (1996)

	Current name of environmental ministry/agency	General environmental law
Panama	Autoridad Nacional del Ambiete (National Environment Authority)	Ley General de Ambiente (1998)
Paraguay	Secretaría del Ambiente (Ministry of the Environment)	Ley No. 1561 (2000) que crea el sistema nacional del ambiente, el consejo nacional del ambiente y la secretaria del ambiente
Peru	Consejo Nacional Del Ambiente (National Environment Council)	Ley General del Ambiente (2000)
Puerto Rico	Departamento de Recursos Naturales y Ambientales	Ley Orgánica del Departamento de Recursos Naturales y Ambientales (1972)
Uruguay	Ministerio de Vivienda, Ordenamiento Territorial y Medio Ambiente (Ministry of Housing, Regional Planning and the Environment)	Ley del Medio Ambiente (1994)
Venezuela	Ministerio del Poder Popular para el Ambiente (Ministry of Popular Power for the Environment)	Ley Orgánica del Ambiente (1976)

Sources: Barcena et al. 2011; ECLAC 2000; FIDA, Inter-American Forum on Environmental Law database of environmental laws in the Americas (www.oas.org/dsd/fida/laws/database.htm).

contemporary with US air and water acts. Panama has gained considerable momentum by emulating its neighbour Costa Rica in some aspects of policy.

As a result of this institutional evolution, today most Latin American and Caribbean countries have dedicated ministries of the environment (see Table 1.1).

Institutionalization

All public policy is shaped by diverse institutional and political factors that are dynamic and so change over time. Since the 1990s, the institutionalization of environmental management in Latin America and the Caribbean has been in considerable flux. Environmental administration was initially accorded low priority and included within pre-existing, established ministries, limiting policymaking in this area (see Mumme and Korzetz 1997). Embedding environmental functions in existing agencies with essentially different missions and competing values created significant bureaucratic impediments to policy progress. By 1995, only three countries in the region (Costa Rica, Brazil and Colombia) had a cabinet-level ministry exclusively dedicated to the environment, and most incorporated environmental affairs in ministries with responsibilities only partially related to the environment, such as natural resource management. But, as attitudes changed, environmental management increasingly became regarded as a separate ministerial portfolio and environment ministries were created with specialist powers and status (see Chapter 6). Costa Rica, for example, became the first Central American country to raise environmental protection to cabinet level with the creation in 1986 of the Ministerio de Recursos Naturales, Energía y Minas (MIRENEM, Ministry of Natural Resources, Energy and Mines) (see Weidner and Jänicke 2010; and Annis 1992). In some cases institutional development was related to the transition to democracy. In Mexico after the defeat of the ruling Partido Revolucionario Institucional (PRI, Institutional Revolutionary Party) in 2000, and in Paraguay after the dictatorship of General Alfredo Stroessner (1954–89), environmental policy processes underwent significant change. Today, most countries in Latin America and the Caribbean have a separate environmental ministry, although even when environmental responsibilities have gained cabinet status in this way, it is no guarantee policymaking will be successful. Institutional changes are also frequently associated with the short-term agenda of a particular administration.

The civil service

Democratizing governments in Latin America and the Caribbean often inherited administrative systems characterized by bureaucratism that limited the ability of environmentalists to influence policy. Traditionally, the region has been seen as one with large yet weak states whose capacity was hampered by the absence of stable, professional civil services. Moreover, the bureaucracy has often been seen as a resource at the disposal of politicians by contrast with an ideal type distinguished by regularized and impersonal procedures and appointments based on qualifications and achievement (see Weber 1947; Stein et al. 2005).

Bureaucracies vary considerably in terms of their autonomy and capacity and have been shaped historically by different political practices. The weakness of the bureaucracy, part of the executive branch of government, has traditionally limited the executive's ability to assert itself over other interests, obstructing a country's development. Countries that benefit from professional and merito-cratic bureaucracies supporting strong and autonomous states tend to have enjoyed more coherent and stable patterns of development. Even so, different sectors of the civil service within one country may behave in diverse and even contradictory ways. The role played by the civil service in policymaking, and the quality of public policy, will be shaped by degree to which it is neutral and professional. Yet the transition from authoritarian to democratic government tended to strengthen mechanisms that subordinated the bureaucracy to political control, reviving forms of "clientelism" – the relationship between a political patron and a client in which the latter gives the former support in exchange for resources. A winning party, for example, may reward members with public sector jobs and try to reduce the autonomy enjoyed by civil servants because this limits their policymaking scope.

The IDB grouped countries in the region into three levels of bureau-cratic development (see Stein et al. 2005). A first group (Panama, El Salvador, Nicaragua, Honduras, Peru, Guatemala, Ecuador, the Dominican Republic, Paraguay and Bolivia) had bureaucracies with a minimum level of development in which the civil service could not attract and retain competent personnel and lacked the management mechanisms necessary to promote efficient performance. A second group (Venezuela, Mexico, Colombia, Uruguay, Argentina and Costa Rica) had civil services that were fairly well structured but that had not established systems of merit or management tools that would allow them to use their capabilities effectively. Bureaucracies in a top group (Brazil and Chile) excelled and were more institutionalized relative to other countries.

A key factor determining the effectiveness of a ministry is the quality of its staff, with officials in an environment ministry more likely to be drawn from technical backgrounds such as the biological sciences than in other areas of public administration. This can give a technocratic sheen to environmental administration, and in Latin America the technocrat – the highly educated bureaucratic official advocating planned technical solutions to problems – has often been a controversial figure. Technocracy was implicated in authoritarian regimes and also the neoliberal administrations of the 1990s that saw economic development as a precursor to political reform. A global vision of technocratic environmental management has taken this idea to a new level in the notion of "green governmentality", which refers to a science-driven and centralized, multilateral form of climate policymaking (see Bäckstrand and Lövbrand 2007; Van der Heijden 2008).

Political institutions

Alongside the formal institutions of public administration, political institutions – presidencies, cabinets, legislatures, judiciaries and parties – are crucial policy actors. In developing regions such as Latin America and the Caribbean, formal political processes have played a key role in shaping both the emergence of environmentalism itself and subsequent environmental reforms (see Hochstetler and Keck 2007). The transition to democracy in Latin America during the 1980s offered new political opportunities for environmental activists, special interest groups and NGOs that had hitherto operated outside formal political processes (see Chapter 5).

The behaviour of political institutions can be examined in many ways. In Latin America, building and maintaining coalitions in congress, for example, is a crucial aspect of presidential activity, especially in countries such as Ecuador and Bolivia where political processes can be unstable. Similarly, the evolving role of legislatures in the region means they are playing an increasingly substantive role in policy formation. Judicial systems have also changed considerably with the consolidation of democracy, and in some countries, such as Brazil, supreme courts no longer fight shy of ruling against the executive, while in others, such as Mexico, it is rare that they do so. In Bolivia, since 2011, members of a quasi-legal environmental tribunal have been among officials formally elected by the people. It is valuable to sketch out the role and powers of political institutions:

The executive. Presidentialism is the norm in Latin America and the Caribbean and there has been much discussion about the problems this has visited upon the region and whether it would be better served by parliamentary systems (see Linz 1994). Presidents are the key actors in policy formation and, although their personal motivations affect how they govern, this is also influenced by institutional norms.

In some contexts a president will seek to act in the interests of society as a whole, in others he or she may pursue personal or political agendas out of step with the public interest. Presidential powers also vary considerably and have been classified as constitutional and partisan (see Scartascini et al. 2011). Constitutional powers determine the relationship between executive and legislature, in particular how a president mobilizes support for policy. Partisan powers relate to the level of support a president may have in congress in terms both of the number of seats his or her own party or coalition holds and how disciplined they are. Most of Latin America is distinguished by multi-party systems, meaning that the capacity of governments to form and maintain coalitions is a key factor affecting stability. Partisan powers have an important bearing on the level of influence minority actors such as green parties will have within presidential systems (see Chapter 4). Where a president may not be able to get his or her way in congress, one tactic can be to call a referendum with the ability to fix its theme and terms of reference. The ways in which natural resources such as water or gas are exploited have been the subject of referendums in Uruguay and Bolivia (see Box 1.3).

The electoral system and the type of mandate a president enjoys will have a bearing on his or her power to push forward policy. In most of Latin America presidents are elected directly by plurality in a single vote or a second round. The level of popular support enjoyed by a president will determine whether he or she will need to forge an electoral coalition to win polls, and this in turn can offer opportunities to smaller parties such as the greens (see Chapter 4). Having to depend on a coalition, which is common in Latin America, can restrict a presidential agenda. Other factors that also influence presidential power include whether presidential and legislative elections are held at the same time: if so, presidential parties may be able to win more votes and minor parties such as the greens may suffer as a result. A president's relationship with his or her party is also a key element of executive power, and a factor shaping this relationship will be how the presidential candidates are nominated. Some party systems can strengthen a president's loyalty to a party while others can foster independents. When party elites control a centralized nomination process it is more difficult for independent candidates to break through. The most successful presidential candidates at the head of green parties in recent years – Marina Silva in Brazil (2010) and

Box 1.3 Water privatization and democracy

In some countries of Latin America and the Caribbean public hostility to the privatization of water has engendered a notion of "water democracy". Access to water is often considered a basic human right and in Latin America privatization of this resource has generated a political backlash. At the heart of the issue of how water is managed is inequality in patterns of access to it (see Barlow 2004). Since the mid-1990s large multinational utilities have targeted the water sector in most countries of the region, with critics arguing that this has exacerbated problems of scarcity, pollution and unequal access. The World Bank and IDB often support the efforts of these companies to enter markets and large loans have been given to transnational water companies to operate private concessions in countries such as Argentina, Bolivia and Honduras. Privatization has positioned Latin American activists on the front line of a global "water justice movement". Critics say shifting responsibility for public services that ostensibly serve the public interest to private companies whose mandate is maximizing profit causes many problems. It has often meant that the large water corporations have faced public opposition to their operations. The critics say privatization can push up prices for services, cut off customers who cannot pay, reduce water quality, and in some cases causes bribery and corruption among officials. In Bolivia, the best-known reaction to water privatization occurred in Cochabamba in 2000 when Bechtel set up its subsidiary, Aguas del Tunari, and immediately raised the price of water by up to 200 per cent. Large public protests forced the government to reverse the privatization, with Bechtel responding by suing Bolivia.

Antanas Mockus in Colombia (2010) – have joined them from other parties at a late stage in the nomination process. If the electoral system assures a majority for a president's party, for example, he or she can form a cabinet composed of party members, but if it is necessary to form a coalition the president will have to negotiate over portfolios. The effectiveness of coalition cabinets is, in turn, influenced by how much power its member parties hold in the legislature. In Brazil, for example, there has traditionally been a strong relationship between the distribution of ministerial portfolios and the number of seats gained by member parties (see Amorim Neto 2002a). President Luiz

Inácio Lula da Silva (2003–10), however, used methods other than cabinet seats to cement legislative coalitions. This meant the cabinet influence of the Partido Verde (Green Party) in his governments was not a direct reflection of their legislative presence, and the Brazilian greens enjoyed greater influence than their legislative representation suggested.

The legislature. The policy role of legislatures is growing in Latin America and the Caribbean, but their effectiveness depends on presidential and their own institutional powers. A number of studies have sought to classify legislatures, for example, according to the extent to which they can be considered "reactive" or "proactive" – the degree to which they initiate or merely shape legislation – or other criteria (see, for example, Cox and Morgenstern 2002). The IDB developed an index of the policy-formation capacities of congresses in Latin America (see Stein et al. 2005). This indicated that countries with congresses that have a high capacity tend to score highly in terms of the effectiveness of public policy. The role of political parties within legislatures is a key factor in their performance and is influenced by the degree to which parties are institutionalized, the nature of the party system as a whole, and the degree of internal party discipline (see Chapter 4). Factors that determine how legislatures behave include the nature of the legislature's committee system and the electoral formula. Committees are powerful actors able to present, modify or even veto policy proposals. A key issue facing Latin American green parties is the lack of committee experience among legislators. The electoral formula influences the characteristics, preferences and stability of policymakers and can also affect fundamental aspects of political life such as the motivations and integrity of lawmakers. Upper chambers are often loaded to ensure minority representation, or may over-represent rural areas, which can have a bearing on the importance given to environmental issues.

The judiciary. The judiciary's role as an arbiter is important to the policy process and, while it acts mainly as a source of veto, it can also nurture co-operation and foster a climate in which political actors shape policy that is stable and adaptable. The judiciary can help to ensure policies are implemented and enforced appropriately so that they work in the interests of the public as a whole. Historically in Latin America and the Caribbean the judiciary has failed to challenge the legality of presidential acts. However, democratization is strengthening the judicial system's involvement in the policymaking process. A key factor determining the judiciary's policy role is its independence, and this is affected by factors such as its budgetary autonomy, the extent to which judges are appointed according to merit, how stable they feel in their positions, and the reach of judicial review powers (the power of a court to declare laws or administrative acts unconstitutional). Judicial independence also depends on whether a president or political parties try to interfere with the courts.

The judiciary plays several roles in policymaking as policy actor, arbiter and representative. As a policy actor, it can be reactive – for example, by vetoing legislation – or proactive, by interpreting a law in a way that ensures a preferred outcome. An independent judiciary that vetoes policy makes it more difficult for legislators to change policy arbitrarily. Judges will often rule according to how they understand the public interest and hence aspire to ensure the common good, making their work highly significant to environmental policymaking. Reactive rulings such as vetoes can have symbolic power: the risk of a veto on a law that judges believe challenges the common good may restrain policymakers even before it is passed. An impartial judiciary acts as an arbiter between competing interests, especially in terms of the practical application of regulations and standards. This provides an important way for organizations and activists to challenge government decisions or draw attention to their environmental consequences. In Chile in April 2012, for example, the supreme court ruled in favour of the large HidroAysén hydroelectric dam project in Patagonia as part of a joint venture by Spanish-owned energy company Endesa and the Chilean company Colbun that will involve damming the rivers Baker and Pascua and flooding 6,000 hectares of land. The court rejected seven appeals filed against the project following a ruling in October 2011 by a lower court, which had also found in favour of the project. Despite the ruling, the project still needed government approval, ensuring that the role played by the court in discussing its environmental consequences would strengthen official and political scrutiny of it. As a representative, the judiciary can provide a voice in the policy process for marginalized actors providing a way for sectors such as indigenous people, the poor and campesinos to influence policies. Indigenous people and their representatives in NGOs have become assertive litigants in Latin America since the 1990s, and many of the cases that hinge on environmental regulations or constitutional provisions have been brought by them (see Chapter 5). Nonetheless, in some countries it can be very difficult for communities affected by environmental degradation to employ the legal system, especially where the rule of law remains fragile. In Guatemala, for example, representatives of displaced communities have found it hard to secure reparation for injustices caused by the project to construct the Chixoy dam (see Johnston 2011b).

The growing prominence of the judiciary in Latin America and the Caribbean has informed a debate among scholars about the "judicialization" of politics in the region. Judicialization means either the expansion of the province of the courts at the expense of politicians or public administration, or the spread of judicial decision-making methods outside the province of the courts (see Tate and Vallinder 1995). In a study of Colombia, Yepes (2007) has argued that a factor propelling judicialization in politics has been the neoliberal policy norms favoured by international financing institutions seeking to provide protection for foreign investment and property.

Decentralization

As environmental responsibilities have been consolidated over time within one ministry or agency, a contradictory development has evolved as Latin American countries increasingly seek to decentralize governance. Decentralization, whereby policymaking and its implementation is devolved either to a range of semi-autonomous auxiliary agencies or, territorially, to sub-national authorities such as state, departmental or municipal councils, has had an important impact on political systems and has shaped the institutionalization of environmental policymaking. Decentralization can solve problems of governance: bringing government closer to citizens can make public administration more efficient, allows collective demands to be communicated more easily, and improves the quality of public services and makes them easier to monitor (see Andersson, de Anda and van Laerhoven 2009). After poverty alleviation, the conservation of natural resources is an important responsibility for local authorities. In Central America, for example, decentralization processes have often aimed most explicitly at granting local governments greater rights and responsibilities over how natural resources are managed. In Guatemala, the Law of Decentralization (2002) is seen as one of the main pieces of legislation to achieve core rural development goals (see Cardona Castillo 2008) Environmental spending is a key area of municipal budgets, as local authorities are usually responsible for the management of household waste collection and sewage treatment. As most countries in Latin America and the Caribbean have decentralized, provincial and local authorities have become key arenas for environmental politics. Most countries now elect mayors, and federal states such as Argentina, Brazil, Mexico and Venezuela, as well as non-federal states such as Colombia, Paraguay and Peru, also elect regional or provincial authorities. Brazil has a highly decentralized public administration comprising three independent levels: the federal government, 27 federated states with their own governments and over 5,000 municipalities, all of which have their own environmental institutions. Even in countries in which the decentralization of environmental responsibilities is mature, this process continues. Colombia was a pioneer of decentralization in environmental management (see Box 1.4).

Arguments in support of federalism have suggested that a federal structure of government can improve the effectiveness of environmental policy because it tends to promote more competition, experimentation and innovation in government; can nurture progressive policies; and is more sensitive to sub-national concerns by providing local groups with access to policymaking (see, for example, Kincaid 2001). Critics of federalism, however, say that while it could potentially improve environmental policy responses, it could also interfere with coherent policymaking and lead to waste and duplication (see Riker 1964). If federalism weakens national government, it can foster conservatism in policymaking and enhance the status quo. Critics argue that regulations to ensure clean air or clean water are best developed at national or supranational levels, and that in decentralized systems standards risk being "bid down" by competing regional and local interests. In Mexico City, where the problem of air pollution and other forms of environmental degradation are shared by surrounding states, sub-national authorities have developed mechanisms to co-ordinate policy implementation. The Comisión Ambiental Metropolitana (CAM, Metropolitan Environmental Commission) was created in 1996 to co-ordinate the work of the federal-level Secretaría de

> **Box 1.4** Environmental decentralization in Colombia
>
> Unlike most Latin American countries where institutions with environmental responsibilities developed at a national level before being extended to the regions, Colombia's environmental management has been decentralized since the 1950s (see Blackman, Morgenstern and Topping 2006). The first of its regional environmental management institutions, known as Corporaciones Autónomas Regionales (CARs Autonomous Regional Corporations) was established in 1954 in Valle del Cauca and was influenced both by ideas about development planning in the US and ECLAC (Economic Commission for Latin America and the Caribbean). A total of 18 CARs were created between 1960 and 1988 with geographic boundaries initially defined by watersheds but, later, by administrative boundaries because each of Colombia's *departamentos* (departments) lobbied for its own. The roles played by CARs initially varied considerably – from electricity generation and transmission to telecommunications, transportation, flood control and sanitation – but most focused their resources on infrastructure, land development and cattle ranching. In 1968, President Carlos Lleras Restrepo created the Instituto Nacional de los Recursos Naturales Renovables y del Ambiente (INDERENA, National Institute of Natural Renewable Resources and Environment), a new national environmental management institution. However, INDERENA lost authority as new CARs were created and had a limited budget in proportion to its responsibilities and in the mid-1980s INDERENA itself encouraged a campaign by Colombian environmentalists and members of the environmental management bureaucracy for decentralization. Continuing debate responded to a simultaneous process of constitutional reform in 1991 that transformed public administration. The environmental proposals and constitutional reforms paved the way for the passage in 1993 of Law 99 which created the Sistema Nacional Ambiental (SINA National Environmental System) redefining the roles and reach of the CARs.

Medio Ambiente y Recursos Naturales (SEMARNAT, Ministry of Environment and Natural Resources), the work of the authorities of Mexico City's central Federal District (DF) and the surrounding State of Mexico (EM).

How institutions are designed under decentralization has an important impact on how services are delivered, and mechanisms to ensure local participation in this process vary considerably. Andersson, de Anda and van Laerhoven (2009) found in an assessment of 390 municipalities in four Latin American countries that local institutional arrangements have a significant effect on the delivery of rural development services. The research in Brazil, Chile, Mexico and Peru suggests that municipalities with a high degree of inclusive and participatory decision-making and implementation that involves local farmers, NGOs and local officials are more likely to deliver effective services.

The influence of state and municipal governments can extend well beyond their jurisdiction to shape national policymaking. They have a number of tools that enable them to bargain with central government and their officials are key players within political parties with influence over nominations that gives them a say over a legislative agenda. Where there is considerable fiscal decentralization to the states or provinces and they have revenue-generating powers, as in Brazil, they can exert significant pressure on national policymaking. Decentralization of environmental management to states and municipalities needs to be accompanied by the devolution of powers to tax and charge for environmental services if it is to enable countries to meet their sustainable development objectives. In Mexico, for example, insufficient federal spending on environmental protection, the limited revenue-raising ability of states and municipalities and a low reliance on external financing all explain why decentralized aspects of environmental policy suffer from a financing gap (see IISD/Stratos 2004a). Fiscal decentralization within Latin America is probably greatest in Argentina, significantly enhancing the role of provincial governors (see Scartascini et al. 2011). Underpopulated provinces can be over-represented in a legislature (malapportionment), strengthening their political power relative to more populated provinces, and as a result these states often receive disproportionately greater resources per capita. However, while decentralization can strengthen local participation in policymaking it can also generate tension between centre and periphery and confusion about which tier of government is responsible for policymaking (see Cardona Castillo 2008)

Constitutional provisions and the development of environmental law

Constitutionalism is a key aspect of Latin American and Caribbean legal and political culture, rooted in legalistic traditions inherited from Spain and Portugal by which great importance is placed upon codified rules of political conduct. Constitutional change has driven the institutionalization of environmental management in the region. Most constitutions compel a government to ensure that its citizens enjoy fundamental rights, such as the rights to life, justice and, increasingly, to a clean and healthy environment, which are then implemented through legislation. Potentially, constitutions provide a powerful tool for individuals or groups seeking to protect the environment. However, even where constitutions do not formally place an environmental duty on the state, courts across Latin America have often recognized environmental rights and duties under other constitutional provisions.

Constitutional provisions that recognize the importance of conserving and protecting natural resources are not new in Latin America. However, it was not until after the Stockholm Conference in 1972 that most countries in the region began to include environmental provisions in their constitutions. Governments have been amending and recognizing environmental rights and duties in their constitutions since then and this has given rise to a significant body of law and jurisprudence guiding the work of institutions. Pioneers of this process were Cuba and Chile. Article 27 of the Cuban constitution of 1976 imposed a duty on the state and society to "protect nature" and stated that it is incumbent on the state and each citizen "to be vigilant in order to maintain clean waters and air, and so that soils, flora and fauna are protected" (see Evenson 1998). Article 19 of Chile's 1980 constitution established the right of citizens to live in a pollution-free environment and imposed a duty on the state to guarantee this.

New obligations on the state of this kind had several effects: they made environmental conservation an explicit objective of government and established environmental rights as legitimate concepts (see Chapter 5), and they began a process of institutionalization that would, eventually, rationalize under one authority the environmental protection duties contained in laws and regulations that had developed separately across distinct ministries. A landmark in the development of constitutional law in Latin America came with the Rio Earth Summit in 1992, after which countries revisited their constitutions or began to amend and expand pre-existing clauses, often through the inclusion of commitments to "sustainable development" (see Chapter 6).

Today all Latin American countries acknowledge in their constitutions environmental protection in some way (see Table 1.2) and the environment is a prominent focus of constitutional reform in the region. Growing environmental awareness has also progressively steered courts to interpret the right to life as meaning the right to a healthy environment in which to live. The most recent constitutional texts in countries such as Venezuela (1999), Ecuador (2008) and Bolivia (2009) articulate environmental rights in a context that requires states to ensure legal, political and economic pluralism to reflect natural and sociocultural diversity (see UNEP 2010).

A criticism frequently made of constitutionalism in Latin America and the Caribbean has been that there is often little relation between what is stated in terms of constitutional provisions and the reality on the ground. Comprehensive constitutions may list extensive rights, but these often have little practical application and, indeed, their ample nature may even complicate the work of public authorities. The gap between what is written in a constitution and its practical application forms the basis of a distinction by the constitutional scholar Loewenstein between constitutions that are normative and nominal (see Loewenstein 1965, 1986). Normative constitutions are really enforced and effective, thereby controlling or governing the political processes within a particular country and the democratic or republican principles it claims to uphold. The contents of nominal constitutions, by contrast, may be juridically valid but do not always correspond to the real policies carried out within a country and are not really enforced. Many Latin American constitutions were nominal in some aspects until recently, meaning that while clauses explicitly pledged protection of the environment, in practice these have not always been followed (see, for example, Tecklin, Bauer and Prieto 2011). However, democratization and institution-building have increasingly enabled these constitutions to become normative texts, a process reinforced by the extension of participation in environmental policymaking.

Table 1.2 Constitutional clauses on the environment

Country	Articles that refer to the environment	Year of first inclusion
Argentina	41	1994
Bolivia	7	2002
Brazil	Section VIII, Chapter VI	1988
Chile	19, 20	1980
Colombia	67, 79–82, 88, 95, 277, 288, 300, 317, 332–34	1991
Costa Rica	50	1994
Cuba	27	1976
Dominican Republic	63, 66, 67,	2010
Ecuador	Section VI, 44–48	1996
El Salvador	69, 117	1997
Guatemala	97	1985
Haiti	253–58	1987
Honduras	145, 274	1982
Mexico	4, 25, 27, 73, 115, 122,	1917
Nicaragua	60, 102	1987
Panama	114–17	1983
Paraguay	6, 7, 8, 268	1992
Peru	66–69, 192, 195	1993
Uruguay	47	1996
Venezuela	15, 112, 127–29, 156, 178, 299	1999

Source: Author.

The protection of human health was a common underlying objective of the early provisions by which many constitutions began to approach the environment. In 1982, for example, Honduras included in its constitution a duty on the state to conserve the environment so that it is suitable for people's health (Article 145). Some of the most important developments in environmental protection in Latin American countries since the early 1990s have also derived from an emerging human rights approach to law. While judges in Latin America and the Caribbean have recognized a number of rights related to the environment as fundamental human rights, it is often unclear whether courts can effectively enforce these (see Bruckerhoff 2008). Often the problem of enforcement can be a result of the constitutional language employed. The Instituto Internacional de Derecho y Medio Ambiente (International Institute for Law and the Environment) based in Spain has examined the development of several environmental rights in Latin America and the Caribbean (see Fabra and Arnal 2002):

- *Right to a healthy environment*. Judges across Latin America have been moving the right to a healthy environment up the hierarchy of human rights, in some cases by recognizing it as a fundamental right, by applying a broad interpretation to it and by giving it detailed content through landmark decisions (see Hill, Wolfson and Targ 2004). Most Latin American constitutions now explicitly recognize the right to a healthy environment.

- *Right to health*. The right to health has also been widely discussed in Latin American courts: where environmental harm threatens life by definition it threatens health.

- *Right to culture*. Courts have established the right of indigenous peoples to their culture and have identified damage to the environment as a threat to cultural survival.

- *Right to property*. The right to a healthy environment is often balanced against a right to property, but some judgments in Latin America have established property rights *in support of* environmental claims or limited the right to property in order to protect environmental rights. In countries such as Nicaragua, recent history has left property rights fragile and contested, meaning that legal clarity is hard to establish in land claims.

- *Right to Privacy*. Latin American courts have ruled that environmental nuisance can threaten the right to privacy.

- *Right to Information*. The exercise of political rights essential to a democracy – such as access to information and the right to participate in decision-making – also have a bearing on protection of the right to a healthy environment. In Latin America there have been cases attempting to enforce laws protecting the right of individuals to environmental information and in Peru, Brazil, Paraguay and Argentina a notion of *habeas data* offers a constitutional remedy designed to protect freedom of information (see UN DESA/UNCSD 2011).

- *Ecosystem and biodiversity rights*. In 2008, Ecuador became the first country in the world to give constitutional rights to nature itself, establishing provisions that recognize legally enforceable "ecosystem rights". It changed its constitution to give nature "the right to exist, persist, maintain and regenerate its vital cycles, structure, functions and its processes in evolution". Yet these rights have not halted oil companies from despoiling biodiverse areas of the Amazon and it was not until 2011 that the first court case to successfully test them was heard. A key area of debate over environmental rights is biodiversity, which several constitutions now also make reference to. Colombia's 1991 constitution, for example, places a duty on the state to "protect the diversity and integrity" of the environment (Article 79). Bolivia's 2009 constitution imposes a duty on the state to ensure that education addresses the need for conservation and the protection of biodiversity, and that what is agreed through international treaties does not threaten biodiversity. Nonetheless, efforts to incorporate biodiversity in constitutional law and environmental rights face significant difficulties of language and interpretation (see Bruckerhoff 2008). One way of overcoming the ambiguities associated with enshrining ecosystem rights in constitutions is to clarify them in statute law. Bolivia's "Law of the Rights of Mother Earth" of 2011 aimed to establish parity between human and natural rights (see Box 1.5) but has provoked disagreement over how this should be applied.

Environmental lawmaking

The early steps Latin American countries took to develop environmental laws originated in the broader effort to regulate the use of natural resources. As environmental awareness and the technical capacity of governments increased, norms and standards were refined and institutions evolved even in the smaller countries of the region (see, for example, Aguilar Rojas and Iza 2009). In general, the pattern of extending public administration to the environment has followed similar lines of top-down change, typically beginning with a new constitutional provision to protect the environment and then by the establishment of a comprehensive general framework law and a strategic policy, from which further detailed legislation flows thereafter (see Table 1.2). Brazil's long history of environmental lawmaking – originating in efforts to regulate forestry, water resources and agriculture – provides a good example of this process (see Box 1.6). The country demonstrates how democratization has propelled the development of an environmental agenda in government that responds to public pressure for more modern policies. It was not until 1985, when military rule ended, that a Ministério do Desenvolvimento Urbano e Meio Ambiente (Ministry of Urban Development and

Box 1.5 Bolivia's Law of the Rights of Mother Earth

In 2010, Bolivia passed the world's first laws stating that nature has equal rights to humans with the so-called Ley de Derechos de la Madre Tierra (Law of the Rights of Mother Earth) which derived from a longer draft bill that remains under discussion. The Law of the Rights of Mother Earth proposed 11 new rights for nature including: the right to life and to exist; the right to continue vital cycles and processes free from human alteration; the right to pure water and clean air; the right to balance; the right not to be polluted; and the right to not have cellular structure modified or genetically altered. The law also stated that nature has a right to not be affected by large infrastructure and development projects that threaten ecosystems and communities. The law formed part of a restructuring of the Bolivian legal system following the changes to the constitution in 2009 and was, above all, a statement of principles lacking legal force that left it unclear what actual protection the new rights will give to nature in court. Although Bolivia's largest social movement, the Confederación Sindical Única de Trabajadores Campesinos de Bolivia, helped draft the law, which aspires to strengthen the regulation of industry, a number of social disputes since 2009 have demonstrated that the government has sought to balance increased regulation with the developmental benefits of continued extraction of natural resources in what has sometimes been called "neo-extractivism" (see Box 6.6). Nonetheless, the law formed an important symbolic backdrop to the case Bolivia has made about who is responsible for climate change – and who must fund efforts to tackle it – under President Evo Morales (2006–), an indigenous president who has been an outspoken critic of industrialized countries. Bolivia hosted a global conference on Climate Change and the Rights of Mother Earth in April 2010. The Law of the Rights of Mother Earth was influenced by an indigenous Andean spiritual world view which places the earth deity, Pachamama, at the centre of all life and considers humans as equal to all other entities (see Vidal 2011; Weinberg 2010a).

Environment) was created, and this eventually became the current Ministério do Meio Ambiente (MMA). Environmental governance has since established a sophisticated array of institutions and gained global prominence.

Similarly, in Chile it was not until the end of the military regime

Box 1.6 Environmental governance in Brazil

In 1981, the Brazilian government's Law 6938 established its Política Nacional do Meio Ambiente (NEP, National Environmental Policy) to establish standards that ensure greater protection for the environment. The NEP created the Sistema Nacional do Meio Ambiente (SISNAMA, National Environment System) to enforce environmental principles and norms which brings together agencies and environmental institutions in the states, municipalities and Federal District. The system is overseen by a governmental council, an advisory body of the Brazilian presidency. Below this, the Conselho Nacional do Meio Ambiente (CONAMA, National Environment Council) advises the government and deliberates over the environmental rules and standards that state and municipal governments must follow. Created as a separate ministry in 1992, the MMA sits beneath this and plans, supervises and controls national environmental policy and guidelines, co-ordinating the work of the various agencies and entities that comprise SISNAMA. Linked to the MMA is the Instituto Brasileiro do Meio Ambiente e dos Recursos Naturais Renováveis (IBAMA, Institute of Environment and Renewable Natural Resources), which formulates and enforces the NEP. At the foot of the SISNAMA hierarchy sit municipal and state agencies responsible for inspecting environmental activities, implementing policies and monitoring them. A large number of state and sub-regional agencies and entities also exist within this hierarchy as well as councils and commissions nominally subordinate to the MMA (see IISD/Stratos 2004b). However, the ultimate arbiter of environmental policy in the country remains the executive, which will always act with political considerations in mind (see above). A good example of this came in 2012 when President Dilma Rousseff (2011–) vetoed divisive elements of a controversial forestry law that relaxed the forest cover farmers must preserve on their land, taking a stand against the country's powerful agricultural lobby that had pushed a more lenient version of the bill through congress (see Hurwitz 2012)

and the return of civilian government in 1990 that meaningful public agencies dedicated to environmental protection were formed. Chile's approach, like other countries in the region, reflects a continuous process of institutional evolution thereafter, and significant reforms to institutions in 2010 have obeyed this trajectory of modernization, centralizing under one authority the direction and co-ordination of environmental policymaking.

Foreign models and the influence of individuals who have spent time abroad or are more open to external ideas have also influenced the evolution of environmental legislation in Latin America. In the early development of an environmental policy culture in countries such as Costa Rica and Bolivia, contact with foreign individuals and organizations was important to the transmission of environmental ideas. Steinberg (2003) argues that key to this phenomenon were "coupling institutions" in which foreign and domestic actors met, thereby nurturing the growth of a bilateral community of activists. In Costa Rica local people were exposed to foreign environmental ideas and scientific and donor networks from the 1940s until the 1970s in organizations such as the Inter-American Institute for Agricultural Sciences, the Organization for Tropical Studies and the Tropical Science Center. These provided an institutional base within the country for foreign conservationists, enabling some to participate in domestic debates. The US has provided influential models of environmental legislation, and influenced Mexico's first consolidated environmental law in 1971 (see Muñoz 1997).

Problems faced by environmental institutions, and institutional reform

The environmental ministries and agencies of Latin America and the Caribbean operate in new democracies that remain weakly institutionalized. An institutional learning process is underway and this, compounded by a lack of continuity between past and present approaches to regulation and by the continuing evolution of democratic norms, can complicate the ability of officials to address environmental issues. Environmental institutions in the region face a range of problems:

Rapid institutional change. Institutional structures in Latin America have in the past been prone to rapid and ill-planned changes that can disrupt their work and obstruct ambitious proposals from being acted upon. In Ecuador, for example, in 2000, the environment ministry was both incorporated within and then later separated from the tourism, trade and industry ministry in the same year. Complex institutional arrangements can lead to regulation that is both confusing and incomplete. In Honduras, for example, the drafting of an ambitious national biodiversity strategy in 2007 highlighted the institutional complexity of devising a policymaking infrastructure across three separate ministries (natural resources and the environment, health, and agriculture and livestock) together comprising 64 departments, dependencies and agencies. Young ministries formally vested with powers that enable them to take decisions affecting other portfolios may lack authority in their dealings with other, more well-established ministries. In Peru, in 2011, the energy and mines ministry was able to veto objections by the environment ministry to the large Minas Conga open-cast gold mine in the Cajamarca region.

Lack of authority and legal clarity. While environmental ministries in Latin American countries have generally coded violations of the law and the sanctions that will be imposed on offenders, they often lack the resources and authority to enforce these. In Mexico, for example, non-enforcement has been the source of much debate in trade relations with the US and Canada. In Honduras, fishing laws establish strict regulations about the activities that can be carried out in coastal areas, but in practice these are rarely applied to environmental violations. In Cuba, the development of a complex, administrative environmental law is not matched by the existence of a clear judicial structure for reviewing the legality of regulations (see Houck 2000). Brazilian enforcement agencies and mechanisms are sometimes held up as an example for the rest of Latin America. McAllister (2008), for example, has argued that institutional reform in Brazil during the 1980s and 1990s resulted in genuine enforcement of environmental law and, as a result, strengthened the rule of law in general.

Regulatory capture. Environmental reform can be a sensitive political process in which policymakers come under pressure from powerful economic interests. A key risk facing environmental institutions is "regulatory capture" in which an agency responsible for developing and enforcing regulations is dominated by commercial interests and ends up advancing these against the public interest. The weaker the institutional framework in which environmental reforms are carried out, the greater the risk of regulatory capture. Environmental agencies need to be strong enough to resist regulatory capture; institutions have to be sufficiently powerful to balance competing interests; and policymakers making recommendations based on an environmental assessment need to have the support of constituencies with sufficient political power to back them. In the mid-2000s, the World Bank began to propose an approach for incorporating environmental considerations in policy formulation founded on the principle of strong institutional support. This acknowledged that to achieve effective policymaking it was necessary to strengthen the structures underlying decision-making processes.

Institutional overlap and co-ordination. A key issue in institutional development in Latin America is the division of labour between ministries and across tiers of government, and where this is distributed unevenly it is sometimes referred to as "bureaucratic fragmentation". In Brazil, for example, McAllister (2008) found that the federal-level environmental agency in the state of Pará had greater political independence and financial autonomy than its state-level counterpart, and hence performed better. Environment ministries often developed by bringing together within one department environmental functions with related competencies such as agriculture or public health, while all the while other ministries were also involved in implementing environmental rules. This often reflects the fact that environmental legislation has sometimes been built around older laws on, for example, health and sanitation and so has been under the jurisdiction of many agencies. Today, most national environmental bodies have been given responsibility for monitoring the sustainable development agenda and often tend to shoulder excessive responsibilities relative to their capacities, undermining their effectiveness (Barcena et al. 2011). A consensus has developed that one of the principal roles of environmental ministries is strategic policy *co-ordination* and that this is best achieved horizontally – co-ordinating the policymaking and regulation of other "sectoral" ministries such as agriculture or water resources, often through interministerial consultation or steering groups overseeing policy design. In its 2012 global environmental outlook, the UN Environment Programme (UNEP) argued that policies need to be designed and implemented in ways that transcend the traditional compartmentalized, sectoral approach that has prevailed in the region (UNEP 2012a). However, institutional hierarchies in Latin America and the Caribbean are often highly centralized and vertical, deferring authority upwards to the executive.

This makes co-ordination difficult, and for it to be effective it may require the strict delimitation of responsibility and authority of different ministries. Ministerial systems in the region generally lack the benefits of a cabinet office at the centre of government to oil the machinery of governance. Moreover, as reforms in Chile since 2008 have attempted to address, legal traditions are grounded in the exercise of authority, not co-ordination. Ministerial systems can also be competitive and rivalry between ministries and agencies can be a major obstacle to effective regulation. Country studies conducted by ECLAC between 2001 and 2005 in Latin America and the Caribbean argued that, given the restraints on funding faced by environmental authorities, improving co-ordination would greatly enhance the efficiency of policies.

Funding constraints. Obstacles to the establishment of effective institutions include funding limitations, and the financing of environmental protection by Latin American states has been erratic. The limited resources set aside for environmental spending fluctuate in line with the state of public finances. In Argentina, for example, the country confronted a critical economic situation in 2001 that had a severe impact on the environmental budget – representing a cut of about 40 per cent for the year (Barcena et al. 2002). Management and control of budgets generally depends not only on an environmental ministry per se, but also on sectoral ministries and sub-national authorities (see above). Throughout Latin America there are also often huge geographic imbalances in how funds are allocated, commonly resulting in regions with the worst environmental problems or highest population density receiving the lowest amounts. The funding of environmental protection in Latin America has also been affected by other trends such as external debt, variations in official development assistance (ODA), and changes in private international financial flows and multilateral grants and loans. The variation in budgets, and a focus on areas that do not necessarily reflect public priorities, have prompted multilateral bodies such as the World Bank to develop a more systematic approach to assessing the effectiveness of public spending on the environment based on expenditure reviews (PEERs).

Corruption and the rule of law. Large corporations are drawn to countries with natural resources such as oil and timber whose exploitation generates large revenues, and they may be tempted to leapfrog environmental regulations limiting extractive activities or imposing costs on them through corruption. Corruption among politicians, law enforcement officials and public officials open to bribery in order to supplement low wages is a problem almost everywhere and Latin America and the Caribbean is no exception. Corruption scandals have been a normal feature of the region's political landscape, often linked to the awarding of contracts by a government, and have reached to the highest levels of administration. There have been many instances of high-level corruption in the region involving natural resource use, although institutions such as the World Bank argue that there is no causal relationship between mineral abundance and high levels of corruption (see Di John 2009). Corruption can reflect institutional weakness while being fuelled by external demand for extractive products. It is considered to be a significant feature of illegal deforestation threatening woodlands in countries such as Honduras (see EIA 2005). Extractive industries such as mining have been at the heart of debates about corruption and the need for greater state and corporate transparency. In Colombia, for example, a complex web of royalties, tax and other payments are made by companies involved in extractive industries to various government ministries and departments, local authorities and quasi-state bodies, but very little information about these payments is made public (see Cook 2011).

Popular participation and accountability. Popular pressure has not been a principal driver of institutional development in Latin American environmental management but has nonetheless grown in importance as civil society enhances its role in ensuring accountability (see Chapter 5). Some authoritarian regimes were quick to realize that environmental initiatives could be valuable in mobilizing the population or legitimizing their rule (see above). In Chile, while popular participation and the democratization of decentralized environmental bodies has improved, these nonetheless have their origins in military rule and the model of environmental protection that has evolved is less a result of dialogue and more one of bureaucratic evolution and lawmaking. At the very least, adequate structures are needed to ensure that marginalized groups are represented in the environmental debate so that it does not remain a preserve of urban intellectuals (see Miller 2007). Today, the presence of an environmental constituency within civil society is seen

as important for ensuring policy continuity. Institutionalizing participation in environmental impact assessment and decision-making has
also risen up the agenda in Latin America and the Caribbean, not
least because of the potential for regulatory capture and the need
for transparency and accountability to ward against corruption (see
above). Multilateral agencies such as the World Bank have concluded
from work trying to support the creation of strong environmental
institutions that engagement with civil society is essential (see
Eltz et al. 2010; McCormick 2007). While the extension of participation in decision-making has clearly become a prominent theme in
Latin America and the Caribbean, formal participatory mechanisms
often remain absent or inadequate. Research into institutions that
enable participation in budgeting or habitat conservation planning,
for example, identifies considerable variations across national and
sub-national levels (Baiocchi 2001; Thomas 2001; Heller 2001; Goulet
2005). Argentine environmental legislation includes a law establishing
the parameters of open access to "public environmental information"
that guarantees the right of citizens to official data about environmental issues. An important element of comprehensive environmental
reforms in Chile in 2010 was to enhance participation, and reforms
to the country's environmental impact evaluation system (Sistema
de Evaluación de Impacto Ambiental, SEIA) aimed to widen the scope
of those who can make representations about a project (see Olivares
Gallardo 2010). Ensuring public participation in decision-making can
highlight the importance of institutional design in environmental
management. Some green thinkers put great store on institutional
design aimed at achieving a more "deliberative" democracy, a notion
that reflects the idea of consensus building through participatory
governance (see Smith 2001; Dryzek 1987). An innovation growing in
popularity that reflects a greater commitment to participation is the
co-management of environmental resources, especially in protected
areas (see Moreno-Sánchez, del Pilar and Maldonado 2008; Aagesen
2000).

Conclusion

Strong institutions are essential for good environmental management,
but too often in Latin America and the Caribbean state ministries and
agencies, and the political institutions that formulate and interpret

policy, have been bedevilled by problems with damaging consequences for the natural environment. These institutions operate in countries with democracies that remain relatively new and are more weakly institutionalized than in the developed world. They face problems of rapid and ill-planned changes that can disrupt their work and often lack the resources and authority to enforce environmental rules, sometimes enabling powerful corporations to dominate them. Such regulatory capture is a significant problem for environmental policy-making in Latin America and the Caribbean, where abundant natural resources create huge incentives to weaken environmental regulations. Ministries and agencies often duplicate each other's work, may compete as rivals for jurisdiction over environmental responsibilities, and in the absence of clear hierarchies may co-ordinate their work poorly. Improving coherence across institutions in how policy is made and implemented has become a prominent feature of reform in the region. Budgets notionally destined for environmental protection may in fact be spread thinly across many bodies, and may not end up being directly allocated to protecting the environment. Corruption and a weak rule of law – persistent features of politics in Latin America and the Caribbean – can be a significant problem, limiting the effectiveness of environmental institutions and eroding public trust in them. Yet in all these areas Latin American and Caribbean countries are making progress, often with the support of multilateral agencies. This has meant that although environmental governance in the region leaves much to be desired, enormous strides have been made in developing effective institutions, particularly in areas such as forestry policy.

Recommended reading:

Barcena, Alicia et al. 2011. "Sustainable Development in Latin America and the Caribbean 20 Years on from the Earth Summit: Progress, Gaps and Strategic Guidelines", LC/L 3346, August 2011, 2011-457. New York: United Nations. Available online at www.eclac.org/rio20/noticias/paginas/9/43799/REV.Rio+20-Sustainable_development.pdf.

Baud, Michiel, Fabio de Castro and Barbara Hogenboom. 2011. "Environmental Governance in Latin America: Towards an Integrative Research Agenda", *European Review of Latin American and Caribbean Studies*, 90 (April), pp. 79–88.

Mumme, Stephen P. and Edward Korzetz. 1997. "Democratization, politics, and environmental reform in Latin America", in Gordon J.

MacDonald et al. (eds), *Latin American Environmental Policy in International Perspective*. Boulder, CO: Westview Press.

World Bank. 2003. *World Development Report 2003*. Washington: International Bank for Reconstruction and Development/The World Bank. Available online at www.dynamicsustainabledevelopment.org/showsection.php [accessed April 2012].

Useful websites:

Asociación Interamericana para la Defensa del Ambiente (AIDA, Inter-American Association for Environmental Defense): www.aida-americas.org/front

Comisión Centroamericana de Ambiente y Desarollo (CCAD, Central American Commission on Sustainable Development): www.ccad.ws/

Commission for Environmental co-operation (CEC) (North American countries): www.cec.org/

Community Environment Legal Defense Fund (CELDF): www.celdf.org/

Earth System Governance Project: www.earthsystemgovernance.org/

Environmental Law Alliance Worldwide: www.elaw.org

Foro Interamericano de Derecho Ambiental (FIDA, Inter-American Forum on Environmental Law): www.oas.org/dsd/fida/

International Institute for Sustainable Development (IISD)/Stratos, National Strategies for Sustainable Development country studies: www.iisd.org/measure/gov/sd_strategies/national.asp

International Network for Environmental Compliance and Enforcement, Directory of Web Sites of Environmental Agencies of the World, Americas and the Caribbean: www.inece.org/links_pages/online resourcesEnvironmentalagencies.html

International Union for Conservation of Nature (IUCN): www.iucn.org

||||||||||||||||||||||||||||||||||||||||||||||||||||||||||||||||||||||||||||||||||||||||||||||||||||||||||||||||||||||||||||||||||

CHAPTER TWO

Policy

WHILE CONSIDERABLE ACADEMIC ENERGY has been focused on the content of public policy in Latin America and the Caribbean and its consequences, there has been less attention to the policy-making process itself and the factors that shape it (Francheschet and Díez 2012). Apart from Mexico and Brazil, few countries in the region have an academic community producing case studies and engaged in theoretical debates on the topic, and within this the specific study of environmental policymaking is even more limited. Public policy – a government's response to public problems – is of fundamental importance to the study of the politics of the environment, not least because it determines among other things the distribution of "public" goods. Nonetheless, a debate continues about how to study public policy in Latin America and the Caribbean between those who believe the region is unique, and therefore demands its own analytical armoury, and those who argue that general theories employed to study other regions of the world – which themselves have evolved significantly over time – can now be applied fruitfully in the region. Francheschet and Díez seek to take a middle ground in this debate, arguing that students of the region must engage with debates in the field of comparative public policy, that often follow theoretical frameworks originating in the US, while also recognizing that there are risks to merely importing theories and concepts uncritically to what is a highly distinctive region. A particular difference in how

Latin American policy processes function, for example, results from presidentialism through which – unlike the US and other developed countries where pluralism often ensures competing policy proposals – the executive retains disproportionate influence over policy preferences. Nonetheless, in recent years interest in public policy has grown among scholars of Latin America and they are now applying general concepts and theories of public policy more frequently. This chapter examines factors that influence environmental policymaking and how that process varies across the region. It looks at how the power of policy elites is shaped through agenda-setting, advocacy coalitions and exogenous change, and how institutions and political practices influence these phenomena. It examines the policymaking tools available to Latin American and Caribbean governments and the political, legal and administrative constraints that can limit the implementation of environmental policies.

Public policy

Francheschet and Díez argue that three aspects of Latin American politics are indispensable for understanding public policy processes in the region:

The state and state–society relations. Debates about the state's role are of importance in determining the degree to which the environment is recognized in development policy and the tools that are used to implement a green agenda. The state also remains at the centre of questions about how best to resolve problems associated with the over-exploitation of natural resources. But Latin American and Caribbean states are often considered weak in terms of their autonomy – the extent to which they can act independently of dominant social groups or powerful international actors – and their capacity to perform basic roles (see Chapter 1). Limited autonomy and capacity, therefore, make the nature of the state and state–society relations key starting points for the study of public policy in the region. Where weak state institutions are dominated by certain interests, public policies tend to serve particular sectors of society rather than the common good. In post-transition Mexico, for example, powerful actors continue to enjoy privileged access to the policy process, often through informal channels to politicians. At the same time, weak state capacity means that no matter how well-intentioned policy may be, it may be poorly implemented, and it can also be obstructed by strong presidents (see Box 2.1). As a result, weak state capacity in Latin America can help to account, among other things, for the judicialization of politics (see Chapter 1), declining faith in representative institutions, and the difficulty of drawing attention to serious problems. Even in countries such as Chile where the state has considerable autonomy, business groups retain privileged access to policymakers, resulting in a bias in favour of existing economic models (see Teichman 2010, 2012; Castiglioni 2012).

The role institutions play in policymaking. Policy outcomes often reflect the historical power relations embedded in institutions, especially where these are highly unequal, and weak and inefficient formal institutions are a key feature of many Latin American countries. Scholars should also pay attention to what O'Donnell (1996) and others have described as "informal institutionalization", whereby institutions operate according to unseen but nonetheless powerful social rules, norms and ideas (see also Helmke and Levitsky 2005). Informal rules and the role of ideas and norms in policymaking have become a focus of "new institutionalism", which places institutions as opposed to social actors at the heart of the study of public policy (see, for example, Hall and Taylor 1996; Pierson and Skocpol 2002). Francheschet and Díez (2012) argue that informal relations are critical to understanding policymaking in Latin America fully, and are exemplified by the prevalence of clientelism – a relationship between unequal political actors in which loyalty is exchanged for benefits. They suggest that ideas, values and beliefs are also important to policymaking in the region even though there has been little empirical research on their role (see Chapter 6). One way in theory that the role played by ideas has been understood is the degree to which they have been embedded in the institutions that structure political processes through, for example, the norms underlying constitutions (see Chapter 1). Ideas are also important in the early stages of policy-making through "agenda-setting" (see below) and, more generally, by underpinning the identities by which groups mobilize (see Chapter 6).

In an overview of policymaking across Latin America and the Caribbean conducted in 2005, the Inter-American Development Bank (IDB) argued that the institutional context in which policies are

> **Box 2.1** Privileged policy access in Mexico
>
> Díez (2012) argues that despite democratization, which has brought about fundamental changes to the distribution of power in Mexico's political system and opened policymaking to more institutions and actors, the presidency remains central to the policy process and there are examples in which the executive has altered environmental policymaking in the interests of producers and against the will of the legislature. Díez highlights the Mexican president's institutional prerogative to draft the regulations through which a law passed in the legislature is implemented. He identifies two instances in which this prerogative has been used to hinder progress in environmental policy. Following the passage of reforms to forestry laws in 1997 that penalized illegal felling, President Ernesto Zedillo (1994–2000) lowered the penalties unilaterally even though these had been agreed on with congress. Both the administration of Zedillo and that of his successor President Vicente Fox (2000–06) failed to enact the implementing regulation that would have put into effect reforms on toxic and hazardous waste disposal passed by congress in the 1990s. Fox both ignored pressure from the country's senate to enact the implementing regulations and in 2004 declared a regulatory moratorium on all policy areas in an effort to foster competitiveness and investment. In both cases it is thought that privileged access to the policy process by powerful industrial groups contributed to these decisions.

formed and implemented, and the processes by which these occur, are crucial to the design of good policy (Stein et al. 2005). It argued that policies gain importance not only because of their technical content but because they have certain characteristics such as stability, adaptability, coherence, efficiency, the possibility of being implemented effectively, and that they aim to work in the public interest.

Inequality. Persistently high levels of inequality are a characteristic feature of Latin American politics, and inequality shapes policymaking by nurturing forms of clientelism; influencing public opinion in ways that can limit the politicization of inequality by suppressing mobilization against it; and determining who participates in policymaking, thereby excluding the weak. In Brazil, for example, there is evidence in state politics that inequality is related to patterns of partisan competition and the professionalization of legislative branches, with a consequent effect on policymaking: policies that are more broadly based and sensitive to public concerns are more difficult to achieve where politics is dominated by personalistic, rather than ideological, factors (see Marsiaj 2012).

Environmental policymaking

Environmental policymaking begins with the reality that natural resources are "public goods" that, in effect, belong to the entire community. Given this, it is the community that bears the cost if natural resources are depleted by minority interests (see Volume 1). One of the main roles of environmental policymaking is to ensure that those interests shoulder the costs of using these resources and do not deplete them for future generations. Nonetheless, those interests will try to protect their use of resources, often in unison, and society may find it hard to counter this. At the same time, many environmental problems are complex and linked to other policy issues, such as trade or development strategy, which do not permit of simple solutions. There are limits to what nation states can do anyway, because many environmental problems are transboundary. Developing nations may lack the scientific expertise needed for effective environmental policy-making, and as a result policymakers may remain cautious, mindful of other issues such as trade rules or economic growth. The role of science in environmental policymaking can strengthen technocratic decision-making that resists the extension of pluralism. Democracy also politicizes policymaking, which can limit its effectiveness and the willingness of politicians fighting elections to pursue long-term solutions. The main trends shaping the context for environmental policymaking in Latin America and the Caribbean are economic reforms, which have enhanced the role played by transnational and local capital in economic policymaking and resulted in cuts to social spending and environmental policies; a neglect of the countryside which has fuelled urban growth and a labour market that is increasingly informal and feminized; and the multiple constraints on policymaking imposed by growing globalization.

The way policymaking elites tend to approach environmental issues is, in general, governed by the "traditional policy paradigm" that tends to give priority to economic growth over environmental protection (see Neil Carter 2010). Policymakers remain committed to ever-growing economies and aim to deal with problems through regulation that does not address the *systemic* underlying causes of environmental degradation. In Latin America and the Caribbean, technocratic perspectives advocating economic modernization have resulted in the creation of environment ministries that are weak in comparison with other sectoral ministries, especially economic departments (see Chapter 1). The traditional policy paradigm is reinforced by key features of Western systems: business (producers) enjoy a privileged position; governments have a sectoral structure; and elites dominate policymaking:

Producers. Latin America offers a valuable laboratory in which to explore the relationship between the state and societal interests because of the strength of "structuralist arguments" that attributed a key role in economic development to the state (see Volume 1). Although business is today a powerful actor, in countries such as Mexico and Bolivia it evolved subject to corporatist relations between bureaucratic governing parties overseeing development policies – in which the state played a dominant role in production – and organized sectors of society such as associations of industrialists and trades unions. For many years in Latin America, corporatism contained private business interests as one of several actors in a mutually beneficial relationship with states under the control of large bureaucratic parties. The position of business within civil society has been the subject of debate and in many countries it was only until recently that the business lobby could be treated as a formal and discrete interest group similar to the environmental lobby itself. Today, in Latin America's most dynamic economies, business has emerged as a dominant interest that can manipulate the policy process. The discourse of producer groups has arguably been strengthened since the early 1990s by elements of the sustainable development agenda (see Chapter 6). Efforts to understand state–society relations that acknowledge the centrality of the state often attribute environmental policy outcomes to its institutional capacity (see, for example, Haas 1992). They suggest that communities of experts in government agencies shape the state's response to environmental problems, and hence differences in policy are determined by how close an institution is to certain social forces (see Silva 1997). By contrast, pluralist approaches that emphasize the role played by society in policymaking point to the role of actors and factors *outside* state institutions that pressure states to adopt or sideline environmental policies. An effort to reconcile these positions would suggest that, while state experts determine policy preferences, external actors and forces – especially powerful private interests – can influence the policy process, especially if policy preferences challenge market-friendly ideas. In Argentina, for example, an alliance between powerful biotechnology producers and a state that has embraced this technology for reasons of food and economic security means that the country has not experienced the protests seen in other countries that produce genetically modified products (see Newell 2009). Newell argues that large agro-food corporations have played a key role in supporting the "biohegemony" of genetically modified organisms (GMOs) in Argentina's agricultural economy (see Box 2.2). In Mexico, by contrast, the discovery of transgenes in maize landraces in Oaxaca in 2001 served to increase awareness in society of the importance of maize diversity and the crucial role of small-scale farmers in maintaining it, leading to debates about the potential impact of genetic engineering (see Antal, Baker and Verschoor 2007). These debates contributed to the regulation of biotechnology in Mexico through legislation on GMOs (see Bellon 2010).

Sectoral administration. In Latin America, in the 1980s and 1990s, a technocratic perspective on environmental policymaking fostered the creation of ministries and agencies that treated the environment as a discrete policy area, yet gave this limited power in relation to other sectoral ministries (see Chapter 1). Technocratic perspectives can reinforce the way governments often divide responsibilities into distinct policy areas with specific responsibilities: "sectoral adminis-tration". This has tended to reproduce a policy climate which encourages economic expansion that is harmful to the environment in the long term. There are several reasons for this: first, sectoral administration implies an institutional hierarchy in which some ministries are more powerful than others. Economic ministries such as finance, industry and energy tend to dominate policymaking and make the decisions that most affect the environment, and environment ministries tend to have much less influence than them. Second, sectoral adminis-tration can hamper co-operation because individual ministries are dominated by elected politicians whose motivations and rivalry can

Box 2.2 GM producer power in Argentina

The Argentine case – where biotechnology corporations operate in a context in which there is strong state support for them alongside an absence of popular opposition to what they produce – offers one example of the potential power of producer interests within the "traditional paradigm" of economic growth. Argentina has become one of the world's leading cultivators and exporters of GMOs, accounting for more than a fifth of global GM production, and is an influential player in the politics of biotechnology globally alongside the US and Canada (see James 2006). Argentina is unusual within Latin America in terms of the lack of opposition it has encountered to the development of GM technology, which in Mexico, Brazil and Peru has sparked significant debate and some opposition. The fact that most of Argentina's GM production is for export, mainly as animal feed, means that it has avoided debates about human consumption, and there has also been little discussion about the environmental impact of GMOs. Supporters of biotechnology point to savings from reduced pesticide use and reduced soil erosion from less intensive tilling. Critics point to continuing use of chemical inputs (such as glyphosate), deforestation associated with land clearing for GM production, land concentration and the impact of the sector on agricultural employment. The focus has been on the merits of biotechnology as a developmental strategy, and successive Argentine governments have maintained a commitment to promote biotechnology, which played a key role in the country's economic recovery after its damaging 2001 debt crisis. One reason Argentina has embraced this technology, according to Newell (2009), is the power of agro-food corporations in the country and their role in sustaining what he terms "biohegemony". Newell argues that this biohegemony is sustained by an alliance of interests that includes big agribusiness producers and traders (such as Cargill), Argentine exporters (such as Bio Sidus, Relmo and Don Mario), multinational biotech firms (such as Syngenta, Dow and Monsanto), commercial banks and supporters within Argentina's state.

make them pursue personal agendas against the greater good. Such a structure can strengthen the influence of producer interests that have strong political connections and access to ministers. This threatens regulatory capture (see Chapter 1) and limits a ministry's commitment to protecting the common good or the environment. The relationship between a sectoral ministry and producers may be so strong that it excludes other interests entirely to the detriment of the environment, as in the case of energy. Ideas about sustainable development challenge the sectoral nature of public administration and it is generally accepted that a strategic overview of policymaking, often referred to as institutional integration, is required for truly effective environmental policies. The need to bridge the divide between institutions that manage economies and those that protect the environment was a prominent theme of the 1987 Brundtland Report on sustainable development. A key role of environment ministries, therefore, is co-ordinating the work of other ministries and aspiring to *transversalization* – integrating environmental perspectives within development policies in general (see Neil Carter 2010; UNEP 2010).

Policy elites. A key concept in the study of environmental politics is that of closed policy networks or "communities" through which producer interests can enhance their influence. These networks may comprise public and private actors dependent on each other for information, funding, expertise or legitimacy. Influential actors within them seek solutions to environmental problems that do not question the principles shared by the policy community. Governments can use policy networks to avoid political damage when they advance plans that are unpopular or difficult to implement, because they give new actors access to the policymaking process in ways that may make them more likely to conform (see Compston 2009a, 2009b). Closed policy communities are common in sectors where environmental issues affect economic interests and the government has close ties with producer groups. The influence of scientists has similarly been analysed through the concept of "epistemic communities" – groups of experts who share common beliefs about environmental issues (see Haas 1992). Scientists influence a political process through their ability to persuade others that their knowledge is important enough to require a policy response. In Latin America and the Caribbean, other features of political development have enhanced the power of policy communities: traditions of corporatism, strong executives and limited accountability in government. Economies reliant on the export of commodities and the political imperative placed on such issues as a secure food supply (food security) have also strengthened the ability of powerful producer groups to dominate closed policy communities in such sectors as hydrocarbon production, mining and agriculture. In Peru, in 2010, for example, producer pressure contributed to the refusal by then president Alan García to sign a law passed by congress that would have given indigenous people more power to stop oil and mining projects on their lands. Policy communities can ensure that policy is not diluted in such a way that it threatens established forms of production or can ensure issues that question established norms are kept off the agenda entirely, as in Argentina's biotech industry. The relative power of policy communities can be contrasted with a small and weak environmental movement struggling to gain access to the policymaking process (see Chapter 5). The creation of environmental ministries powerful enough to disrupt policy communities dominated by producer interests offers green groups the ability to influence governments, and this is made easier where policymaking is more pluralistic.

The policy process

The way policymaking is conducted will vary according to factors such as the profile of the main actors, the institutional structure, the sector in which policy is being developed and the strength of the traditional policy paradigm and sustainability discourses. Silva et al. (2002) identify four prominent discourses on sustainable forestry that offer different diagnoses of problems and policy prescriptions:

- the "market friendly" policy narrative that views government intervention as the main problem in forestry and advocates freer markets based on clear property rights;

- the developmentalist narrative that views forestry issues as technical problems best left to officials and favours government planning and regulation to help guide forest industries;

- the social narrative that rejects both free markets and traditional government bureaucracies and insists that local communities should control forests and benefit from them;

- the conservation narrative, which emphasizes the environmental services of forests and is divided between those who favour market-friendly strategies, those who support government intervention, and those who look to the grassroots.

Reforms to forestry laws in Bolivia provide an example of contrasting approaches to policymaking and the complex processes that this can involve (see Box 2.3).

Three main elements shape how the power of policy elites is exercised – agenda-setting, advocacy coalitions and exogenous change.

Agenda-setting. Levels of public and media attention to the environment fluctuate and interest groups, the media and politicians engage in "agenda-setting" to control the policy process. However, a policy community may be strong enough to ignore an issue or a challenge to existing policy. A comparison of forestry policy in Chile, Venezuela, Mexico and Costa Rica in the late 1990s suggested that in most cases national forestry policy leaned towards a market-friendly approach even where government experts influencing policy preferred more progressive, environmentally friendly or developmentalist policies (see Silva 1997). Scholars ask why some issues make it on to governmental agendas while others do not (see, for example, Kingdon 1995). Others note that what citizens see as problems rise and fall on both public and governmental agendas, often independently of the type of problem itself (see Downs 1972; Cobb and Elder 1983; Hilgartner and Bosk 1988; and Baumgartner and Jones 1993). Even if they attract attention, problems that do not have clear solutions may not make it on to the agendas of officials (Kingdon 1995). Alternatively, they may rise up the agenda only to then fall in public importance (Downs 1972). Sustained agenda-setting over time can change a "policy culture" – expectations about what the government will do in a particular area (see Steinberg 2003). Throughout Latin America growing public interest in environmental protection, and the rise of environmental policy cultures, is reflected in an increase in news coverage of green issues (see Figure 2.1). In an examination of the policy cultures of Costa Rica and Bolivia, Steinberg (2003) noted that whereas there was once indifference towards environmental issues, now biodiversity, sustainable development and other green themes are popular topics creating a source of new policy proposals.

Advocacy coalitions. Shared ideas and information may create coalitions that compete to dominate the work of a policy community, especially where an issue is technically complex or politically contentious (see Sabatier and Jenkins-Smith 1993). In Latin America and the Caribbean, where ideas and information have overturned

Box 2.3 Forestry policy in Bolivia

Reforms from 1990 to 1996 to forest policy in Bolivia – which has large forests and substantial timber sectors – offer insights into how a range of actors influence the policy process. After 1986, structural adjustment policies encouraged non-traditional exports and the rapid expansion of forest products (see Volume 1). A 1996 forest law reflected efforts to seek compromise among a large number of stakeholders and actors. Forest policy reform under President Jaime Paz Zamora (1989–93) was initially dominated by a coalition of legislators, international organizations and state institutions with the support of environmentalists, and focused on the congressional Comisión del Ambiente y Recursos Naturales (COMARENA, Natural Resource and Environment Committee). Early drafts of the bill reflected the technocratic preferences of the UN's Food and Agriculture Organization (FAO) and Bolivia's environment ministry. In 1992, a consultation process enabled social groups, logging interests and local governments to participate. Loggers recommended the privatization of forests but local governments sympathized with small-scale forest users and gained the support of environmental groups that championed the cause of indigenous peoples. A bill presented to congress in December 1992 isolated timber interests by proposing to prohibit round log exports and a share in timber revenues for local government. However, the detailed formulation of policy between 1992 and 1996 was drawn out as actors lobbied to block each other, resulting in several presidential interventions to break deadlock. President Gonzalo Sánchez de Lozada (2002–03), an advocate of the free market, took office in 1993 and appointed consultants for the logging lobby to positions in the new Ministerio de Desarrollo Sostenible y Medio Ambiente (MDSMA, Ministry of Sustainable Development and the Environment). This gave them an institutional base from which to build support in congress behind the idea of establishing 40-year renewable forest concessions that could be bought and sold, a measure that was approved in 1994 by the lower house. However, continuing disagreement bogged down the bill in the senate by divisions for two and a half years, and in 1994 the president allied with the Proyecto de Manejo Forestal Sostenible (BOLFOR, Bolivia Sustainable Forest Management project), funded by USAID, to seek a compromise. A new forestry law was eventually approved in 1996 representing a compromise between all the main actors.
(*Source*: Silva et al. 2002)

Figure 2.1 Environmental news stories in Costa Rica and Bolivia

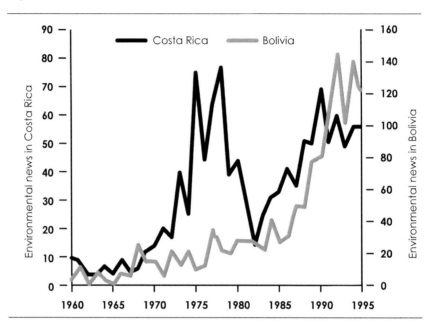

Source: Paul F Steinberg, "Understanding Policy Change in Developing Countries: The Spheres of Influence Framework", *Global Environmental Politics*, Vol. 3, No.1 (February 2003), pp. 11–32 © 2003 by the Massachusetts Institute of Technology.

existing policy communities these have often originated from outside the region within a multilateral development agency or a developed country such as the US. The idea of climate change, for example, was slow to gain momentum in the Latin American policy community until the 1992 Earth Summit in Rio, whose work was dominated by multilateral bodies and international environmental non-governmental organizations (ENGOs). Environmental policymaking is a complex process bringing together many issues in bodies representing different actors with conflicting goals. In Latin America, public policy is formed and implemented in systems populated by a diverse array of participants from politicians, opinion leaders and business groups to local and indigenous communities. It has been common for issue-oriented local coalitions of groups to work closely with policymakers and officials in addressing environmental problems. Successful cases of policy implementation have often involved the participation of urban social movements such as neighbourhood associations (see

Lemos and Looye 2003). These coalitions cut across classes and the state–society divide and usually form around a specific problem affecting a locality (see Chapter 5). Hochstetler (1997) points out that issue-based environmental coalitions often play a "representation" role in which they pursue an objective without directly challenging political institutions. Their success is defined by their acceptance as legitimate interlocutors in policymaking, and in terms of the policy outcomes (see Lemos and Looye 2003). The cities of Porto Alegre and Belo Horizonte in Brazil provide examples of successful popular participation in local decision-making that leads to improved account-ability and local empowerment.

Exogenous change. Natural disasters or new issues such as climate change for which the dominant members of a policy community have no response may provoke radical change. Changes in international conditions – such as new treaties or economic recession – can disrupt a policy community's work (see Chapter 4). International agreements impose external standards that may require a government to override powerful local interests. Privatization in Latin America and the Caribbean in the 1990s, for example, weakened existing corporate interests and disrupted previous policy norms. Moreover, environ-mental policy innovation in the region has been driven by international "policy diffusion" – the convergence of regulatory patterns, ideas, approaches and institutional innovations in environmental policy-making across the world (see Jörgens 2001; Steinberg 2003; Chapter 3). Multilateral bodies or think tanks, consultancies and foundations act as agents of diffusion. The growth of new social movements and, in particular, indigenous groups in countries such as Ecuador, Bolivia and Brazil, has leveraged green issues on to an international agenda and made it harder for local policy elites to ignore them (see Chapter 5). The growing prominence of ENGOs with international clout such as Greenpeace has also tested the power of existing lobbies on a range of issues, and ENGOs have had considerable influence in areas such as forestry (see Humphreys 2004). An example of how internal and external factors combine to challenge the outlook of established policy communities in Latin America can be found in Bolivia. Steinberg (2003) envisaged two "spheres of influence" affecting environmental policy in Bolivia: international and domestic. Those with access to the resources of the international sphere affect national policy by deploying financial and scientific resources, while those with access to the resources of the domestic sphere influence policy with political resources such as social networks, knowledge of institutional relationships and political engagement. The weight of domestic politics in a policy issue varies. In Mexico and Costa Rica, for example, international factors have been important in shaping forestry policy (see Silva 1997). Chilean forestry policy and the country's relationship with bodies such as the OECD suggest that international factors strengthen market-friendly approaches to policymaking.

Institutional and political influences

The complex interactions of participants in a policy process will also be shaped by institutions and political practices, which affect the roles, incentives and transactions of these actors in different ways. Policy formation is determined to a significant extent by the political institutions of a country and such factors as the nature of relationships between the executive and legislature, electoral rules, the federal structure and the judiciary's level of independence (Scartascini et al. 2011; see Chapter 1). The presidency and the committee system in the legislature play a key role in this process. In Chile, for example, the consensual nature of democratic politics means policies are more likely to be stable, adaptable and well implemented in areas in which there is less disagreement among the actors involved. When they are polarized, it is more likely that one actor will veto policy. Of great importance is how institutions can nurture the ability of diverse participants to co-operate, and certain conditions shape co-operation (see Stein et al. 2005):

- *Benefits*. Non-co-operation between actors is more likely if it generates benefits. In Argentina, for example, fiscal rules mean provinces may have an incentive not to co-operate in reaching spending agreements with the federal government.

- *Number of actors*. It is difficult to achieve co-operation when there are a large number of political actors. Ecuador, for example, has one of the most fragmented party systems in Latin America and hence unstable and turbulent politics.

- *Time periods*. Levels of co-operation are influenced by how interactions between politicians and officials develop over time. If relationships tend to last, then it is in the interests of each party to be co-operative in the short term. Where legislators serve for longer, as in Uruguay, Chile and Brazil, public policies tend to be of higher quality.

- **Delegation**. Delegating policymaking to autonomous agencies, as is common in countries such as Ecuador, nurtures co-operation by removing party politics from the equation.

Institutional practices and norms will determine how priorities are set, how stakeholders are represented, the accountability of policy-makers, and how policy "learning" takes place. Cultural, historical, institutional and political influences determine how decision-makers set environmental priorities. These include public opinion, development agency priorities, international agreements, judicial decisions and the results of technical studies and risk assessments (see Ayres, Anderson and Hanrahan 1998). Powerful interests have a disproportionate influence over policy processes making it essential to have mechanisms representing weaker stakeholders in discussions. Policymakers need to be aware of who is vulnerable, but determining this can be difficult. While more plural systems favour efforts to build consensus on policy – especially in countries such as Costa Rica, where there is a tradition of bringing marginal groups into the political process – if a government is not fully committed to consulting vulnerable groups it will not respond to their needs. Participation can help policymakers set priorities but can also serve as a means of legitimizing policies that have already been determined in advance (see Box 2.4). An analysis of public participation in the Barrancones environmental conflict from 2007 to 2010 – in which opposition halted plans by GDF Suez to construct a power plant near Punta de Choros, Chile's main marine reserve – suggests that innovations in environmental law to enable citizen participation have had an ambivalent impact, both legitimizing policies favourable to producers while influencing the emergence of collective action resisting these (Spoerer 2013).

It is not enough to ensure that interests are balanced by enabling different viewpoints to be represented in decision-making, In order to guarantee that policies are actually implemented and endure, it is necessary to ensure *accountability* – the obligation on officials to account to citizens for their plans and results. Citizens themselves can hold states to account by monitoring public services, employing the

Box 2.4 Policy tools: participation

Since the 1990s, most Latin American and Caribbean countries have incorporated mechanisms to enable some form of citizen participation in environmental policymaking and have created a variety of consultative councils (Gaventa and Valderrama 1999). Although national and local regulations establish standards about how public participation should take place through instruments such as public hearings, implementing these effectively can be challenging (see UNEP 2012a). Innovative mechanisms to improve participation include Participatory Poverty Assessments (PPAs) which can be a useful tool for consulting the poor then relaying the findings to policymakers who do not have regular contact with them. PPAs do not rely on such traditional methods of social analysis as household surveys and use a variety of methods to seek opinions combining visual techniques such as mapping and diagrams and verbal techniques such as interviews and discussion groups. Alongside these, Poverty and Social Impact Analysis (PSIA) takes a broader approach to analysing the distributional impact of policy changes on different social sectors. PSIA aims to ensure that a country retains "ownership" of the policies advanced by multilateral agencies by informing public debate about ways of combining growth with poverty reduction. Although PPAs do not rely on the traditional household survey, surveys remain a useful way of assessing environmental priorities. Surveys used by the World Bank in Colombia, for example, revealed that the environmental priorities of citizens vary with income, with poorer groups tending to favour better air quality, noise reduction and the reduction of risks from natural disasters, such as flooding and landslides, and richer groups tending to prioritize global environmental issues, biodiversity and urban conditions (see Sánchez-Triana, Ahmed and Awe 2007). Other innovative participatory tools used by environmental policymakers include an interactive website created by Panama's Autoridad Nacional del Ambiente (ANAM, National Environmental Authority) giving the public access to documents (see Calvache, Benitez and Ramos 2011).

media or through participatory mechanisms such as social auditing or independent budget analysis. A key mechanism for reinforcing accountability is ensuring people have access to the judiciary to address issues such as pollution (see Chapter 1; see also Blackman et al.

2005). Organizational "learning" is essential if environmental policies are to improve over time, and organizations gain the experience that influences their practices by repeating routines and searching for new ideas. Once policies have been formulated and implemented, how can they be judged? The key characteristics by which public policy can be assessed include the extent to which it either promotes the common good and public interest, or benefits individuals, factions or regions (see Cox and McCubbins 2001).

Policymaking tools

As the countries of Latin America have developed their environmental agendas, they have refined an array of policy tools. These are selected according to technical criteria but also politically, because decisions are shaped by competing interests. Policy instruments used to address environmental problems can be classified as: regulatory; managerial and institutional; economic (government expenditure and market-based instruments); and social (education, culture, consumption and public participation).

Regulatory tools. The bedrock of environmental policy in Latin America and the Caribbean is the system of general framework laws from which regulations are derived. Regulation is the most widely used policy instrument and represents the attempt of a government to influence behaviour by specifying and enforcing standards to control issues such as pollution. It is also the main instrument used by international bodies to address global problems. Policymakers like regulations because they can be applied quickly, do not require complete information about a problem and so are administratively efficient, and are relatively cheap. As they apply to everyone equally and should in principle be hard to manipulate because they have the backing of the state, they also appear legitimate to citizens. Advocates of the free market often criticize the "regulatory burden" that they say limits the competitiveness of companies, but in sectors such as mining, for example, environmental regulations are considered essential because of the serious impact mining can have (see Jiménez, Huante and Rincón 2006).

The quality of regulation in Latin American and the Caribbean varies considerably but, in general, shows consistent improvement since the

1990s. The World Bank's governance indicators, for example, measure among other things regulatory quality. Figures compiled in 2009 show a high quality of regulation in countries such as Chile, Uruguay and Argentina but much lower regulatory quality in the poorer and smaller countries of the region such as Nicaragua, Honduras and Haiti (WGI 2009). Yale and Columbia universities also produce the Environmental Performance Index (EPI), which ranks countries on 25 performance indicators tracked across 10 policy categories, covering both environmental public health and ecosystem vitality. The effectiveness of regulation is determined by a country's judicial or administrative procedures, with different countries adopting distinct regulatory "styles" (see Neil Carter 2010). Some are formal and legalistic, stressing judicial oversight; others are more administrative and discretionary, avoiding the prescription of rules and standards (see Bennett 1988). Enforcement styles also differ, with some systems more confrontational and coercive and others more voluntaristic and co-operative. A coercive style can strain relations between enforcement agencies and the industry and result in more law-breaking. In Peru, for example, legislation aiming to make it easier to enforce penalties for illegal mining generated violent protests in the city of Puerto Maldonado in clashes between miners and police in 2012.

Regulations are usually based on national environmental standards – particularly those imposed on traded goods – which apply to the whole pathway of a product, from the extraction of raw materials through processes of manufacturing, packaging and distribution, to sale, use and disposal. Standards seek to ensure producers, traders and consumers internalize environmental costs in their decisions (see below). However, standards are not effective by themselves and work best as part of a broader management strategy. If they are too demanding they can threaten livelihoods: in Mexico, for example, the need to meet demanding environmental standards in order to achieve "certification" as a producer of a natural forest product has compounded problems faced by small chicle producers (see Forero and Redclift 2006). Regulation has been the preferred policy response to air pollution. In the Metropolitan Area of São Paulo, for example, the Programa de Controle das Emissões Veiculares (PROCONVE, Vehicular Emission Control Programme) was implemented in 1986 establishing emission standards for new vehicles, and since then pollutants have fallen significantly.

International trends also play an important role in Latin American regulation, especially in efforts to encourage energy efficiency. International standards have, for example, been applied to the use of new energy-efficient technologies and renewable energy sources such as biofuels. Argentina has pioneered energy-efficiency labelling schemes in Latin America and Brazil has promoted voluntary comparative and endorsement labelling programmes. A popular form of regulation is certification ("eco-certification") by which commercial producers are certified for adhering to environmental production standards.

Managerial and administrative policy tools. Latin American governments use a wide range of managerial and administrative tools in environmental policy, with the basis of all policymaking being environmental impact assessments (see Chapter 1).

Environmental assessment. A key concern of any assessment process is achieving scientific consensus, and the difficulties involved in this can be illustrated well by examining the example of forest cover. To evaluate the effectiveness of environmental policies, officials must resolve key problems of nomenclature: while there are numerous definitions of what a forest is, there is no consensus between the scientific community and stakeholders on a definition that can be used as the basis for remote sensing studies (see UNEP 2010). The challenge of securing accurate information is a perennial obstacle to policymaking in Latin America and the Caribbean and there is a persistent lack of relevant, up-to-date information and expertise. Multilateral officials believe that the adoption of integrated environmental and economic accounting systems is a particular priority (UN 2010; UNEP 2010). Environmental accounting is growing in importance as a planning tool, and concepts such as the "ecological footprint" have been taken up enthusiastically by countries and cities developing sustainable development strategies. Scientific research is often closely linked with public policy and a more integrated approach to information management is emerging throughout Latin America and the Caribbean (see, for example, Ballve 2003).

Planning. Different forms of policy planning are undertaken in Latin America and the Caribbean. Land-use planning is an approach to how land should be used in a way that provides an overview of all the resources and dimensions involved in development. It is often participatory, involving the stakeholders who, ultimately, must put plans into effect on the ground. Participatory planning, an approach employed in Costa Rica, strengthens the power and roles of local organizations and communities and establishes forms of co-ordination and co-operation between different stakeholders. In rural areas, which harbour considerable biodiversity, land planning should not only help local stakeholders to solve problems but also address attitudes in urban government circles that affect rural development policies. A so-called "territorial approach" to rural land planning aims to take a holistic view of rural issues to account for such factors as cultural practices. Bitter divisions over land use in the Brazilian Amazon and policy changes in 2010 allowing for more development offer an example of what can be at stake politically and economically in land-use planning (see Box 2.5). Territorial approaches to land-use planning that are focused on rural areas have been employed extensively in Mexico. In recent years, many cities have strengthened their planning systems and the region is making efforts to institutionalize urban environmental planning and management. In order to boost co-ordination Brazil, for example, created a Ministério das Cidades (Ministry of Cities).

Ecosystem management. Ecosystem management, in which Latin America has been a leader, adopts a long-term, integrated view of how to benefit from ecosystems. It aims to take into account inter-relationships between pressures on the environment; institutional change; and the impact of development on ecosystem services and human well-being. In Bolivia, after 1997, for example, the Climate Action Project in the biodiverse Noel Kempff Mercado National Park in Santa Cruz was considered a pioneering example of ecosystem management. A tool used to implement this approach is payment for ecosystem services (PES), which identifies an ecosystem service such as the maintenance of water quality produced by a watershed, then aims to balance the needs of the service providers (those living in and maintaining a water basin) and the beneficiaries (towns or industries that use the water). Another area in which the ecosystem approach has been applied is REDD – Reducing Emissions from Deforestation and Forest Degradation – a UN-led initiative to tackle climate change based on payment for ecosystem services schemes. The UN-REDD programme has worked with pilot countries that include Bolivia, Panama and Paraguay. Carbon credits generated by

Box 2.5 Brazil's new forestry code

Disputes over land-use planning in the Amazon became a prominent issue in Brazilian politics in 2012 during debates over a controversial forest law that culminated in the legislation being passed by congress in April. Under the country's previous forest code, dating back to 1965, landowners had to conserve forests on a percentage of their terrain – ranging from 20 per cent in some regions to 80 per cent in the Amazon. However, in practice, the law had not been widely enforced and an estimated 20 per cent of the Amazon rainforest has been cleared through logging and farming. The new code proposed to ease rules on how much land farmers must preserve as forest, enabling them to cultivate land closer to hilltops and riverbanks which are vulnerable to erosion if trees are cut, and granting an amnesty from fines to those famers with land of up to 400 hectares who illegally cleared trees before July 2008. Small-scale landowners, who comprise most of Brazil's farmers, were to be exempted from having to replant deforested land. The legislative proposals created the classic division between those who see development and economic growth as the top priority against those who argue that conservation is the most pressing issue facing the Amazon. The division also reflected a cleavage that has existed in Brazilian government and society over Amazon policy since the 1990s between a nationalistic current oriented toward a more state-regulated economy and inclined to exercise classical military sovereignty over the Amazon, including the exploitation of natural resources, which includes conservatives and socialists; and globalists favouring an open economy, large-scale international co-operation in the Amazon and restrictions on human settlement, which includes neoliberals and social democrats (see Viola 1997). The changes had been proposed by Brazil's Communist Party (PCdoB), which argued that the existing rules prevented small farmers from using their land to its full potential and hence stopped them from escaping poverty. The legislation was strongly supported by Brazil's powerful farmers' lobby, which argued that the changes will promote sustainable food production and that the status quo had undermined investment in agriculture. Environmentalists and scientists, however, said the new forest code would lead to further destruction of the Amazon and would represent a step back after Brazil had made progress slowing deforestation with the use of satellite monitoring, for example (see Ballve 2003).

REDD schemes are luring the private sector into forest conservation. BioCarbon – a company set up by Australia's Macquarie Bank, the International Finance Corporation (the private sector investment arm of the World Bank) and the US-based Global Forest Partners, a forestry investment fund – has indicated that it will invest its $25 m of equity in conservation projects that qualify for the UN's REDD scheme that may include forest areas in the Brazilian Amazon.

Ecosystem management has also been used in eco-tourism initiatives and in Cuba has been employed to develop sustainable socio-economic activities in the country's largest wetland areas, the Ciénaga de Zapata Biosphere Reserve and a Ramsar Site in Matanza. In Costa Rica it has played an important role in the reversal of past damage to the environment through reforestation. So-called "set-aside" policies can work alongside the management of protected areas but also highlight the difficulty faced by governments trying to find alternatives to extraction. In 2007, for example, Ecuador floated unprecedented plans to leave underground a fifth of its oil reserves (846 m barrels) in the Ishpingo, Tambococha and Tiputini (ITT) oilfields beneath the Yasuni National Park if, in return, the international community came up with $350 bn, half of the oil's market value. This would have avoided the emission of 407 m tonnes of CO_2 and provided funds to develop national renewable energy initiatives. However, in 2013, Ecuador abandoned the scheme blaming lack of international support, after financial commitments reached only a small fraction of the amount needed.

Infrastructure management. Infrastructure drives development but economic factors and a short-term outlook often mean large projects result in environmental damage. In recent years, infrastructure development in Latin America and the Caribbean has had more to do with regional or global imperatives than local needs. The large infrastructure projects envisaged under the Puebla-Panama Plan (PPP) or the Initiative for the Integration of the Regional Infrastructure of South America (IIRSA) respond, above all, to a developmentalist agenda that prioritizes economic growth (see, for example, Rivera 2008). Nonetheless, policy innovations are making their mark.

- *Waste disposal*. Although recycling is still inadequate in the region, local governments, sometimes in partnership with social groups and companies, have implemented important initiatives. In Ecuador, in

1998, the city of Loja, with support from the German Development Service (DED, now GIZ), launched a waste-management programme in which biodegradable garbage, after being processed in an earthworm composting plant, is sold as fertilizer to farmers and citizens or used in parks.

- *Transport*. Most Latin American urban authorities dedicate considerable effort to public transport initiatives, often concentrating their attention on introducing bus rapid transit systems (see Wöhrnschimmel et al. 2008). Shipping provides an example of the potential for effective infrastructure management to respond to environmental problems. In Panama, officials and scientists have developed a plan to constrain shipping lanes into and out of the Panama Canal in order to protect humpback whales (see Black 2012).

- *Water*. Watershed management concentrates on guaranteeing the supply of water for agriculture, human consumption and hydroelectric power. The prevailing approach has tended to consider the environmental needs of water basins in isolation and not to manage water with air, land and desertification policies in mind. However, an ecosystem approach is increasingly being adopted and countries are co-operating in watershed management. Participatory mechanisms have also been a prominent feature of Brazil's approach to water management (see Keck 2004).

- *Protected areas*. Establishing protected areas is a valuable administrative tool for safeguarding biodiversity and Latin American and Caribbean governments have a good record of creating national parks. Marine protected areas are also being created off the coasts of Latin America, bringing complex management challenges. In the Galápagos Islands Marine Reserve, for example, authorities have to manage invasive species by establishing protocols to protect against the risk posed by tourist and freight vessels. There has been considerable debate regarding the effectiveness of protected areas and concerns that many do not, in fact, protect biodiversity from human activity. Climate change is also calling into question the ability of protected areas to ensure conservation by, for example, altering the distribution of endangered species. While biodiversity conservation is a key goal, it can sometimes conflict with the needs of local people to use natural resources for their livelihoods (see Orlove 2002; Fraser 2003; Moreno-Sanchez and Maldonado 2008).

- *Coastal and fisheries management*. Environmental management is essential to protect marine and coastal resources and to respond to climate events. Over-fishing is a major problem in the region, often reflecting weak port control and monitoring mechanisms that do not scrutinize industrial fishing activities and do not ensure fleets comply with quotas. In the 1980s, social groups began to press for fisheries management that reflected multilateral treaties, and policy innovations since then have had concrete results. In Chile, the government established Áreas de Manejo y Explotación de Recursos Bentónicos (AMERB, Management and Exploitation Areas for Benthic Resources) giving artisanal fishermen rights to use portions of the seabed in a co-management deal with the state and today, there are about 700 AMERB in the country.

Economic policy tools. Support for the use of economic instruments as a more efficient alternative to regulation has grown in recent years and a range of tools can be employed to protect the environment, from traditional government spending to sophisticated instruments that harness the behaviour of the market, market-based instruments (MBIs). There are various MBIs and these all apply the "polluter pays" principle aiming to ensure that the price of a good or service incorporates the cost of environmental or "public" goods such as air and water. An important requirement for assessing the use of economic policy tools is to place a value on the contribution the environment makes to development, and the concept of "environmental accounting" aims to achieve this (see above). However, Latin America has relatively little experience in using these instruments, and the principles of environmental protection are still viewed by productive sectors with suspicion. Where economic instruments are now being used, it is usually in countries with well developed institutions. Some of the principal economic tools in a government's environmental toolbox are: infrastructure spending aimed at improving the environment such as investing in renewable energy or "green industries"; subsidies to encourage producers and consumers to change their ways; eco-taxes on pollution or goods whose production causes pollution; tradable permits that combine regulation with a financial incentive, and offer companies flexibility to reduce pollution in the most cost-effective way; and payments for environmental/ecosystem services (PESs, see above). Macroeconomic policies can also be used strategically to achieve environmental policy objectives, trade policy has been increasingly associated with environmental concerns, and multilateral borrowing has also become crucial in financing green initiatives (see Volume 1).

Social policy tools. Policymaking can seek to change attitudes with the long-term aim of nurturing more sustainable practices, and governments can use a range of social policy tools to achieve this.

Extending participation in environmental policymaking can improve its quality and offers a way of resolving conflicts (see above). However, the relationship between democracy and environmental policymaking is complex, and policymakers in competitive, democratic systems may resist introducing radical changes such as restrictions on car use for fear of alienating voters. While environmental groups can use consultation exercises such as public inquiries to draw attention to issues, this is no guarantee of environmentally friendly outcomes. Where projects under discussion relate to sustainable development initiatives, such as hydroelectric power, they may also divide environmental lobbies. Although governments are undertaking consultation exercises more frequently, producer interests have a natural advantage in a consultation forum. Nonetheless, the participation of the private sector in policymaking is important if there is to be a reduction in the damage caused by production. Environmental initiatives designed to interact with the industrial, trade and business sectors often go beyond concrete measures such as eco taxes to more subtle approaches such as developing corporate environmental responsibility. In Brazil, corporate responsibility schemes until the 1990s were limited to addressing poverty but have since been transformed through the pressure of interest groups. Initiatives such as the Conselho Empresarial Brasileiro para o Desenvolvimento Sustentável (CEBDS, Brazilian Business Centre for Sustainable Development) are examples of how members of the business community can support environmental objectives. Some countries in Latin America are also promoting the notion of sustainable forest management, often by devolving this to local communities. Vaccaro, Zanotti and Sepez (2009) suggest that communal exploitation of a commodity can improve ecological conditions. Latin America has also become a global leader in environmental education (see, for example, O'Neill et al. 2008). Costa Rica has been a regional leader in environmental education and environmental topics were first introduced in the country's national curriculum in 1977 (see Blum 2008).

Climate change policy tools. Climate change has significant implications for policymaking and is a theme of unparalleled complexity that creates multiple conflicts between interests. Just one example of this is the uneasy relationship that scientists and political interests are required to forge in an effort to come up with viable policies (see Dessler and Parson 2006). Climate change policies are usually characterized as those that aim to decrease global warming or its effects, *mitigation*, in particular through action to reduce the concentration of greenhouse gases (GHGs) in the atmosphere; and those that aim to help society and ecosystems adapt to global warming and its effects, *adaptation*. To the extent that mitigation aims to reduce the release of carbon into the atmosphere, above all through changes in energy policies in order to reduce GHGs, this can be understood as a separate policy area. A broad range of other measures to fix climate change policy into overall development strategies is also being deployed (see Gupta 2001; Schneider, Rosencranz and Niles 2002). Global action on climate change is complex and multifaceted, and has evolved considerably since the 1980s when it rose up the agenda of multilateral forums. The science of climate change is well-established and policy tools already exist that could significantly reduce GHGs without being prohibitively costly (Stern 2007). However, policy measures so far have failed to reverse the rise in emissions, partly because the main obstacles to robust action on climate change are political: governments and other political authorities are reluctant to take decisive action (see Compston 2009a, 2009b; Hale 2010).

Latin American and Caribbean governments have begun to develop their own distinctive analysis of climate change and ways of responding to international initiatives seeking low-carbon development (see De la Torre, Fajnzylber and Nash 2009). Responses in the region to the climate change agenda have been framed by two tensions within the global bargaining process. First, the developed world has been divided over its willingness to make firm commitments, largely as a result of different levels of access to stable energy supplies. Second, a north–south divide in negotiations has resulted in disagreements about the principle of "common but differentiated responsibilities", with many developed countries unwilling to fund mitigation efforts in the developing world and unlikely to share their technology without compensation. NGOs from the developed world have often worked in support of the position taken by Latin America and the Caribbean states.

Given the strong tradition of government intervention in economic decision-making in Latin American and the Caribbean, governments in the region have been expected to take the lead in confronting climate change. They have gained a prominent international profile in negotiations, helped by their status as rapidly developing countries. Latin America has also played a key role in hosting conferences that have led to some of the most important developments in global environmental governance, such as the Earth Summit in Río; its politicians have occupied important positions in multilateral environmental governance institutions; and regional figures have made significant contributions to the design of key climate change instruments. Since 2010, the executive secretary of the United Nations Framework Convention on Climate Change (UNFCCC), for example, has been the Costa Rican Christiana Figueres, who has been one of the principal promoters of Latin American participation in the convention. Latin American countries have adopted a varied menu of domestic policies to tackle the challenges posed by climate change. Some have utilized or amended legislation and regulations in order to use existing laws to address climate change (see above). Others have established sustainable development ministries or departments to ensure that this issue influences overall development policy (see Chapter 1). Most have taken a mixed and evolving approach to policy that takes in multilateral developments, a good example of which is Mexico (see Box 2.6).

The climate change policy areas that have gained most attention in Latin America and the Caribbean are as follows:

Reducing emissions. Price and market mechanisms can be employed to make producers and consumers internalize the environmental costs of the emissions that cause climate change. Policies usually employ two ways of doing this: taxes on GHG emissions ("carbon taxes"), and emission-trading schemes (see Volume 1).

Energy policy. Energy policies have evolved to guarantee the supply of cheap power for industries and homes while ensuring fuel diversity to avoid dependence on imports. Urbanization and industrialization is pushing up demand for energy rapidly. According to the International Energy Agency's World Energy Outlook (2009) under its "reference" (business as usual) scenario, the likely growth in primary energy demand in Latin America between 2007 and 2030, at 1.7 per cent, is above the world average (1.5 per cent), albeit significantly lower than non-OECD energy growth (see Table 2.1). Demand for oil for

Box 2.6 Climate policy in Mexico

Pulver (2007) has examined the evolution of climate policy in Mexico and argues that this has four distinguishing features: first, the initial agenda for action was developed by scientists in the national university and bureaucrats in the environment ministry; second, as UN climate talks gained prominence other ministries began to engage in the policy process, and bureaucratic politics hindered progress, such that after 1995 Mexican climate policymaking became erratic; third, industry actors themselves and, notably, the state oil monopoly Pemex were advocates for precautionary action on climate change; and fourth, Mexican ENGOs were largely absent from climate debates. Attention to climate change was initially concentrated among scientists and environmental bureaucrats at the Universidad Nacional Autónoma de México (UNAM) and the Instituto Nacional de Ecología (INE), the research agency of the Secretaría de Medio Ambiente y Recursos Naturales (SEMARNAT, Ministry of Environment and Natural Resources). After the 1992 UN Framework Convention on Climate Change was agreed, INE and UNAM's Centro de Ciencias de la Atmósfera (CCA) established a programme to co-ordinate research with financial support from the US. This generated information on Mexico's vulnerability to climate change and led to the country's initial national communication to UNFCCC in 1997. The process brought together scientists and bureaucrats working on climate change in Mexico and key individuals gained policy leadership roles. After the UNFCCC entered into force, the climate issue was increasingly viewed in the context of broader policy. However, there has been significant disagreement between different agencies and the government's interest in the issue has oscillated. In 1997, prior to the Kyoto negotiations, climate change rose up the political agenda and Mexico hosted a session of the Intergovernmental Panel on Climate Change (IPCC). More actors and agencies became involved as climate change became a focus of the ministries of agriculture and rural development, commerce and industrial development, communications and transport, energy, and social development. Concerned about the potentially negative impact of international regulation on Mexico's oil economy, the Secretaría de Energía (SENER) joined Mexico's delegation to Kyoto. Politicization of the climate issue resulted in institutionalization of the informal group of scientific policy advisers into a formal Comité Intersecretarial de Cambio Climático (Inter-ministerial Climate Change Committee). The Mexican senate's decision to ratify Kyoto in 2000 was the result of a struggle between SEMARNAT – advocating climate regulation – and SENER, which opposed ratification. President Ernesto Zedillo decided to ratify, partly as a result of the influence of Pemex, which advocated action on climate change largely to showcase a position of adopting the best practice of global oil majors. In 2000, Vicente Fox of the opposition Partido Acción Nacional (PAN, National Action Party) became president and gave a lower priority to climate change. In 2001, the US withdrew from the Kyoto Protocol negotiations, delivering a blow to Mexican expectations that it would benefit under the clean development mechanism (CDM) from a US–Mexico emissions trading partnership. However, the EU's ratification of Kyoto in 2002 revived CDM possibilities in Mexico. After 2002, competition between federal agencies over control of the climate issue obstructed progress. INE lost its policy role in 2000 and concentrated its attention on generating GHG data. Policy decisions were discussed in the Comité Intersecretarial, but new activities on climate change were driven by bilateral initiatives. In 2003, the US and Mexico formed a Bilateral Working Group on Climate Change. Mexico has continued to play a prominent role in the climate change agenda and in 2010 hosted the UN Climate Change Conference in Cancún. President Felipe Calderón (2006–12) made significant unilateral commitments on emissions reductions. (Main source: Pulver 2007)

transportation accounts for much of this, and demand for electricity is actually projected to decrease by 4 per cent by 2030. Greenpeace and the European Renewable Energy Council (EREC) have argued that, while CO_2 emissions in Latin America will increase under business as usual scenarios by a factor of four up to 2050, with the correct mix of policies they could decrease from 800 million tonnes in 2003 to 440 million tonnes in 2050 (EREC/Greenpeace 2007).

Despite the comparatively modest consumption of energy in Latin America and the Caribbean, CO_2 emissions from fuel combustion have been rising consistently. Countries in the region have made limited progress in improving energy efficiency by reducing consumption yet have significant potential to do so. Greenpeace and EREC have argued that the share of renewables can be dramatically increased in the region if governments limit the growth of primary energy demand. The mere existence of energy efficiency regulations does

Table 2.1 Latin America's primary energy demands*

Region/country	1980	2000	2007	2015	2030	2007–30 (percentage)**
Latin America	292	457	551	633	816	1.7
OECD	4,050	5,249	5,496	5,458	5,811	0.2
US	1,802	2,280	2,337	2,291	2,396	0.1
EU	n/a	1,684	1,757	1,711	1,781	0.1

* Mtoe (million tonnes of oil equivalent), under the "Reference Scenario".
** Compound average annual growth rate.

Source: World Energy Outlook 2009 © OECD/IEA 2009, Table 1.2, p. 76 (www.worldenergy-outlook.org/media/weowebsite/2009/WEO2009.pdf).

not guarantee results because of difficulties states face in punishing illegal behaviour, and there are also economic and historical reasons explaining why energy efficiency measures are not properly enforced, such as the custom of paying less for services through subsidies than the real market prices (see ECLAC, OLADE and GTZ 2009). The region faces considerable challenges in developing renewable sources such as hydroelectric, wind, solar, wave and biomass energy because of an absence of public policies and a lack of investment in new technologies. In 2008, Latin America and the Caribbean attracted just 12 per cent of the $155 bn invested worldwide to develop renewable solar, geothermal, wind and small-scale hydropower (Bloomberg New Energy Finance/UNEP 2011). Nonetheless, renewable energy sources now account for 27 per cent of its primary energy demand. Biomass (wood and bark), mainly used for heating, is the main renewable energy source, followed by hydropower. Few countries other than Brazil boast a significant renewable energy sector, although in 2011 Mexico took the lead in Latin America where investments, mainly in wind but also in geothermal, grew close to 350 per cent; Argentina saw investment grow nearly sevenfold to $740 m; and investment also grew in Chile, Peru and Venezuela (Bloomberg New Energy Finance/UNEP 2011). Hydroelectric power is important throughout the region but its growth potential is increasingly constrained by political opposition to the damage to habitats and communities caused by large dams. Obstacles to the development of other renewable sources include the existence of powerful energy producers, competitive liberalized energy markets, discriminatory fossil fuel subsidies and technological challenges.

After hydroelectric power, wind is the largest renewable energy source in Latin America and the Caribbean, and the total capacity for wind production in the region is considerable (see GWEC 2011). Growth has been rapid in recent years in Brazil, Mexico and Chile. The Organización Latinoamericana de Energía (OLADE, Latin American Energy Organization) launched a comprehensive investigation into the market for solar thermal energy in the region in 2010–11 with a view to greatly expanding the use of solar power in place of gas to heat water, and identified serious regulatory and institutional obstacles to expansion (see Noboa 2011). Latin America also produces 40 per cent of the world's biofuels and Brazil is a global leader in the use of them with 35 years of experience in producing ethanol from sugarcane. Wave power also has great potential as a large and predictable source of energy in the region, but as in other parts of the world remains in its infancy. A newly prominent sector that may have a global impact, with its epicentre in South America, is lithium, which has the potential to produce non-polluting and safe energy. Renewable energy also makes sense as part of a wider strategy of diversifying supplies away from fossil fuels or imports in order to foster "energy security" and avoid periodic shortages. In Brazil, for example, wind power is seen as a useful complement to inconsistencies in the energy provided by hydroelectric power, which at times suffers from water shortages. In recent years cuts in Chile's supply of natural gas from Argentina exposed the country's energy vulnerability, when the reductions were followed by one of the worst droughts in decades and by the rise in oil prices in 2008. Energy security and the desire to diversify sources is also driving the region's nuclear power sector, and in Argentina and Brazil nuclear energy has grown as an environmental issue.

Transport policy. Climate change requires radical changes to transport policy, and vehicles need to generate lower emissions and traffic volumes need to be reduced. Ways of doing this include making cars more efficient by incorporating anti-pollution devices or using alternative fuels such as ethanol or methanol. Nonetheless, the impact of clean technology is often limited and does little to address growing volumes of traffic. Strategic planning is needed to develop transportation systems that limit car use and encourage public transport, cycling or walking. Governments in Latin America and the Caribbean have relied heavily on the construction of roads to fuel economic growth and the ownership of cars has long been considered an indicator of development. Cars in cities generate unacceptable levels of air pollution, and tackling this problem in a metropolis such as Mexico City is highly complex. Mexico City has become notorious for its air pollution problems, and transportation accounts for 37 per cent of emissions within the Mexico City federal district (Simms and Reid 2006; see Box 2.6). The policies that have been undertaken to address urban transportation issues have frequently concentrated on the air pollution generated by vehicles. City planners and transport officials have a key role to play and cities such as Curitiba in Brazil have pioneered urban transport solutions aimed at getting people out of their cars. In Mexico City, the ProAire 2002–10 air quality management plan aimed to cut pollutants through policies such as the replacement of 80,000 old taxis through a subsidy to owners that enabled them to buy a new, cleaner vehicle and dedicated bus lanes and high-capacity buses (UNEP 2010). Toll roads can be found throughout much of Latin America and the Caribbean, but the railway infrastructure in the region is limited and train use is low.

Limits on policy implementation, compliance and enforcement

Democratization has improved the political prospects of environmental groups and, as they have grown, ecology parties have emerged. However, they are handicapped in their ability to influence policy by the persistence of limitations that often reflect incomplete democratic consolidation in Latin America and the Caribbean (see Chapter 4). Among the political, legal and administrative constraints that shape and can limit the implementation of environmental policies are the following:

- *Restrictions on representation and obstacles to participation.* Formal aspects of the political process in some Latin American countries – from electoral laws and the legal thresholds of support that parties must reach in order to register for elections, to censorship of the press – limit the efforts of environmental groups to ensure their concerns get on to the policy agenda (see Chapters 4, 5). The inability of mainstream political parties and party systems to represent large sectors of the population has also been a barrier to full democracy. In Ecuador, indigenous groups have found it more effective to articulate

environmental concerns through the national Confederación de nacionalidades indígenas del Ecuador (CONAIE, Confederation of Indigenous
Nationalities of Ecuador) than through mainstream parties.

- *Co-option*. Governments have long co-opted their opponents and
  critics in order to defuse the political threat they pose, and this creates
  a serious problem for environmental organizations. Co-option – the
  process of absorbing actors into policymaking structures to neutralize
  them as a threat – has not disappeared with democratization, which
  has extended new opportunities to become involved in politics to
  previously marginalized interests. In resource-rich countries, politics
  is oiled by the distribution of patronage, whereby political leaders
  can manipulate natural resource policies to reward allies. Corporatist
  models of representation that bring into policymaking the most well
  organized sectors of society also have deep roots in Latin America and
  the Caribbean. As non-traditional actors in policymaking, environmental groups may be particularly susceptible to overtures that offer
  inclusion in government-dominated policy forums. In Mexico, for
  example, many environmental activists were dismayed when leading
  figures opted to join the new administration of Carlos Salinas de
  Gortari in 1989 (see Chapter 4). However, some ENGOs deliberately
  amend their goals to take advantage of co-optive opportunities.
  Ecuador's most influential ENGO, the Fundación Natura (FN, Nature
  Foundation), has consciously pursued what might be viewed as a
  co-optive alliance with the state in exchange for concrete influence
  over natural-resource policy (Mumme and Korzetz 1997).

- *Inherited policy biases and regulatory capture*. Policy biases inherited
  from authoritarian regimes continue to influence national agendas
  throughout Latin America and the Caribbean. Conservative interests
  and parties are more likely to favour market approaches to environmental protection and democracy naturally gives them a tool to
  limit efforts to reform policy. Established interests once favoured by
  authoritarian regimes continue to exert considerable influence within
  conservative parties throughout Latin America. In Brazil, for example,
  influential military leaders with strong connections to parties on
  the right continue to express reservations about conservation in
  Amazonia. Government actions are sometimes also determined by
  regulatory capture when powerful corporate interests wield undue
  influence over regulators, especially in extractive sectors such as
  mining or oil (see above). A government's failure to stand up to
  business interests can stoke social conflict. In Honduras, there have
  been recurrent disputes over forestry policy between farmers seeking

to protect water sources and public authorities that have turned a blind eye to destructive illegal practices by timber concessions. At the same time, a "green business lobby" itself is developing in Latin America to represent companies taking advantage of new opportunities in eco-tourism, organic food, recycling and sustainable forestry production (see Volume 1).

- **Legal formalism and administrative backwardness**. Until recently, the enactment of legislation for symbolic reasons or a failure to implement laws has been a feature of Latin American and Caribbean environmental law. Legislation can create the appearance of responsiveness that enables unaccountable officials to deflect criticism while keeping control over policy implementation. A legacy of bureaucratism, institutional fragmentation and the inappropriate allocation of environmental responsibilities to sectoral ministries can mean green issues get lost in the system. Embedding environmental responsibilities in the work of strong ministries can increase the bureaucratic obstacles to policy implementation because green issues then have to compete with a ministry's main priorities.

- **Limited access to information**. Administrative obstacles to environmental policymaking are made worse by inadequate information about the environment. Throughout Latin America, government information is not disseminated or easily accessed by citizens or groups and often a bureaucratic bias persists in granting only privileged interests access to information. However, the right to information has risen up the agenda and freedom of information laws, and in some cases the inclusion of constitutional principles guaranteeing data, have been passed in recent years. However, at the same time, privacy legislation has grown rapidly in Latin America and by 2011 five countries – Argentina, Uruguay, Mexico, Peru and Costa Rica – had enacted laws that also enable authorities to deny access to information.

The degree to which environmental policy is enforced, or to which social sectors comply with it, varies considerably across Latin America and the Caribbean. While countries have developed detailed legal and institutional frameworks aimed at protecting the environment and promoting sustainable development, compliance with and enforcement of these laws and regulations often remains inadequate. Some Latin American countries have established environmental protection agencies modelled on that of the US federal EPA that have become powerful cross-sectoral bodies. Mexico's Procuraduría Federal de Protección al Ambiente (PROFEPA, Federal Environmental

Protection Agency) was created in 1992 to enforce environmental regulations as a by-product of the institutional reforms under the North American Free Trade Agreement (NAFTA) that created new environmental oversight mechanisms (see Chapter 3). Research into the enforcement of Mexican environmental law since the signing of the environmental side agreement to NAFTA has drawn attention to a lack of transparency and public participation in this area of policy, and to the fact that international priorities can lead to a lack of vigorous enforcement (see Behre 2003). Brazil's autonomous Instituto Brasileiro do Meio Ambiente e dos Recursos Naturais Renováveis (IBAMA) is seen as a powerful potential enforcement model for other countries. Other states have opted for weaker or more consensual forms of enforcement, depending on their own institutional traditions and legal and political systems (see, for example, Avina 2011). Environmental framework laws often outline what is forbidden, but not how sanctions will be implemented or by whom, which can inhibit levels of compliance. In Honduras, for example, the general environmental law establishes a comprehensive framework for designing and administering protected areas and stipulates what is forbidden in these, but does not outline mechanisms for implementing these rules.

A key issue of debate has been the indicators that countries develop and use as part of their environmental compliance and enforcement (ECE) regime. In 2004, a World Bank project on ECE indicators in Latin America was piloted in Argentina to ascertain compliance and enforcement indicators for air and water quality and concluded that a systematic approach was lacking (see Di Paola 2004). Enforcement is particularly difficult if many people are reliant upon illegal activities, such as gold panning in rivers, for their livelihoods. Where the rule of law is fragile, limited enforcement can again penalize vulnerable sectors of society that already have limited political and legal recourse (see Johnston 2011b). Few Latin American environmental groups have the resources to pursue legal action, and judicial processes sometimes do not recognize environmental associations as legal entities. Evidential "burden-of-proof" requirements, especially in cases where pollution may have multiple sources, create serious obstacles for plaintiffs (Mumme and Korzetz 1997).

International laws may not always be enforceable in Latin America and the Caribbean, may not specify an enforcement mechanism or may rely on voluntary targets that lack sanctions and effective monitoring systems. Moreover, some developing nations do not consider themselves bound by all international laws. Critics of Brazil, for example, argue that it inflamed tensions over dam projects on the Madeira River by ignoring transborder dispute-resolution mechanisms (see Clemons 2009). Yet there are also examples in which an international or regional body has ruled against a national state on environmental matters and obliged it to change its law. An instrument of particular importance is the American Convention on Human Rights, which is interpreted by the Inter-American Court of Human Rights. In 2001, for example, the Mayagna (Sumo) Awas Tingni indigenous community located on the Atlantic Coast of Nicaragua took their government to the Inter-American Court of Human Rights in a dispute over road construction. The court ruled that the Nicaraguan state had violated the community's rights to judicial protection and property and ordered restitution.

Institutions are more likely to be able to hold corporations to account in countries with developed legal frameworks and if they have independent enforcement institutions, a receptive judiciary and an active civil society. In Brazil, for example, the Ministério Público (interior ministry) has played a key role in promoting compliance with and enforcement of environmental regulations in the country (see Mueller 2009; Eltz et al. 2010). Throughout Latin America and the Caribbean, court decisions have generated a body of legal enforcement precedents, and there are many examples of judges ruling against polluters or using the precautionary principle to prevent environmental degradation. Organizations such as ECOLEX, a global environmental law database operated jointly by the FAO, IUCN and UNEP, offer a significant resource (see websites below). The National Law Center for Inter-American Free Trade at the University of Arizona in Tucson has also developed a database of laws, regulations and source materials for countries in the Americas. Governments are showing signs of being more willing to enforce regulations against large corporations extracting natural resources. In February 2011, for example, a court in Ecuador ordered the US oil company Chevron to pay $8.6 bn for pollution caused in the Amazon since the 1960s.

However, environmental enforcement agencies can be as vulnerable to political interference as other institutions. In Brazil, in 2011, for example, the president of IBAMA, Abelardo Bayma Azevedo, resigned amid pressures from the energy ministry to give final approval for construction to begin on the huge hydroelectric dam at Belo Monte in the rainforest. His departure removed any obstacles to the approval needed for the project to move forward (see Messenger 2011; Box 5.2). In 2012, Brazilian federal judges ordered the immediate suspension of work on the dam after ruling that indigenous communities should have had the right to comment on its environmental impact.

Conclusion

Although today environmental issues are routinely taken into account in development policies, green policies have generally been insufficient to halt ecological destruction in the region. This is, first, because policy-makers do not generally call into question economic models based on the export of raw materials and the pressure these place on natural resources; and, second, because the benefits of conserving ecosystems and the services they offer have not been formally included in the costs of production, that is, they have not been "internalized". Yet, in Latin America and the Caribbean conflicts that have environmental implications are multiplying – sometimes escalating into violence – and are likely to require ever greater state interventions. The impact of development on the environment is often so serious that states lack sufficient regulatory and administrative capacity to address it. Although in principle Latin American and Caribbean countries have access to the same environmental policymaking tools available throughout the world, distinctive political, legal and administrative constraints limit what they can do in practice. Democracies that are not yet fully consolidated, and exaggerated presidentialism, have meant that powerful producer interests retain privileged access to – and environmentalists are often unable to influence – those that make and shape policy. In some countries environmental activists can be further limited by aspects of the political process itself – such as press censorship or clientelism – which can work against policies aimed at the public good. Policy biases inherited from authoritarian regimes can also be exacerbated by regulatory capture, especially where institutions are weak and the state's autonomy to act remains restricted, as well as a consensus that economic growth takes priority over sustainability. Less formal factors such as ideas and norms, as well as a generalized lack of information about environmental problems among the public, can also limit effective policymaking. Moreover, while Latin America and the Caribbean has often occupied a prominent position in international efforts to improve policy enforcement and compliance, this varies considerably across the region. Given the limitations of their states, some of the international laws that Latin American and Caribbean politicians have embraced so publicly may simply not be enforceable or may rely on voluntary targets without meaningful sanctions. Even where legislatures have enthusiastically passed environmental laws that enjoy public support, there are examples of these being subsequently blocked or delayed by presidents prepared to heed powerful economic interests at home and abroad. Although courts are showing signs of taking a more proactive role in the interpretation and shaping of environmental policy, their independence is not always guaranteed, and environmental enforcement agencies can also be vulnerable to political interference. Research on all these phenomena as part of the study of public policy in Latin America and the Caribbean more generally remains in its infancy, and it has only been in recent years that scholars have begun to apply to the region theories and models from the developed world in a meaningful way.

Recommended reading

Dessler, Andrew E and Edward A Parson. 2006. *The Science and Politics of Global Climate Change: A Guide to the Debate*. Cambridge: Cambridge University Press.

Díez, Jordi and Francheschet, Susan (eds). 2012. *Comparative Public Policy in Latin America*. London: University of Toronto Press.

Steinberg, Paul F. 2003. "Understanding Policy Change in Developing Countries: The Spheres of Influence Framework", in *Global Environmental Politics*, Vol. 3, No. 1 (February), pp. 11–31.

Tecklin, David, Carl Bauer and Manuel Prieto. 2011. "Making Environmental Law for the Market: The Emergence, Character, and Implications of Chile's Environmental Regime", *Environmental Politics*, Vol. 20, No. 6 (November), pp. 879–98.

Useful websites

Brazilian Wind Energy Association: www.abeeolica.org.br

Charles Darwin Foundation and Galápagos National Park: www.hear.org/galapagos/invasoras/temas/manejo/marina/index.html

Chilean Renewable Energies Association: www.acera.cl/v2/

Conselho Empresarial Brasileiro para o Desenvolvimento Sustentável (CEBDS, Brazilian Business Centre for Sustainable Development): www.cebds.org.br/

Earth System Governance Project: www.ieg.earthsystemgovernance.org/

ECOLEX database on environmental law (FAO, IUCN and UNEP): www.ecolex.org

Fundación Ambiente y Recursos Naturales (FARN, Environment and Natural Resources Foundation), Argentina: www.farn.org.ar

Global Solar Thermal Energy Council: www.solarthermalworld.org/

Global Water Partnership, Integrated Water Resources Management (IWRM): www.gwp.org/en/The-Challenge/What-is-IWRM/

Global Wind Energy Council: www.gwec.net/

Instituto Brasileiro do Meio Ambiente e dos Recursos Naturais Renováveis (IBAMA, Institute of the Environment and Natural Renewable Resources), Brazil: www.ibama.gov.br/

Instituto Ethos de Empresas e Responsabilidade Social, Brazil: www1.ethos.org.br/EthosWeb/Default.aspx

Mexican wind energy association: www.amdee.org

National Law Center for Inter-American Free Trade at the University of Arizona in Tucson database of laws, regulations and secondary source materials for countries in the Americas: www.natlaw.com

Procuraduría Federal de Protección al Ambiente (PROFEPA, Federal Environmental Protection Agency), Mexico: www.profepa.gob.mx

REDD-monitor.org: www.redd-monitor.org/tag/cdm/

UN Millennium Development Goals update, "Goal 7: Ensure Environmental Sustainability": www.un.org/millenniumgoals/environ.shtml

UNESCO Decade of Education for Sustainable Development 2005–14 http://unesdoc.unesco.org/images/0014/001416/141629e.pdf

CHAPTER THREE

International relations

THE GLOBAL PROFILE assumed by the Amazonian rainforest in debates about climate change is evidence of how some of the most pressing environmental challenges of our era transcend the traditional structures of governance by which relations between states have been organized. It confirms that environmental change can test traditional concepts of sovereignty, and hence the very notion of the nation state, something already placed on notice by economic globalization and the emergence of a comprehensive network of multilateral bodies developing forms of global "governance" that individual states find impossible to ignore. Yet, although there are often common responses in Latin America and the Caribbean to these powerful forces – and although many of the environmental problems faced by countries in the region are similar – there also remain considerable differences in how the environment is dealt with in the foreign relations agenda of each country. This chapter examines how the environment influences Latin American international relations and foreign policymaking. It examines the transboundary nature of many environmental issues and how this poses challenges to good neighbourly relations yet also offers opportunities for unprecedented levels of co-operation. The study of environmental foreign policy is nascent and has attempted to draw upon existing theory in international relations and political economy, but several international factors emerge as having a partic-ularly important role in environmental policymaking in Latin America and the Caribbean, not least trade liberalization and financial flows. Policymaking in the region has responded to the growing body of environmental law thrashed out by multilateral treaties, embracing key global principles such as precaution and sustainable development. Latin America and the Caribbean itself has participated actively in this process, and the region has taken a prominent role in shaping some of the most important environmental treaties of our age.

Key themes

Several key themes in the region's relationship with the outside world have helped to determine both the character of environmental degradation and how environmental governance has developed.

Foreign investment and dependency. Since the Independence era, the relationship between Latin American and Caribbean countries with those outside the region has been shaped by the way natural resources have been exploited for export and the role this has played in the consolidation of states. Foreign investment has been the most influential factor shaping development and its impact continues to be profound. A discussion of export-led development in Latin American and the Caribbean of necessity addresses the rise of capitalism associated with the global expansion of the great powers. Many of the foreign corporations that have developed Latin America's extractive sectors have been based in industrialized countries such as the US, which has exercised power sometimes characterized in terms of imperialism (see Box 3.1). There are many examples of environmental degradation in Latin America and the Caribbean as a result of export booms associated with the activities of foreign interests (see Miller 2007). In Cuba, for example, the expansion of the sugar industry following the establishment of US military rule on the island after 1898 caused rapid destruction of forests in Camagüey. In Nicaragua, the Somoza dynasty pursued uncontrolled development in association with foreign companies that deforested extensive areas. Foreign direct investment (FDI) flows to Latin America and the Caribbean have grown rapidly since the late 1980s and the export of natural resources has risen accordingly. However, discourses encouraging foreign investment have often overlooked its environmental consequences or the limitations of export-led development (Offen 2004). States have competed over which can provide the most favourable conditions for investment, such as low wages and limited environmental restrictions. Industries were often attracted to Latin America because they could pollute, dump wastes and extract resources with minimal state interference. Large US pharmaceutical companies were lured to Puerto Rico in the post-war period, for example, by weaker environmental regulations than in the continental US (see Meyn 1996). Today, mining, oil and financial interests continue to exert significant influence over policies in the region, especially in countries that have explicitly globalized their economies to take advantage of FDI, such as Chile. The power exercised by foreign corporations today is mostly evident in the form of regulatory capture (see Chapters 1, 2). Their activities in sectors such as forestry and mining continue to provoke political struggles, even in stable countries. In Costa Rica, for example, an international forestry, pulp and paper project promoted by the US-based Stone Container Corporation and its local representation Ston Forestal generated significant protests (see Van den Hombergh 2004).

Multilateral agencies. Foreign models are often diffused by multilateral bodies, which have played a significant role both in the development of environmentalism within Latin America and the Caribbean and in how its states have internalized core principles of environmental policymaking. To a large extent, this reflects a global convergence of governance patterns in environmental policymaking (see Kern, Jörgens and Jänicke 2001; Jörgens 2001). Chile's environmental institutions introduced in 2010, for example, are explicitly modelled on what the OECD sees as best practice, reflecting acceptance of principles in environmental law founded in the concept of globalization (see Olivares Gallardo 2010). The acceptance of developed world environmental norms by countries such as Mexico and Chile when they join bodies such as the OECD reinforces governance according to the models, structures and legal systems that underpin globalization. Increasingly, those structures view a lack of rigour in environmental policymaking as an *obstacle* to economic liberalization. Similarly, multilateral action to reduce greenhouse gas emissions has had a significant influence on policymaking since the 1992 Earth Summit in Rio, which established the UNFCCC infrastructure. Latin American and Caribbean countries have been participants in all the subsequent negotiations on multilateral responses to climate change, on other

Box 3.1 Foreign investment and "imperialism"

Production in large sectors of Latin America's economy has recurrently been dominated by foreign corporations, which have gained huge power in the countries in which they have operated. In Venezuela, for example, foreign companies controlled the oil industry until the Second World War (see Wilkins 1998). Into the early twentieth century the corporations of different world powers competed for the allegiance of individual states against their commercial rivals. In Ecuador, in the early years of oil development, for example, British oilmen sometimes competed against US interests with the help of the state. The way in which foreign interests in Latin America have conditioned environmental change has often been interpreted through the notion of "imperialism" or "dependency" (see Volume 1). Imperialism has been hotly debated in political philosophy and in Latin America and the Caribbean leftwing thinkers have often used the term to complement their understanding of dependence. Marxist theories of imperialism argue that it consists mainly in the economic exploitation of one region by another. The term has also been used to describe the behaviour of the US towards its neighbours since the assertion of the Monroe Doctrine in 1823, by which the emergent US claimed the role of a guarantor of sovereign republicanism in the Americas. Interactions between the US and the region have been shaped by asymmetry in military and economic power and a recurrent problem in relations has been the US tendency to act unilaterally from its position of strength. A tendency to intervene in Latin American affairs or indifference towards developments in the region has ensured that relations have often been characterized by confrontation and distrust (see Rivarola Puntigliano 2008). However, recent contributions to debates about imperialism have taken the concept of globalization as the basis for a new, decentred supranational capitalist order in which the US is only one actor alongside transnational corporations. Theories of a "new imperialism" stress the transnationalization of capital and the role of supranational institutions in imposing capitalist domination upon a vulnerable inter-state system (see, for example, Robinson 2007; Hardt and Negri 2000). In the 1960s and 1970s, many Latin American intellectuals and political leaders also embraced dependency theory to explain underdevelopment. This argument stated that their countries were poor because industrial states appropriated their economic surplus. Some Latin American environmentalists have embraced ideas of "eco-dependency" in which extraction of surplus takes the form of environmental pillage. They argue that transnational corporations earn greater profits in the region than in the industrialized world because they are free to ravage the environment (Dore 1996a).

protocols such as the Montreal Protocol, and in the Doha negotiations on trade and environment (WTO/UNEP 2009). The region's participation in these initiatives is an inevitable consequence of the emergence of a system of international environmental management since the 1970s (see Ivanova 2010). Foreign governments and multilateral agencies have also shaped economic norms in the region in ways that have had damaging ecological consequences. In the 1980s, for example, "neoliberal" reforms became an article of faith among lending agencies with significant environmental implications (see Volume 1). Under pressure to comply with macroeconomic conditions imposed by multilateral banks, Latin American governments pursued strategies that damaged the environment (see Dore 1996a).

National integration and socio-political change. Foreign capital has shaped the administrative development of states in Latin America and the Caribbean through an alliance with local elites that has excluded popular classes from politics. Since the nineteenth century, elites have seen foreign investment as a prerequisite both of economic progress and the incorporation of territory under state control. A reflection of this have been the persistent territorial struggles between nation states and indigenous people, often over access to natural resources. Elite discourses have stressed that the need to exploit resources rationally within a global market is essential for the development of modern nation states and the integration of marginal sectors of society within these – "national integration" (see Chapter 5). In areas such as the Mosquitia of eastern Nicaragua, for example, the weak Nicaraguan state's imperative to "incorporate" the area during the nineteenth century depended on significant investment by foreigners, while discourses meant to encourage this foreign investment overlooked the environmental limitations of the export economy (Offen 2004). Today, similar ambitions are frequently expressed by politicians who disregard questions of sustainability. Foreign consumption habits have also influenced how the state has organized production and export and industrial policies, with consequences for the environment. US consumer demand for coffee, for example, was key to ecological transformation in late nineteenth-century Brazil, and demand for beef had significant consequences in northern Mexico. US car makers such as Ford and GM created consumer demand for cars in Latin America, lobbied for government-funded road building, and established the first car, tyre and road-building companies.

Key themes in international relations

Any discussion of the foreign policies of Latin American and Caribbean states cannot begin without acknowledging the traditional importance of the US. Relations between states in the region for most of the twentieth century were conducted under the umbrella of US predominance. A key factor in the recent evolution of those relations was the Cold War, which limited the ability of Latin American states to act autonomously in international arenas. The end of the Cold War and democratization greatly expanded the opportunities open to countries to co-operate, and since the 1990s key themes steering foreign policymaking in the region have been autonomy, integration and globalization, often enshrined through membership of supranational bodies such as the World Trade Organization. Since 2000, US influence in the region has declined and the creation in 2010 of the Comunidad de Estados Latinoamericanos y Caribeños (CELAC), which excludes the US and Canada, is a potent symbol of this. Enhanced activity by multilateral institutions, non-state actors and transnational corporations, social movements and NGOs have further complicated a picture of relationships traditionally based on sovereign nation states. Options available in foreign relations are also shaped by differences between individual countries and sub-regions such as the Andes and the Southern Cone. The effects of globalization have been uneven and processes of regional integration are widening differences, suggesting each country will pursue its own interests as it seeks greater insertion in the world economy. For example, Ecuador, Costa Rica and other Central American nations joined forces with the US banana industry in a lawsuit at the WTO that had important repercussions for the industry in the Caribbean. An international system characterized by globalization has consequences for policy: economic integration means domestic decisions have *international* implications and the international community can modify domestic policies (see Hochstetler and Keck 2007). Links between domestic and foreign policy have prompted some scholars to develop a notion of "intermestic" issues that affect both foreign and domestic policy.

A central question in globalization research is whether it leads to the convergence of political institutions, policies, the legal order and societal structures, or whether domestic responses to global challenges will continue to be determined by existing national structures (see, for example, Guillén 2001; Meyer et al. 1997; Barrios, Görg and Strobl 2003; Knill 2001; Kahler and Lake 2003). Research suggests that the diffusion of environmental policy innovations across borders occurs regularly (see, for example, Busch, Jörgens and Tews 2005). Competition theory is also divided over whether globalization drives regulatory or environmental standards up or down (see Oates and Schwab 1988; Vogel 1995). An analysis of 24 OECD countries found that there is a trend of convergence in environmental policies and towards stronger regulation (see Holzinger, Knill, and Sommerer 2011). Nonetheless, the nation state continues to structure global environmental policy, although globalization is testing existing concepts of national identity (see Trittin 2004).

Although many of the problems faced by Latin American and Caribbean countries are similar, there are considerable differences in how the environment is dealt with in their foreign relations agendas. The Durban summit in 2011 and the Rio+20 summit in 2012 offered examples of how governments approached the same issue from different perspectives. Brazil was at the heart of the so-called Basic group – comprising Brazil, South Africa, India and China – that criticized the timetable for the establishment of mechanisms for proceeding with emission-reduction targets after 2012. Members of the Alianza Bolivariana para los Pueblos de Nuestra América (Alba, Bolivarian Alliance for the Peoples of Latin America) criticized the developed world for not living up to its promises on climate reduction funding. Colombia and Guatemala put forward their own proposal for reform that stressed the need to combat poverty, change consumption patterns and enhance energy security.

Key themes in the analysis of Latin American international relations that have an important bearing on understanding how the environment influences foreign policy include the following:

Sovereignty. Globalization is changing traditional understandings of sovereignty that reject outside interference in the domestic affairs of a nation state. This view has long been a defining characteristic of foreign relations in Latin America and the Caribbean and was enshrined in Article 18 of the Charter of the Organization of American States (OAS). However, the impact of globalization is making the concept of sovereignty relative: economic interdependence, the extension of the discourse of human rights, the desire for legitimacy in international arenas, the emergence of transnational corporations, NGOs and social movements and shared concerns about our planet have all tested the traditional position once cherished by nation states. The evolution of a complex structure of international treaties, institutions and laws also requires nation states to concede authority to supra-national bodies. Political scientists have debated the implications for the nation state of global environmental change (see Box 3.2). This is likely to transform politics in Latin America: for example, the erosion of national sovereignty can take power even further away from communities and indigenous peoples, whom many environmentalists argue should be at the centre of sustainable development initiatives.

It has also been argued, for example, that the global importance of the Amazonian rainforest and biodiversity makes necessary the active intervention of industrialized countries to stop Brazilians from carrying out policies they deem to be destructive, such as deforestation (see Fearnside 2000; Hall 2000). The determination of governments in the region to defend sovereignty has been a bone of contention in environmental diplomacy: Brazil has at times resisted international pressures over Amazon deforestation, explicitly on the grounds that what it does there is a sovereign affair.

Latin American countries are also often hostile to suggestions about how they exploit their resources, helping to explain why multilateral environmental agreements (MEAs) rarely include sanctions. However, in contemporary international law, the concept of absolute territorial sovereignty is no longer recognized and relations are more likely to be determined by such notions as "good neighbourliness" (see Mendis 2007). While states could once use resources freely, it is now accepted that a state cannot alter the natural conditions of its own territory to the detriment of a neighbour. International law thereby places on states a duty to consult and negotiate. A distinction has sometimes also been drawn between the obligations a state has towards the international community as a whole and those arising vis-à-vis another state. Global environmental problems such as the loss of biodiversity, the pollution of international waters, and climate change were identified as the common concern of mankind in the 1992 UNFCCC and Convention on Biodiversity, implying that states have a duty towards the international community to uphold them (see Mendis 2007).

Box 3.2 Environmental change and the nation state

The concept of the nation state has been inherited from the nineteenth century and has been increasingly challenged by international institutions and forms of global governance. While these do not threaten the continued existence of nation states, they limit their capacity to act in isolation. This challenges established notions of sovereignty and tests the methodological norms of disciplines such as international relations in which the nation state is the building block of the inter-state system. Global environmental change adds considerably to the challenges facing the nation state. Biermann and Dingwerth (2004) argue that global environmental change challenges the nation state in two ways: first, it adds to stresses on nation states by increasing the demand for adaptive and mitigative activities that reduce their resources and hence their administrative, organizational and technological capacity. This diminishes a state's ability to fulfil basic functions such as guaranteeing security, protecting civil rights and ensuring political participation, stretching the capacities of developing countries in particular. Second, the transboundary nature of global environmental change reduces the ability of nation states to act without the co-operation of other states and/or non-state actors – businesses, NGOs and the scientific community – which have assumed an increasingly prominent role in transnational environmental politics. Even powerful states cannot ignore the transboundary nature of ecological issues and global environmental change creates new forms of interdependence because of the shared impact of phenomena such as climate change. Nation states still try to act unilaterally and through international treaties, but policy diffusion (see above) and the influence of international treaties increasingly means that national environmental policies are becoming globalized, fostering global environmental governance. New legal approaches are being developed to constrain the behaviour of nation states on the basis that environmental threats are a common concern of humankind. The role of the nation state is now being conceived of as a public trusteeship whereby public trust may be transferred from a national to a global level (see Sand 2004). Environmental governance is becoming "collaborative" and "post-sovereign" and Karkkainen (2004) argues it has three distinguishing characteristics: it is "non-exclusive", "non-hierarchical" and "post-territorial".

Multilateralism. In the 1990s, following the end of the Cold War, there was a global shift in favour of multilateralism, an approach to issues in which states collaborate based on shared interests. Domínguez (2000) identified several types of multilateral activity in Latin America and the Caribbean: commercial multilateralism, which refers to the growth in intra-regional trade agreements; political multilateralism, which refers to shared support for democratization and human rights (see Van Klaveren 2001); and security multilateralism, which refers to growing co-operation on issues of security. To these forms of multilateral co-operation can today be added the notion of *environmental multilateralism* – the extension since the 1970s of international environmental agreements to which Latin American states subscribe. Growing interdependence between states is generating rules that respond to what the region considers its international environmental responsibilities.

International environmental co-operation can be hard to achieve because the global system is fragmented and it is difficult to co-ordinate policy or enforce compliance with agreements (Carter 2007). It has also been hampered by the pressure wielded in powerful states such as the US by strong economic interests resisting change, such as the oil industry. The nature of environmental issues themselves also determines the progress that can be made: it may be easier to agree on protecting "common-pool" resources, such as fisheries stocks which provide a source of concrete benefits to those who have use of them, than "common-sink" resources, such as clean air, which are affected by the extent to which individual actors make use of them to dispose of waste (see Carter 2007). However, since 1973 there has been agreement on a number of international environmental treaties, support for about 200 MEAs, and the creation of institutional structures to monitor, enforce and strengthen these. At the Latin American and Caribbean regional or bilateral levels, about 1,000 environmental agreements have entered into force, constituting a large body of law (see UNEP/IISD 2005). This has been made possible by rising multilateral attention to Latin America's environmental priorities by mechanisms such as the Global Environment Facility (GEF), a fund administered by the World Bank, UNEP and UNDP. Latin America and the Caribbean has played an important role in the negotiation of MEAs and in all of the major environmental agreements and amendments negotiated between 1985 and 1995, states in the region have influenced outcomes. They have been key players behind agreements and institutions dealing with ozone depletion, hazardous waste, climate change and biodiversity.

Regionalism and integration. Regional integration is a cherished aspiration of Latin American political elites and is an important theme in local relations. A first wave of integration initiatives began in the 1960s as an effort to boost industrialization but by the mid-1970s these had lost momentum. With the end of the Cold War a new spirit of continentalism was evident and its latest manifestations are the creation of CELAC and, most recently, the Pacific Alliance (Alianza del Pacífico) aiming to create a free trade zone, oriented towards Asia, between Chile, Colombia, Mexico and Peru. Trade has driven integration, but the desire for greater influence in a multipolar world has also become key to this process, and large infrastructure and media projects that transcend national borders are also driving intra-regional co-operation, with major consequences for the environment. In 2000, for example, the Initiative for the Integration of the Regional Infrastructure of South America (IIRSA) was launched with the participation of the 12 countries that form the Union of South American Nations (UNASUR). Killeen (2007) studied IIRSA proposals and argued that they could have far-reaching environmental consequences.

Natural resources and security. Multilateralism has eased military competition and bilateral strains in Latin America and the Caribbean, although territorial and maritime border tensions have not disappeared and there are disputes over natural resources. In 2005, for example, Costa Rica filed a lawsuit against Nicaragua at the International Court of Justice (ICJ) in a dispute over who should control the San Juan river, and in the same year Peru and Chile squabbled over fishing rights in the Pacific. A recent source of tension has been energy, and in particular the need for countries to secure stable supplies. Energy resources are not distributed evenly: some countries have significant resources and six states in the region are oil exporters while others, such as Chile, have meagre reserves and are net importers. Bolivia and Peru are important sources of natural gas, a resource that has had a significant influence on Bolivia's political development in recent years. Brazil is a major producer of hydropower from dams, and has had success diversifying energy supplies through biofuels. But even energy diversification is no guarantee against blackouts: in 2009, for example, Ecuador rationed electricity after a drought caused water shortages at the country's main hydroelectric plant. Blackouts are not uncommon and major power shortages in several Latin American countries in 2009 increased concerns that the region faces a serious energy crisis. Recognition that energy policy is a potential source of tension promoted the Inter-American Development Bank to establish a programme promoting collaboration on energy policy in the Americas.

The transboundary nature of environmental issues. Environmental problems do not respect national frontiers and threats to endangered wildlife, natural habitats and marine life are usually transboundary issues, meaning conservation strategies must emphasize co-operation. In June 2013, for example, the Brazilian government mobilized its navy after oil from a damaged pipeline in Ecuador leaked into the River Coca, passed through the Peruvian Amazon region of Loreto, and threatened to head downstream towards the Brazilian Amazon. Problems that may once have been considered sub-regional – such as deforestation, desertification and water shortages – are now seen as international. This can complicate the ability to protect some areas, as illustrated by the case of forestry (see Humphreys 2006). Conservationists have identified "bioinvasion" – in which species responding to ecosystem changes migrate into new areas and thereby threaten established species – as a key transboundary issue. Globalization and global warming are increasing the likelihood of bioinvasion and Stoett (2007) argues that this poses a considerable challenge to global environmental governance structures, which generally lack legal authority and policy co-ordination mechanisms. Despite the transborder nature of this issue and the existence of multilateral organizations studying it, the main preventive measure remains border control, which is administered at a national level (see also Bright 1999; Van Driesche and Van Driesche 2000).

The cross-border nature of environmental issues in Latin America is also reflected in the creation of transboundary protected areas. These are examples of a contemporary challenge to the notion of sovereignty, demand new forms of co-operation, and can even help in resolving disputes. There are now at least 29 transboundary protected areas in Central and South America, six that involve three countries

(Sandwith et al. 2001). Transnational protected areas offer important environmental benefits: a larger area better safeguards biodiversity; and they allow for economies of scale and so can be cheaper to manage, allowing better control of hazards such as wildfires (see Sandwith et al. 2001). They can also offer concrete political benefits: since 1997, the IUCN has promoted a "Parks for Peace" initiative to enhance regional co-operation. Sub-regions such as Central America have explicitly used cross-border co-operation of this kind in reconciliation efforts following periods of tension.

The transnational environmental movement. International ENGOs have played an important role in the policy response of governments in Latin America and the Caribbean to the environmental agenda, and have extended their activities throughout the region (see Chapter 5; Kaimowitz 1996). Following the 1972 Stockholm Conference, northern environmental movements began to press governments and international agencies to support progressive policies in Latin America and the Caribbean. Activism provoked by the construction of large dams in Brazil nurtured the emergence of one of the first movements involving both local and international groups (see McCormick 2007; Srinivas 2001). Forest destruction in the Amazon also helped to make tropical deforestation a major theme on the agenda of ENGOs in developed countries since the 1980s. The work of multilateral agencies has provided the focus for global co-ordination among ENGOs. In 1995, UNEP's governing council began to give NGOs input into project design, implementation and evaluation through the United Nations Non-Governmental Liaison Service (UN-NGLS).

Prominent international NGOs working in Latin America or financing the activities of local environmental organizations include Conservation International, the Nature Conservancy, the IUCN and the World Wildlife Fund. Voluntary organizations such as Greenpeace and the World Resources Institute (WRI) promote natural resource projects and provide technical help to Latin American ENGOs. Northern ENGOs have also broadened their focus from conservation to themes such as economic development and governance (see also Chapter 5). Some of these organizations employ full-time lobbyists to influence politicians. Lobbying enabled environmental organizations to convince the US government to negotiate an environmental side agreement to the North American Free Trade Agreement (NAFTA), for example (see Box 5.6). A regional environmental movement has also emerged in Latin America since 1989 with the establishment in Brazil of Vitae Civilis (the Vitae Civilis Institute for Development, Environment and Peace) and in 1990 of the Fórum Brasileiro de ONGs e Movimentos Sociais para o Meio Ambiente e o Desenvolvimento (FBOMS, Brazilian Forum of NGOs and Social Movements for the Environment and the Development) to give social movements a voice at the 1992 Rio summit. In 2011, about 60 organizations participated in the Forum's meeting. Similar organizations exist at an international level such as the Stakeholder Forum and the Northern Alliance for Sustainability (ANPED). Alongside ENGOs, the transnational indigenous movement that has developed in Latin America has had considerable influence in environmental policymaking (see Chapter 5; Tilley 2002).

Policy options

The study of environmental foreign policy is nascent and has attempted to draw upon existing theory in international relations and political economy, in which perspectives are often developed in terms of realism and institutionalism.

Realist arguments assume the existence of an international arena without order characterized by inter-state conflict and the self-interested pursuit of power by sovereign nation states (Tulchin and Espach 2001). In the absence of a framework within which this pursuit of power can be managed – such as that provided by the Cold War rivalry between the US and Soviet Union – the world is dangerous, and where international institutions exist it is because dominant parties believe they are useful. In these terms, the environment is primarily an issue of *security*, and a key threat to it arises from conflicts over resources. Climate change will exacerbate these conflicts and create environmental refugees, threatening further insecurity.

Institutionalist approaches hold that a country's influence is partly determined by its involvement in international institutions. Such perspectives point to growing interdependence and shared interests and values among states. Power is "soft" – defined not by military might but by economic competitiveness, skills, and the ability to exert influence. International institutions benefit less powerful states in two ways: they offer them a more equal forum for the pursuit of their interests, enabling them to enhance their relative influence; and they restrain powerful countries from acting unilaterally. Environmental regimes – the regulations, conventions and structures created by treaties and agreements to enforce environmental rules – may enhance the capacity of weaker states and strengthen their sovereignty by transferring finance and technologies to them. Institutionalist approaches are usually seen as offering the most plausible way of assessing Latin American policy options in the context of globalization (see Tulchin and Espach 2001). The rise of multilateralism, changing attitudes to sovereignty and a strong impetus towards regionalism combine with the essentially transboundary nature of environmental problems in Latin America and the Caribbean to further strengthen the institutionalist perspective.

Literature on international environmental politics often addresses how states co-operate in managing common problems, the impact of global political economy on the environment, and how treaties are made. Nonetheless, the policies and actions of individual states shape these processes and determine the success of treaties, etc. This means that to understand international environmental politics it is often necessary to look at *national* foreign policies and policy processes. Barkdull and Harris (2002) have argued that existing theories and approaches to foreign policy and international relations can be of value in exploring how it is formulated. They argue that the first step is to consider why a state adopts a particular policy orientation on international environmental concerns.

A number of international factors influence and constrain environmental policymaking in Latin America and the Caribbean:

Economic liberalization. Economic reforms promoting foreign trade and investment have meant that corporations play a significant role in determining environmental quality. Critics of neoliberalism have argued that corporations search out countries with weak environmental regulations in which to invest in order to reduce production costs. However, multinational corporations have often adopted better environmental practices and transferred cleaner technologies to Latin American countries, and it is often smaller local firms that employ inefficient processes. Governments have not created the incentives for these companies to use raw materials and energy less wastefully. Export markets can strengthen industries based on the extraction of resources whose production methods are damaging to the environment. In Chile, for example, commercial plantation forestry, which has enabled large local timber and paper groups to emerge, has been criticized for damaging both native forests and biodiversity while weakening efforts to strengthen conservation measures in forest management law (see Silva 1997). However, export markets can also increase the competitive pressure on local industry to find more efficient, and hence cleaner, production methods. As export markets demand better environmental performance of them, the sectors of industry that cater to these will be obliged to modernize production and improve environmental management (MacDonald and Stern 1997).

Globalization. Latin America's economic dependence has weakened as it has grown as an exporter of primary commodities in a multipolar world market characterized by the diversification of trade and investment relations. Rising demand for commodities has buoyed export earnings, and countries from the region are taking a more prominent role in international financial institutions such as the G20 and IMF (Baud, de Castro and Hogenboom 2011). The main driver of economic globalization – and associated environmental change – has been the growth in international trade (UNEP/IISD 2005). Globalization is a contested idea and its impact on the environment is similarly disputed. Economic liberals argue that it is beneficial because, by increasing overall global wealth, it will fund environmental improvements. Critics suggest that, by fuelling rapid economic growth, globalization is responsible for over-consumption and creates waste. In developing regions such as Latin America and the Caribbean, it reinforces the move towards intensive agriculture for export to supply northern markets, with a consequent impact on soil erosion and ecosystems (Carter 2007). Moreover, globalization may be nurturing new forms of economic dependency. China's increasing engagement with Latin America in recent decades, for example, has increased the region's specialization in primary products (see Jenkins 2010). The alpaca offers an example of the impact globalization can have on a country's natural resources (see Box 3.3). A compromise between critics and supporters of globalization would recognize that it will have detrimental impacts but that environmental problems can be tackled through the institutions of global environmental governance.

Box 3.3 Alpacas and globalization

Peru's alpaca herders, or *alpaqueros*, raise their animals in one of the world's most isolated regions on the grasslands of the Andean plateau at altitudes above 3,500 m. The country has 4.5 m head of alpaca out of an estimated global total of 6.5 m, and neighbouring Bolivia is also a large alpaca producer with about 1 m head, making it a regional competitor. Alpacas are the main source of income for about 120,000 families in the highlands of Peru, Bolivia and, to a lesser extent, Chile. Their fine fleece fetches high prices on world markets and Peru's annual production of about 6,500 tonnes of alpaca fibre earns the country about $50 m in export income. Intermediaries tend to purchase by weight and offer no premium for quality, meaning that herders have no incentive to produce higher quality fibre at a time when international markets favour fine, light fibres such as mohair and cashmere. This has led to a steady decline in the quality and value of Peru's alpaca fibre and has favoured new alpaca farms in Australia, New Zealand and – alarmingly for Peru – now even China. These countries are emerging as strong competitors through their own breeding programmes, processing technology, quality standards and investment in research. The main purchaser of Peru's alpaca fibre, China, began importing alpacas to create a domestic fibre industry. Fibre from Australian-born alpacas raised in farms in Shanxi province is already being used in the rapidly growing Chinese fashion sector. In 2004, Australian producers exported alpacas to collective farms in Qinghe as part of a project by the Xinjiang regional government to provide local people with a source of income. Australia's alpaca producers are also exporting fibre and woven products to the Chinese market. A major problem facing Peru is that there is limited scope to expand alpaca production in the Andes, due to lack of grazing land. Herds in the US, Canada and Australasia are expanding rapidly. In 2011, the issue of alpaca smuggling from Peru was raised by the organization Proyecto Especial Camélidos Sudamericanos (PECSA, South American Camelids Special Project). The organization said there was evidence that at least 2,000 thoroughbred alpacas had been smuggled out of the country via Bolivia and Chile for onward export to Australia, Canada, the US and China.

Aid and multilateral development banks. Development aid from countries and regional bodies has played a key role in supporting environmental initiatives in Latin America and the Caribbean and has influenced environmental policymaking. In 2011, members of the OECD provided $133.5 bn of official development assistance (ODA) globally, representing 0.31 per cent of their combined gross national income (OECD 2012). The European Union has provided significant levels of aid and technical assistance to Latin America and the Caribbean to support environmental initiatives (see EU-LAC 2008). Individual countries also support many environmental initiatives in Latin America. The UK, for example, has made several environmental aid commitments to Ecuador under its Darwin Initiative.

After the 1972 Stockholm Conference, international aid programmes were slow to incorporate environmental considerations, but a new consensus developed with the 1987 publication of the World Commission on Environment and Development's report, *Our Common Future*, that embraced the concept of sustainable development (Brundtland et al. 1987). This made new assistance available for projects aimed at transforming development strategies. In 2002, the International Conference on Financing for Development held in Mexico agreed the so-called Monterrey Consensus – a partnership between developed and developing countries to find ways of financing efforts to meet the Millennium Development Goals (see UN 2003). To date, multilateral development banks (MDBs) have been the principal source of environmental aid in Latin America and the Caribbean and have provided support for infrastructure such as water supply, sewerage, air-quality improvements and solid-waste disposal projects. Latin America and the Caribbean has been one of the main beneficiaries of MDB lending globally, and agencies routinely apply environmental criteria in their appraisal of projects. The region also enjoys the most comprehensive network of regional multilateral banks in the developing world: the Inter-American Development Bank (IDB), the Andean Development Corporation (ADC), the Central American Bank for Economic Integration (CABEI), the Caribbean Development Bank (CDB) and the Latin American Reserve Fund, all of which promote sustainable development. Concessionary international multilateral funds, such as the Global Environment Facility (GEF) and the Montreal Protocol Multilateral Fund are also distributed in the region. A key form of multilateral

Box 3.4 The small grants programme (SGP) in Peru

The small grants programme (SGP) is funded by the Global Environment Facility (GEF) and implemented by the UNDP, and its activity in Peru – where projects are the most diverse in the entire programme – has been seen as a success story. Since 1998, when it was launched, SGP Peru has financed 214 projects worth $6.6 m. It currently has projects in 23 regions of the country related to the conservation of forests; the sustainable use of medicinal plants; the sustainable management of wetlands; biodiversity protection; the recovery of traditional knowledge; eco-tourism; and coastal marine ecosystems. The programme is aimed at helping poor communities protect their natural resources at a local level as part of the overall aims of the Millennium Development Goals and is supported by the country's Ministerio del Ambiente (Environment Ministry). Direct funding of this kind aims to avoid resources being wasted on bureaucracy, and to give communities the opportunity to control their own development. The local focus and the effort to sidestep bureaucratic intermediaries are considered by experts to be the programme's principal strengths.

funding for biodiversity projects has come though the UNDP's small grants programme, which has had considerable success in countries such as Peru (see Box 3.4).

Increasingly, companies developing clean technology have turned to multilateral initiatives such as the GEF for funds and credit lines. Financing for environmentally friendly projects – "green financing" – is also being provided by private equity funds operating in the region (see Volume 1). The Montreal Protocol Multilateral Fund has backed efforts to promote industrial technology substitution for environmental purposes in Latin America, and the Kyoto Protocol's CDM encourages private-sector involvement in energy-efficiency projects.

However, most multilateral funding has tended to target "brown" urban pollution problems and health issues at the expense of "green" natural resource conservation projects (see Nielson and Stern 1997). Political factors also influence how countries borrow funds and what they use these for. In borrowing countries where electoral rewards for direct spending are greatest, the proportion of brown-to-green (environmental infrastructure versus conservation) projects should be greater (Nielson and Stern 1997). This is because where political systems and electoral rules reward the construction of narrow rather than broad coalitions politicians are likely to prefer projects that enable them to funnel scarce resources to their political clients. But where national parties are strong, they favour policies that reward broad coalitions that provide public goods, such as green projects. The larger and more institutionalized a country's environmental movement, the more likely it is that policymakers will pursue environmental borrowing.

Trade and environmental policy

The trend toward globalization has reduced barriers to growing international trade and investment flows. The volume of world trade today is nearly 32 times greater than it was in 1950 (WTO/ UNEP 2009). Trade policy has huge implications for the environment because most economic activity originates in natural inputs (metals and minerals, soil, forests and fisheries). The natural environment provides the energy needed for production and receives the waste products of economic activity. However, the environment and trade represent two distinct bodies of international law, with environmental law embodied in multilateral agreements and as national and sub-national regulations and trade law embodied in such structures as the WTO and regional and bilateral agreements. These are interacting and overlapping: increasingly, international environmental law defines how countries structure economic activities and trade law defines how they design domestic policies in areas such as investment and environmental protection (UNEP/IISD 2005). The impact of trade liberalization on environmental regulation has long been a source of debate (see Box 3.5).

A key feature of trade opening in Latin America has been the proliferation of regional integration initiatives such as NAFTA. Since NAFTA came into force in 1994, countries in the Americas have included environmental provisions in many bilateral and sub-regional trade agreements (FIDA 2008). Bilateral agreements are often based on environmental assessments but only three countries or supranational bodies regularly monitor their free trade agreements: the US, the EU and Canada. The European Commission developed the

Box 3.5 Trade and the environment

The complex interrelationships between trade and environmental issues such as climate change has risen up the agenda of multilateral organizations, and in 2010 the WTO and UNEP published a report bringing together thinking on this relationship (see WTO/UNEP 2009). In itself, trade liberalization is neither good nor bad for the environment and its effects will depend on the extent to which environment and trade goals can be complementary. Evidence suggests that, on balance, conventional growth rooted in the expansion of production factors is associated with environmental deterioration, but that consistent growth beyond a certain level creates economic and political pressures that can result in positive environmental changes. Research has indicated that during the 1970s and 1980s pollution rates rose in Latin American economies that grew rapidly but were relatively closed to trade (protectionist) whereas in more open economies they fell (see Birdsall and Wheeler 1993). The case of Chile does not support the thesis that economic liberalization transforms countries into havens for pollution, with data suggesting that trade opening tends to have both positive and negative impacts on the environment in different sectors (see Muñoz 1997). Moreover, support for the thesis that economic liberalization has a positive impact on the environment argues that it is likely that, as incomes rise, citizens demand higher environmental standards. While this may be true within a national context, it may not apply internationally. In some circumstances trade opening may foster *political* conditions more favourable to environmental protection. In Latin America and the Caribbean, it has contributed both to the development of environmental movements and to their institutionalization as political parties (see Chapters 4, 5). Debates within Mexico over its participation in NAFTA before 1992 and in Chile over its initial desire to join NAFTA, and subsequently to negotiate a bilateral trade agreement with the US, spurred the development of ENGOs and activism in these countries. Trade opening in Latin America has resulted in a raft of bilateral, regional and multilateral trade agreements, and these have also placed states under pressure to account for the environmental impact of liberalization. Anticipatory green policies are often intended either to facilitate a country's entry into more competitive markets that enforce higher ecological standards or to make it easier to negotiate free trade agreements with countries that have stricter standards. Criticisms of countries that have surfaced during free trade negotiations have also generated reactive environmental policies (Muñoz 1997).

Sustainability Impact Assessment (SIA) methodology which was used to carry out an assessment of the EU-Chile and EU-Mercosur trade agreements, for example (UNEP/IISD 2005). The EU also examined the likely effect of an Association Agreement with Mercosur (Mercado Común del Sur, Southern Common Market) and concluded that the impact on climate change would be mixed: there would be a small reduction in greenhouse gas emissions from the reallocation of production between the EU and Mercosur; a free trade agreement could lead to less energy consumption during production because the energy-intensive parts of the manufacturing sector would be largely transferred to Europe; and lower energy consumption and increased use of natural gas would lead to a small reduction in the total CO_2 emissions from production in both Mercosur countries and in the EU (University of Manchester 2009). However, there is significant variation in the scope of environmental measures incorporated into integration mechanisms, with some prominent agreements such as Mercosur remaining weak in comparison with NAFTA (see Hochstetler 2003).

The WTO and Doha

While the relationship between free trade and the environment remains contested, there is recognition that policy imbalances favour the interests of large corporations at the expense of environmental protection. In practice, this means that institutions responsible for governing trade are more powerful than those protecting the environment. The General Agreement on Tariffs and Trade (GATT) made few references to the environment but its general exceptions clause (Article XX) allows trade restrictions where they are "necessary to protect human, animal or plant life or health" or where they relate to the "conservation of exhaustible natural resources". The limitations of these rules were reflected in early decisions under GATT's disputes procedure that prioritized unrestricted trade over environmental protection, such as that on the tuna-dolphin dispute between Mexico and the US. The US stopped selling Mexican tuna, citing complaints that the fishing techniques used by its neighbour were threatening dolphins, but a dispute panel concluded GATT rules did not allow one country to take trade action for the purpose of attempting to enforce its own domestic laws in another country through what is known as "extra-territoriality" – even to protect animal welfare or conserve resources. This has led many environmentalists to condemn the GATT/WTO for failing to protect the environment (see Carter 2007).

The WTO has gradually been giving more attention to climate change and refining its rules on the environment (see WTO/UNEP 2009). However, it argues that it is not the appropriate forum for environmental discussions and has strengthened its working relationship with UNEP and the secretariats of multilateral environmental agreements and agencies to manage these issues (see UNEP/IISD 2005). A key theme in the trade-environment debate concerns the relationship between WTO rules and these international environmental regimes. About 20 of the most significant MEAs contain trade restrictive measures that address transboundary ecological problems. These appear to conflict with WTO rules, and powerful trading nations such as the US have refused to ratify various MEAs (Carter 2007; see Brown 2002). Critics of the WTO say only one trade-restricting measure – on sanitary and phytosanitary standards – incorporates the precautionary principle. However, there have been cases in which the WTO has taken decisions that support environmental protection, and the preamble to the agreement establishing the body lists sustainable development and environmental protection among its objectives. In past cases, a number of policies have been found to fall within the realm of Article XX – aimed at reducing risks to human, animal and plant life and health. For instance, in the Brazil Retreaded Tyres case, the WTO found that an import ban on retreaded tyres supported an import ban on waste tyres, which could prevent the accumulation of waste (WTO/UNEP 2009). The Doha Round of world trade talks gave further impetus to efforts to link trade and the environment (see WTO 2004).

International environmental law

Both the Stockholm Declaration of 1972 and the Rio Declaration of 1992 set out general principles of international law that apply to the environment (see Clemons 2009). While not *formally* binding, these are considered to embody customary international law and, as such, are *effectively* binding. More than 200 MEAs that involve two countries or more have been reached as well as over 1,000 bilateral agreements. MEAs have driven legal reform in Latin America and the Caribbean, and the 1992 Rio process prompted some countries such as Cuba, to undertake radical environmental reforms. The main kind of multilateral instrument containing binding obligations is a convention or treaty, and a framework convention is negotiated outlining principles and aims in anticipation of later protocols that spell out specific targets. The structure of international environmental regimes follow several core principles:

- *Prevention*. It is expensive and difficult to rectify environmental damage once this has occurred so it is better to avoid it in the first place.

- *Subsidiarity*. Decision-making should occur at the lowest level of government or political organization that can act effectively.

- *Common but differentiated responsibility*. Not all countries are equally to blame for past environmental damage, and they have different capabilities for tackling it.

- *"Polluter pays"*. Polluters should pay for the environmental damage they cause.

- *Precaution*. While Latin American and Caribbean countries must often make environmental policy in the face of uncertainty, a lack of scientific evidence cannot justify inaction.

- *Openness*. Transparency and public participation in policymaking are necessary for good environmental management.

Other international rules and structures on the environment have also been accepted throughout the region. In 1977, UNESCO established a world network of 564 protected terrestrial and coastal marine reserves in 109 countries under its Man and the Biosphere (MAB) programme. Of these, 104 are in Latin America and the Caribbean, and Mexico has the largest number in the region at 40. More recently, Latin American governments have taken their cue from the UN's Millennium Development Goals to improve environmental services, such as biodiversity and carbon sinks, as well as social circumstances. Many intra-regional initiatives have also been established, often under the auspices of multilateral agencies. Since 1989, UNEP has convened the Forum of Ministers of the Environment of Latin America and the Caribbean. In 2002, this adopted the Iniciativa Latinoamericana y Caribeña para el Desarrollo Sostenible

(ILAC, Latin American and Caribbean Initiative for Sustainable Development) to co-ordinate a common environmental agenda. This ambition is also reflected in regional consultations on sustainable consumption and production (SCP) since 2003 as part of the so-called Marrakech Process, which led to the Latin American and Caribbean Regional Strategy on SCP backed by a council of government experts. Mercosur joined the Marrakech Process and launched its own SCP Action Plan in June 2008. Multilateral bodies have fostered many other examples of regional co-operation such as the International Network for Environmental Compliance and Enforcement (INECE, see Chapter 2). Sub-regional initiatives have been established such as the Comisión Centroamericana de Ambiente y Desarrollo (CCAD, Central American Commission for Environment and Development). The Summits of the Americas process co-ordinated by the OAS plays a key role co-ordinating the work of 12 inter-American and international institutions (see JSWG 2010a, 2010b). All the multilateral bodies support environmental initiatives in Latin America and the Caribbean either through the Summits process or as a routine part of their work (see Box 3.6).

Principles of environmental law

Environmental law is a large and growing area of national and international jurisprudence for which considerable resources are now available (see websites below). The Instituto Internacional de Derecho y Medio Ambiente (International Institute for Law and the Environment) based in Spain and the IUCN's Environmental Law Initiative have taken a pioneering role in assessing environmental law (see Barreira, Ocampo and Recio 2007). Some of the basic principles of this branch of law are as follows.

- **Sovereignty.** The Stockholm and Rio Declarations assert that states have "the sovereign right to exploit their own resources pursuant to their own environmental policies" but requires them to ensure this does not damage their environment or that of other states (see Clemons 2009).

- **Co-operation.** States have a duty to co-operate on environmental issues and to be good neighbours. The duty to co-operate is a key principle underlying international water law, for example, without which it would be impossible for states to fulfil obligations under treaties.

Box 3.6 Multilateral bodies and the environment

Since the First Inter-American Meeting of Ministers and High-Level Authorities on Sustainable Development in 2006, the 34 OAS member states have been working to an ambitious agenda inspired by the "Declaration of Santa Cruz+10" and the Inter-American Programme on Sustainable Development. The OAS has also played a key role in biodiversity protection through such initiatives as the Inter-American Biodiversity Information Network (IABIN). The Economic Commission for Latin America and the Caribbean (ECLAC) has focused on the relationship between economic growth and environmental protection and increasingly on climate change. ECLAC also helps governments improve policy towards natural resources aimed at achieving sustainable development, and has developed some of the main environmental indicators in Latin America and the Caribbean. The Pan-American Health Organization (PAHO) has overseen planning for protecting health from climate change in the Americas and issued guidelines for assessing vulnerability and adaptation. The World Bank has financed efforts to develop alternative energy resources and introduced programmes in Mexico, Brazil and Peru to support the drafting of climate change strategies. The Inter-American Institute for Co-operation on Agriculture (IICA) promotes the conservation of natural resources and environmentally friendly agricultural practices, and it has supported efforts to develop policies aimed at addressing climate change. The Central American Bank for Economic Integration (CABEI) and the Global Environment Facility (GEF) operate Project CAMBio (Central American Markets for Biodiversity) that promotes biodiversity-friendly enterprises (SMEs). The UNDP focuses on helping countries in Latin America and the Caribbean create conditions that attract investment in lower carbon technologies and sustainable land management and access funds for climate change projects. The Corporación Andina de Fomento (CAF, Andean Development Corporation) has a Programa Latinoamericano del Carbono, Energías Limpias y Alternativas (PLAC+e, Latin American Carbon and Clean Alternative Energy Programme). Its Biodiversity Programme (BioCAF) promotes the sustainable use of ecosystems, natural and genetic resources, and biodiversity. An environmental agenda was also established at the creation in December 2011 of CELAC as a potential successor to the OAS (see CELAC 2011).

- *Equitable utilization*. Environmental diplomacy has been dominated by questions of equity, yet this concept is contested and at the heart of haggling over such issues as binding emission-reduction targets. Equitable utilization is the cornerstone of international law on transboundary watercourses (see CSIS et al. 2003).

- *Precautionary principle*. Global environmental politics has strengthened the importance of the precautionary principle that instruments such as the Cartagena Biosafety Protocol and those on ozone and climate change have applied to problems still characterized by scientific uncertainty. The precautionary approach does not halt harmful action but lowers risk.

- *Sustainable development*. This has become an important concept in international environmental law, asserting that states have an obligation to develop in a way so as to preserve resources for future generations (see Chapter 6).

A major problem in law and the design of treaties is *ambiguity*, even if this can be a *deliberate* part of the process by which a treaty secures the agreement of many parties – sometimes called "constructive ambiguity". Studies on water negotiations, for example, have emphasized that settling a water dispute where there is ambiguity in how resources should be shared can worsen conflict (see Fischhendler 2008). Another problem with international treaties is that the principles they enshrine may clash. The UN Convention on the Law of the Non-navigational Uses of International Watercourses, for example, implies both the principle of equitable utilization and that of "no significant harm" and there have been debates about which holds precedence (see Clemons 2009). Finally, multilateral environmental agreements may still have a limited effect on resolving problems because of issues of implementation. Although the International Whaling Commission was created in 1946, for example, it only became truly effective in 1986 after anti-whaling countries had gained control of it (see Carter 2007).

International institutions

Latin American and Caribbean countries have been prominent in international environmental forums, which they have approached from diverging and sometimes conflicting positions.

CFCs and the ozone layer

In 1985, the Vienna Convention for the Protection of the Ozone layer established a framework intended to foster scientific exchange but media attention to the ozone hole over the Antarctic and increasing use of CFCs created a sense of urgency and in 1987 negotiations over the Montreal Protocol established schedules for reducing CFC production. Latin American countries played an important role in deliberations on this agreement, with some such as Brazil initially hostile to it but others, such as Mexico, strong advocates. Mexico would become the first country both to sign the protocol and to complete ratification of it (see MacDonald and Nielson 1997; Carter 2007).

Hazardous waste trade

The introduction of environmental rules in industrialized countries heightened the temptation to dump waste in the developing world. In the 1980s, there was growing attention to dumping and the trade in hazardous waste and it became clear that regulations were required. Many developing countries, including those in the G77 group of nations such as Brazil, wanted to ban the North–South movement of hazardous wastes entirely. Developed countries wanted to establish regulations for waste trading, which developing countries feared would legitimize the trade. In 1987, UNEP adopted guidelines for managing hazardous wastes safely which became the basis for the Basel Convention. This imposed limits on trading, but left loopholes by allowing trading for recycling. Initially, Mexico accepted the position of the industrialized countries and opposed a complete ban, but its position changed as a result of environmental diplomacy from its Latin American neighbours and it supported the developing-country bloc opposing trade completely.

Biodiversity

Concern about declining biodiversity grew in the late 1980s and a consensus developed that action was needed. Pharmaceutical and biotechnology industries were prominent supporters of action because genetic resources are essential to their profitability. Developing countries argued that if their resources were of commercial value they should benefit from their use. While governments in developed nations such as the US defend intellectual property law robustly, many developing countries say such protection has not been extended to their biological resources that form the basis for many pharmaceutical and agricultural innovations. The Convention on Biological Diversity (CBD) signed in 1992 at the Earth Summit in Rio established as one of its three objectives the fair and equitable sharing of the benefits arising out of the utilization of genetic resources. Brazil, Colombia, Costa Rica, Mexico, Peru and Venezuela all backed the idea of such a convention. Brazil, Mexico and Venezuela had also been developing their own biotechnology industries. In 2010, parties to the CBD adopted the Nagoya Protocol which aims at sharing benefits from the utilization of genetic resources fairly. Although powerful countries such as the US have still not ratified the CBD, corporations that engage in bioprospecting have begun to make genetic property payments. Some Latin American countries took a pioneering position by agreeing mutually profitable deals with multinationals. In 1991 Costa Rica's National Biodiversity Institute (INBio) signed a contract with the pharmaceutical multinational Merck worth \$1.1 m and future royalties that gave the corporation the right to screen a catalogue of all plants and animals in the country.

Global environmental governance

Latin American countries have had an important influence on the evolution of environmental institutions, particularly the GEF and the Commission on Sustainable Development. During the UNCED negotiations over Agenda 21 – the UN's sustainable development action plan of 1992 – differences emerged between developed and developing nations over the financing of conservation. Industrialized countries proposed that financing for UNCED agreements be carried out through the GEF, the grant-awarding arm of UNEP and the World Bank. As the GEF was governed through voting by donor countries, this limited the influence of developing nations. Argentina and Brazil advocated a new "Green Fund" focused specifically on the needs of the developing world. The GEF was retained as the UNCED funding mechanism but reformed and voting rights were changed, giving developing nations more influence (MacDonald and Nielson 1997). Latin American states also played a prominent role in negotiations on the Cartagena Protocol on Biosafety addressing trade in genetically modified organisms (GMOs), that came into force in 2003, although mainly as exporter countries *resisting* regulation (see Falkner 2004; Andrée 2007). Argentina, Brazil, Paraguay and Mexico have significant GMO sectors, and Argentina is a key player in the global politics of biotechnology (see Box 2.2). The case of Mexico typifies the tensions between public concerns and development policy that characterize the biotechnology debate (see Box 3.7).

Developing countries also successfully lobbied for the establishment of an international body to oversee global sustainable development efforts. In meetings prior to UNCED in 1992, Venezuela proposed the establishment of an intergovernmental co-ordinating body to oversee the implementation of Agenda 21 and propose subsequent agreements, to be called the Commission on Sustainable Development. Despite opposition among developed countries such as the US to the creation of the new body, the commission was established (MacDonald and Nielson 1997).

International environmental regimes involve complex interactions between the parties, and it often takes rounds of negotiation before something effective emerges. Many factors determine the success of bargaining, during which a powerful state or states may take a leadership role, seeking the support of other states for a regime or pressing weaker states to support it. Domestic political pressure from ENGOs, a green party, the media, or public opinion may prompt a government to become a lead state (see Chasek et al. 2006). Brazil and Mexico have adopted leading positions in this way, often with a regional focus. A state that blocks or slows down negotiations on an agreement, or stalls its implementation, is sometimes called a veto state (see Carter 2007). States usually use a veto in order to protect vital economic interests or because a government has been lobbied by powerful corporations. Brazil and Mexico played veto roles in an effort to extract important concessions in the ozone negotiations, for example.

Box 3.7 GMOs and Mexico

In a comparison of biotechnology policies in Mexico, China and South Africa, Gupta and Falkner (2006) suggested that policy choices are being driven by market and trade dynamics and a concern with technological leadership and competitiveness. The Mexican state's approach has been to promote biotechnology according to a free-market perspective that has been resisted by ENGOs as well as peasant and labour unions, with the country's environment ministry emphasizing the need for caution. The 1982 debt crisis changed Mexican agricultural policy prioritizing self-sufficiency in maize production and the country liberalized trade and reduced state support for small-scale agriculture. Biotechnology policy has obeyed this neoliberal approach, but the use of genetic engineering in agriculture remains contested and there have been conflicts over genetically modified maize, with imports of transgenic maize from the US for the animal feed and food-processing industry provoking disputes. In 1988, a presidential decree declared a moratorium on the release of transgenic maize into the environment and in 2001 the issue gained global attention after an article in *Nature* magazine alleged transgene ingression into indigenous maize varieties in Chiapas. Mexico participated actively in negotiating the Cartagena Protocol on Biosafety, which it ratified in 2003, as part of a group of OECD countries that were neither in the EU nor part of the Miami Group of GMO-exporters opposed to a biosafety regime that included the US and Canada. Gupta and Falkner suggest that, given the position of the US and Canada, which have not ratified the protocol, explanations for why Mexico chose to do so included the ability to give its policy-makers a weapon to withstand NAFTA and trade imperatives and reflected the environment ministry's newfound potential to influence Mexican legislators. Mexico has permitted field-testing of transgenic crops including corn, canola and soya since 1988 but officials creatively interpreted the law to portray large areas as experimental, thereby allowing the planting of transgenic cotton. However, public fears about transgene ingression into indigenous maize varieties resulted in an amendment to the Mexican Penal Code in 2002, making it a criminal offence to store or release transgenic crops into the environment. This prompted biotechnologists to lobby for a comprehensive biosafety law clarifying what was allowed, which was passed in 2005. Mexico's ratification of the Cartagena Protocol obliged it to implement the agreement through its national biosafety framework under the 2005 law but critics among ENGOs argued that this was not up to the task and would not foresee a precautionary approach. Mexico's membership of NAFTA has also been used by indigenous groups and ENGOs to press their case for caution relating to transgenic maize imports. These groups lobbied NAFTA's Commission on Environmental Co-operation in 2002 to analyse the impact of transgenic maize on biodiversity.

Environmental disputes and conflict management

Although modern Latin America has largely escaped the devastating wars and border disputes of other regions of the world, there are tensions in the region. Transboundary environmental disputes have occurred and security discourses since the end of the Cold War have shifted from traditional issues of war and peace towards "environmental security". In Uruguay in 2011, for example, the former president, Tabaré Vázquez, let slip that he had considered going to war with Argentina in a bitter dispute over the construction of the Botnia paper mill in Fray Bentos on the Uruguay River (see Box 5.3). The project had generated vociferous opposition in Argentina over contamination risks and was referred to the International Court of Justice which resolved it with the establishment of joint monitoring. Disagreements about the environment can provide the touch paper for existing disputes or discord. A factor contributing to Uruguay's stance on the Botnia mill, for example, is the country's sensitivity about energy dependence on neighbours well-endowed with resources. In the late 1990s, for example, Uruguay fell out with Brazil over air pollution from the President Medici power station, and in 2011 with Argentina over access to Paraguayan electricity. Cross-border disputes can also snowball: when Ecuador quarrelled with Colombia over the impact of US-funded aerial coca fumigation, it dragged neighbouring countries into the row. Institutional weakness can further exacerbate disputes: the Botnia disagreement reflected the weakness of regional institutions for economic co-operation and consultation as much as it did the environmental nature of the problem.

At the root of most environmental tensions is competition over access to natural resources among economies with high levels of poverty and dependent on commodity exports. One of the region's poorest countries, Bolivia, for example, has alarmed environmentalists with the development of the El Mutún iron ore deposits near the Pantanal wetlands, which are mainly in Brazil but extend to Bolivia and Paraguay. Where competition over resources is acute, the environment can fuel other grievances. On the contentious frontier between Ecuador and Peru in the Cordillera del Cóndor, the site of Latin America's most serious recent border conflict, both governments are still competing to grant mining concessions in resource-rich areas that have been past flashpoints. Migration resulting from land exhaustion or climate change is another potential source of conflict, especially if it brings peoples with pre-existing tensions into contact. A factor contributing to tensions over El Mutún, for example, is growing demand for food and biofuel that has driven occupation of the Upper Paraguay River watershed in Brazil, destroying forest and threatening pollution.

The UN system has been edging towards "green peacemaking" to address the potential for environmental conflict but some campaign groups believe mechanisms for resolving disputes over resources and pollution are lacking in Latin America (see Conca and Dabelko 2002). Observers have even called for a regional version of the Espoo Convention, the 1991 European pact on transboundary environmental impact assessment.

Access to water resources is seen as a key potential source of conflict in an area where most of the major river basins are shared between two or more countries. In 2006, legislators in Latin America adopted the Panama Declaration on Water, which specified that there is a clear need in the region for a permanent framework to manage shared water basins and develop common strategies for their sustainable use (UNEP/OSA/UNA 2007). The potential for water disputes to stoke conflict is likely to be exacerbated by climate change. Friction between Bolivia and Chile over the Silala River illustrates how disputes can also touch raw historical nerves, and longstanding border tensions between Nicaragua and Honduras have been complicated by the impact of Hurricane Mitch in 1998, which changed the flow of the Negro River. Hydroelectric power can raise tensions, as the Madeira River case illustrates (see above). Opponents of Brazilian mega-dams on the Madeira River warn they will also affect Bolivia and Peru. The potential for dams on the Usumacinta River has been a focus of

Table 3.1 Water flashpoints in Latin America

Risk	Location/Countries	Risk factors
High	*Silala Basin* Bolivia Chile	Existing diplomatic situation Lack of treaty Lack of management structure Historical context Lack of agreement on whether the basin is international
Medium high	*Orinoco Basin* Brazil Colombia Venezuela	Lack of treaty Lack of management structure Increasing pollution Border tensions between Venezuela and Guyana
Medium low	*Amazon Basin* Bolivia Brazil Colombia Ecuador Guyana French Guinea Peru Suriname Venezuela	Increasing pollution Large basin Young organization
	La Plata Basin Argentina Bolivia Brazil Paraguay Uruguay	Increasing pollution Hidrovia Project (navigation) Population increase by 2025
	Lake Titicaca Basin Bolivia Peru	Increasing pollution Young organization Social unrest
Low	*Remainder of Basins*	

Source: UNEP/OSA/UNA 2007.

tension between Mexico and Guatemala. Fear of pollution can add to strains, as in the Botnia dispute between Argentina and Uruguay. A number of potential flashpoints over water exist in Latin America (see Table 3.1).

The politics of water management, "hydropolitics", is often understood primarily as a form of conflict management. Many experts recognize that the international law governing water is out of date, often contradictory and usually unenforceable. Unilateral actions to construct a dam or divert a river in the absence of a treaty or institutional framework to safeguard the interests of neighbouring countries sharing a basin can be destabilizing and generate longstanding hostility. Most water-related tension between countries is generated not by shortages but by the unilateral exercise of control over an international river by a regional power, as in the case of Brazil and the Madeira River. In the case of the shared water resources along the 2,000-mile semi-arid Mexican–US border, for example, asymmetries in power between the two countries and recurrent droughts have exacerbated institutional weaknesses in how resources are managed (see Box 3.8).

The importance of water governance has been reflected in reforms that gained momentum in the 1980s throughout the region (see Box 1.3). However, efforts to strengthen legal or institutional frameworks have often fallen foul of disagreements within countries that bog them down in legislative processes (see FIDA 2008). Nonetheless, researchers at Oregon State University examined interactions between countries where water had a formative influence upon events in the past 50 years and found that, despite the potential for dispute in international basins, the record of conflict is insignificant when considered alongside that of co-operation (see Wolf, Yoffe and Giordano 2003).

The transboundary nature of environmental issues coupled with the potential for jurisdictional disputes in border areas make avoiding conflict a high priority. Attempts to apply domestic laws extra-territorially, as in the case of the US–Mexico tuna dispute (see above), can have serious foreign policy implications. The OAS Charter establishes that dispute resolution should be peaceful and institutional initiatives have also been undertaken, such as principles drawn up by UNEP in 1977 on how states should act when resources are shared. International and regional agreements provide different forums and procedures for dispute resolution and addressing damages, and the UN system has an extensive set of dispute-resolution mechanisms. The OAS has identified conflict avoidance and the need for negotiation among countries as a priority and its Inter-American Forum on Environmental Law (FIDA) has developed best practices for countries dealing with disputes over shared resources (see FIDA 2008). The International Court of Environmental Arbitration and Conciliation (ICEAC) was created in Mexico in 1994 with the aim of resolving conflicts by negotiation. There are also many bilateral and regional agreements on resources among countries that share borders.

Box 3.8 Water management on the Mexico–US border

Water management is one of the most complicated issues in US–Mexico bilateral relations and involves all levels of government – federal, state, and local – on both sides of the 2,000-mile border. It is complicated by competition between agricultural interests and local authorities for limited water resources (see CSIS et al. 2003). Scarcity along both sides of the border has been exacerbated by: a semi-arid climate; rapid population growth and urbanization resulting in rising water consumption; rapid industrialization because of the maquiladora industry and NAFTA; pollution of water sources through the runoff of wastewater, sewage, pesticides, fertilizers and herbicides; high salinity; and aquifer depletion as demand has risen. Climate change is likely to aggravate these factors. In recent decades, droughts resulting in the under-delivery of water from Mexico to the US under existing agreements, causing disputes, have underscored the importance of developing a strategic approach. Mexico has been trying to resolve its own problems in order to meet its treaty obligations, but political pressures have meant that domestic priorities have sometimes overridden its treaty obligations. The International Boundary and Water Commission (IBWC, which in Mexico is called CILA) is responsible for applying the water treaties between the US and Mexico but growing public concern about its inadequacy fostered the establishment of other institutions. In 1983, the US–Mexico Border Environmental Co-operation Agreement (the La Paz Agreement) gave the environmental ministries of both countries authority over water quality matters. In the 1990s, a Border Environmental Co-operation Commission (BECC) was created under NAFTA (see above) to assist border infrastructure projects. Garcia-Acevedo (2004) has argued that despite the existence of these mechanisms water management has reflected the asymmetries of power between the US and Mexico in which the interests of powerful groups take precedence over equity and conservation. She argues that although the institutional arrangements for dealing with transboundary water problems are among the strongest in the world their performance has been poor and reflects a piecemeal, incremental approach by both governments. (Main sources: CSIS et al. 2003; Garcia-Acevedo 2004; IBWC 2007)

Conclusion

International factors have played a formative role in the economic and political development of Latin America and the Caribbean and have driven environmental management in the region. The key factors that have shaped the region's relationship with the outside world over centuries include the role played by foreign investment and dependency – sometimes discussed by scholars as part of a wider debate about "imperialism" or in terms of an alliance between local and foreign elites – as well as by foreign models for institutions and politics diffused by the multilateral bodies that have played a disproportionate role in Latin American and Caribbean development. The study of international relations in the region begins with an acknowledgement of the singular importance of the role played by the US in shaping the political and economic agenda, especially during the Cold War era. But, as the role of the US has declined in relative terms, it must also now take account of the emergence of a multi-polar world in which solutions to problems are sought through multilateralism and, in turn, the comprehensive impact of globalization on Latin America's politics and society. Moreover, as it grows more prosperous the region itself is accelerating its efforts to create structures that respond to its own long-held aspiration for integration. Yet, although literature on international environmental politics addresses global themes, it is often necessary to look at national and regional foreign policies and processes to understand these. Participation in global trade and the expanding reach of international environmental law enshrined in multilateral and bilateral agreements have transformed the context in which national policy is made, yet at the same time have responded to the priorities advanced by individual countries. One effort to characterize the ways in which domestic and international issues overlap has been development of the notion of "intermestic" issues that affect both foreign and domestic policy. Environmental foreign policy in Latin America and the Caribbean has been both a reflection of a wider international agenda yet also an increasingly powerful force shaping it. Countries such as Brazil, Mexico and Argentina have become heavyweight participants in international environmental forums in which they are stamping their own experience on global outcomes.

Recommended reading

Barkdull, John and Paul G Harris. 2002. "Environmental Change and Foreign Policy: A Survey of Theory", *Global Environmental Politics*, Vol. 2, No. 2 (May), pp. 63–91.

Chambers, W Bradnee and Jessica F Green (eds). 2005. *Reforming International Environmental Governance: From Institutional Limits to Innovative Reforms*. Tokyo: UN University Press.

Chasek, Pamela S, David L Downie and Janet Welsh Brown. 2006. *Global Environmental Politics*, 4th edn. Boulder, CO: Westview Press.

MacDonald, Gordon J, Daniel L Nielson and Marc A Stern (eds). 1997. *Latin American Environmental Policy in International Perspective*. Boulder, CO: Westview Press.

Useful websites

Commission for Environmental Co-operation of North America (CEC), covering the NAFTA countries of the US, Mexico and Canada: www.cec.org/

Comunidad de Estados Latinoamericanos y Caribeños (CELAC, Community of Latin American and Caribbean States): www.celac.gob.ve

ECOLEX information service on environmental law: www.ecolex.org.

Environmental dispute resolution within the UN system: www.scribd.com/doc/2634846/Environmental-dispute-settlement-within-the-United-Nations-System

EU EUrocLIMA programme: http://ec.europa.eu/europeaid/where/latin-america/regional-cooperation/euroclima/index_en.htm

EU relations with Latin America: www.eeas.europa.eu/la/index_en.htm

Fórum Brasileiro de ONGs e Movimentos Sociais para o Meio Ambientye e o Desenvolvimento (FBOMS, Brazilian Forum of NGOs and Social Movements for the Environment and the Development): www.fboms.org.br

Organization of American States (OAS), Department of Sustainable Development, Integrated Water Resources Management Section (IWRM): www.oas.org/dsd/WaterResources/

Stakeholder Forum, an international organization working to advance sustainable development and promote stakeholder democracy at a global level: www.stakeholderforum.org

UN Non-Governmental Liaison Service (LIN-NGLS): www.un-ngls.org

UNESCO searchable list of biosphere reserves: www.unesco.org/new/en/natural-sciences/environment/ecological-sciences/

UNFCC: http://unfccc.int/2860.php

Vitae Civilis (the Vitae Civilis Institute for Development, Environment and Peace): www.vitaecivilis.org.br/

World Trade Organization, trade and the environment: www.wto.org/english/tratop_e/envir_e/envir_e.htm

CHAPTER FOUR

Actors – green parties

D EMOCRATIZATION in Latin America and the Caribbean during the 1980s and 1990s spawned new green parties throughout the region, but these have not been studied in detail and their electoral record has varied considerably. Political parties are crucial components of democracies, offering a means of representing citizens and enabling them to shape policy. But there are many factors that determine whether a party survives and thrives, not least how it is organized, relations between its members and other social forces, and the nature of the political system itself. In Latin America and the Caribbean, parties more generally face a specific set of circumstances that impose constraints – and offer opportunities – that cannot be found elsewhere because of the region's unique political history. There are common elements to the emergence of green parties within the wider process of democratization, some of which have become solidly established, yet also crucial local differences that often reflect the geographic and social diversity of Latin America and the Caribbean. This chapter examines the emergence and characteristics of green parties throughout the region, and introduces ways in which these can be assessed by students of politics. It explores why some parties have had a greater impact than others, and looks at indigenous organizations that are also important political actors. It considers some of the ideas that informed the activity of these green groups and key challenges that they face.

Democratization

Any examination of green parties in Latin America and the Caribbean confronts a major lack of research into both their characteristics and their role in government, a problem also encountered in Europe (see Müller-Rommel 2002). Comparative research and scholarly debates on the greens in Europe have focused on three topics: their rise and development; their organizational and ideological strength; and their success in elections. None of these themes has been addressed in detail in the study of Latin American and Caribbean politics and nor has there been research into the role of green parties in government. Key questions for a research agenda are to what extent have greens in government been able to change politics, and has incumbency changed them? A comparison of the record in government of green parties in Belgium, Finland, France, Germany and Italy concluded that those who feared losing support because they would inevitably disappoint or betray their supporters were wrong, yet serving in government nonetheless required acceptance of the constraints of domestic and international policymaking even it meant alienating activists (see Poguntke 2002).

In Latin America and the Caribbean, democratization provided the context for the emergence of green parties by permitting new political forces and activism to converge, especially around the 1992 Earth Summit in Rio (see Hochstetler and Keck 2007). Authoritarianism had taken various forms and this had a bearing on the timing and nature of democratization in each country. Efforts to explain the shift from authoritarian regimes to competitive party systems have studied the initial "transition" to democracy and its subsequent "consolidation", categories still of value in comparative politics. Transition represents an uncertain process of regime change, where the rules of political competition are up for negotiation and it is not clear what the outcomes will be (see Agüero 1998). Theoretical literature on transition drew attention to the political, economic and international factors that contributed to regime change and shaped the type of democracy that emerged. If democracy is understood primarily as an electoral phenomenon, there is no doubt that great progress has been made towards the establishment and deepening of democratic rule in Latin America and the Caribbean since the 1970s. However, the region has faced recurrent problems of instability and during the 1990s attention began to turn to the consolidation of its new democracies with a focus on the conditions needed for democratic governance to persist and stabilize. Scholars have argued that democracy is consolidated when all political actors consider the democratic state to be the only legitimate means to settle competition for office and formulate policy, by putting their faith in institutions and adhering to democratic rules (see Przeworski 1991). Consolidation can be understood in terms of respect for laws, rules and procedures (see Linz and Stepan 1996). The conditions necessary for consolidated democracies are: a vibrant civil society; free and fair elections; the rule of law; a modern and impartial state apparatus; an economy in which property rights are protected and markets function properly; and effective governance (see Diamond 1999; Diamond et al. 1999). The study of democracy in Latin America today tends to concentrate on three themes: institutions and their efficiency and accountability; participation; and gender, race and ethnicity (see O'Donnell et al. 2008).

Parties and party systems

Democratization put parties at the centre of political activity in most of Latin America and the Caribbean. Parties exist to compete for power, are the main agents for representing social interests, and offer citizens the ability to hold governments to account for what they have done (see Scartascini et al. 2011). Parties influence policy by aggregating interests in society, impose order on competing groups and demands, offer voters a choice between rival policies, and enable communication between a government and society. In legislatures, they organize business and influence the conduct of representatives. They act on the policymaking process by advancing political programmes and influencing relations between executive and legislature (Scartascini et al. 2011).

Political parties have usually been examined as elements within a *system* in which various parties compete for power (see Sartori 1976; Carey 1997; Foweraker 1998). A key characteristic of democratic consolidation is the emergence of a party system that represents all the main tendencies. Parties and party systems are of importance to the "institutionalization" of democracy – how it is rooted in society through structured forms of participation and competition that set rules for political actors. Institutionalization is an important theme in the study of the ecology movement because it influences: the profile of small, new parties; the behaviour of parties with strong environmental associations such as green and indigenous parties; and the degree to which parties work to benefit their supporters or broaden their appeal by offering public goods for everybody, such as environmental improvements. Institutions establish predictability, and so weak institutionalization is associated with uncertainty in which political actors put short-term gains before good policymaking and can worsen ideological polarization, making it difficult to maintain stability (see Randall and Svåsand 2002; Scartascini et al. 2011; Stein et al. 2005; Mainwaring and Scully 1995).

Chile has the oldest party system in Latin America and this helps to explain why, in spite of its presidentialist constitution and the 17-year dictatorship of General Augusto Pinochet, after 1990, parties reasserted their role as the backbone of democracy. Mexico's party system has undergone a slow transition despite having some of the oldest parties in the region. Parties were traditionally less well organized in Argentina and Colombia, although in the latter they have grown in strength; and in Bolivia, Ecuador, Peru and Guatemala party organization has traditionally been weak, personalism has prevailed, and there has been electoral volatility. In Guatemala, there persist large numbers of small, ephemeral parties. Brazil's party system has been characterized by fluidity, resulting in frequent coalition realignments. However, the ruling Partido dos Trabalhadores (PT, Workers' Party) is imposing greater institutionalization.

A number of party system characteristics influence the nature of parties and the interaction between the executive and legislative branches of government, including the following:

- *Party discipline*. Party discipline – the consistency with which political elites maintain or stay loyal to a party line in the legislature – is a key factor behind the capacity of a president to push forward a policy agenda and will be influenced by internal party factors, such as the role party leaders play in selecting candidates, and by the electoral system which determines how loyal candidates remain to those leaders. Party discipline is stronger in some countries than in others. In Chile, the multi-party centre-left Concertación coalition which dominated government for two decades after the return of democracy in 1990, has been able to maintain discipline out of fear of a return of authoritarianism. It has done so by ensuring that aspects of the programmes of constituent groups including the greens are incorporated within policy. Brazil traditionally had undisciplined parties unable to sustain strong coalitions, thereby frustrating the legislative agenda (see Amorim Neto 2002b). However, the PT's domination of the political process since 2003 has engendered greater discipline among parties. The PT itself can be seen as a broad coalition often working in tandem with the green party, Partido Verde (PV), that has made political inroads as a result of its legislative discipline. A counterpoint to party discipline is party switching, which was once common. Until recently in Brazil, politicians would often switch parties. Fernando Gabeira, for example, was a founding members of the PV, left the party in 2002 to join the PT, but in 2010 rejoined the greens.

- *Representation*. A key problem faced by Latin America's democracies is the limited ability of parties to represent citizens effectively, and one way of illustrating how parties may not be functioning well is the sheer number of them: in 2008, at least 11 Latin American countries had 10 or more parties in their lower houses (see Latinobarómetro 2008). Ways of illustrating dissatisfaction with the way parties represent demands include levels of turnout and abstention in elections, electoral "dealignment", the degree to which the loyalty of citizens to a preferred party erodes, and electoral "volatility", the change in the vote shares of all parties from one election to the next. Non-identification on a left–right axis is often seen as a symptom of dealignment. Such factors can sometimes work to the advantage of small and new groups, such as green parties. Party system fragmentation, in which there are a large number of parties, may be due to electoral institutions or an indicator of dealignment, and often means that a government's viability depends upon the formation of a coalition. Fragmentation allows new interests to gain representation while lowering barriers to the emergence of new and small parties. It nurtures electoral alliances, giving smaller parties more clout and a chance to gain access to government office (see Van Cott 2005).

- *Party nationalization*. The degree to which parties are national, and hence receive similar levels of support throughout a country, influences a party system. A nationalized system implies that parties act with a common national orientation rather than being divided by regional issues. This is important for policymaking because it affects the number of players who interact in a policy process and the relationship between an executive and a legislature (see Scartascini et al. 2011). Green parties in Latin America have mostly developed from regional bases and are still in the process of nationalizing. In Brazil, the greens developed regionally before nationalization took place, whereas in Costa Rica they have remained regional. In highly nationalized party systems, legislators will focus on national issues to advance their careers and an executive can push through an agenda more easily by negotiating with fewer party leaders. If a party's support is spread evenly across different areas and sectors, it is easier for politicians to unify these behind policies and more likely that they will concentrate on achieving national public goods such as environmental protection. Where nationalization is weak, party leaders may not speak for the whole party and hence may be unable to deliver its legislative support. Denationalized party systems may reflect strong federalism or the existence of regional strongholds within parties, and this will result in uneven influences on policy (see Scartascini et al. 2011). Parties tend to be less nationalized in larger countries or those that are geographically diverse, such as Peru, Argentina, Venezuela and Brazil (see Stein et al. 2005).

Electoral systems

The method by which candidates are elected has implications for the number, characteristics, preferences and stability of the actors and groups charged with policymaking. Latin American and Caribbean electoral systems vary considerably, but in most cases the president is elected by an absolute majority and the legislature through proportional representation in multi-member constituencies (see Catón and Tuesta Soldevilla 2008). Highly representative electoral systems are those in which political groups gain seats in proportion to the votes they win, but voting systems vary considerably. Upper chambers in countries such as Argentina and Brazil are elected in ways that tend to over-represent less highly populated areas and, where over-representation is significant, this can result in sub-national interests being favoured over the national interest. In Brazil, for example, legislators from Amazonian states have sometimes joined to exercise pressure against federal environmental policies (see Hochstetler and Keck 2007). As infrastructure investment tends to be an important source of demands by sub-regions upon the centre, if politicians exist in a more clientelistic relationship with powerful groups in their constituencies this can weaken the ability of environmental groups to resist or amend large projects (Stein et al. 2005).

Electoral rules have a bearing on how policymaking responds to environmental concerns. Systems with strong party leaderships, for example, are more likely to pursue public goods such as environmental protection, while those with more autonomous politicians will pursue particularistic policies. If electoral rules are "party-centred" – putting a party's interests above those of members – then policy will tend to favour public goods and encourage greater attention to environmental protection (see Nielson and Stern 1997). The greater the level of control over candidates for election exercised by party leaders – who must protect their party's image – the greater the incentives to provide public goods. Mexico and Costa Rica, for example, have party-centred electoral systems in which party leaders have significant control over nominations, and both countries also have relatively strong environmental movements and policymaking. However, "candidate-centred" electoral systems – those that give ordinary members considerable autonomy – often yield policy choices that benefit a politician's "clients" rather than the common good: individual candidates need to win office through their own efforts rather than on a party's reputation and so develop a personal vote by distributing benefits to potential supporters, an incentive that works against the promotion of public goods (Nielson and Stern 1997). Colombia and Brazil have candidate-centred systems, although their environmental movements vary considerably. Brazilian politicians often display individualism vis-à-vis their parties, resulting in politicians switching allegiance (see above), rivalry within a party, clientelistic promises to voters and the lobbying of business for funding. In Colombia, leaders often do not control nominations, competition between candidates in a party is common, and they often cut local deals with party bosses for blocs of votes.

Legislature and executive

Most Latin American democracies are multi-party systems that make it more difficult to achieve stability by complicating coalition-building, and as the number of parties increases the likelihood of a presidential majority diminishes (see Foweraker, Landman and Harvey 2003; Mainwaring 1993). However, stable competition between two or three parties or blocs in congress is now common in some systems, and, even when there are many parties in a legislature, one dominant traditional party such as the PRI in Mexico, the Peronists in Argentina, and the PT in Brazil will impose order on competition. The characteristics of parties and the extent to which their members back shared goals also influences the behaviour of legislatures. Party unity is important because it determines whether a leader can enforce discipline on legislators and this, in turn, affects how a party behaves in congress and its reliability as a coalition partner. If internal divisions weaken unity, this limits a dominant party's effectiveness and determines what kind of legislature a president has to deal with (Morgenstern 2002). In Argentina, the Peronists have dominated legislative politics yet have also suffered persistent factionalism. When presidents can count on the support of a disciplined majority or coalition, the legislature's role in policymaking can be limited. For example, despite having relatively weak constitutional powers, Mexican presidents before 1997 dominated policymaking, since they could always count on solid majorities for the governing PRI in congress. When the Partido Acción Nacional (PAN), which took power thereafter, lacked a majority, the legislature became more active in policymaking (Stein et al. 2005). Yet strong congresses do not necessarily mean better environmental protection: in Costa Rica, congressional resistance to the administration of President Oscar Arias (1986–90) forced the newly created Ministerio de Recursos Naturales, Energía y Minas (MIRINEM) to work on environmental planning without the formal approval of congress (see also Torres 1997).

Ideology

Ideology is important to party unity and central to the idea of a functioning democracy is a notion of parties that are ideologically coherent. Ideological programmes are an important factor in structuring party systems in Latin America and the Caribbean and play a key role in the behaviour of legislatures (see Kitschelt et al. 2010). The degree to which parties drift from the centre to more extreme positions – "ideological polarization" – will affect a president's ability to build coalitions in a legislature, with less polarization making coalitions more likely. The extent of polarization is also related to the number of parties, and two-party systems tend to push political actors towards the centre (see Sartori 1976). In a measure employed by Morgenstern (2002) some parties such as Brazil's PT and Chile's Socialists (PSCh) have been ideologically cohesive over long periods. The PT has been ideologically coherent even though it is a heterogeneous coalition of positions often based on strong regional identities. That coherence may derive from its political mobilization in the later years of the military regime: a strong green agenda has co-existed with developmentalism within the party by virtue of the role environmentalists played in protests against the military. The success of legislators belonging to minor parties should vary according to their ideological positions. Centrists and independents tend to be at an advantage over more-extreme parties because of their value to a president when seeking broad support. Electoral rules will influence the degree to which different ideologies – as well as minorities and local interests (localism) – are represented. Some electoral systems make it easier for small parties such as the greens to win seats in the legislature (Scartascini et al. 2011)

Green parties in Latin America and the Caribbean

Green parties began to emerge in Latin America during the processes of democratization that began in the late 1970s. In some of the larger countries, such as Mexico and Brazil, they rapidly became a feature of the political landscape, and in some cases have had a significant impact on politics. Yet their fortunes have wavered, and in most of the region green parties remain minor or yet to obtain legislative seats. Nonetheless, greens have become potent advocates of environmental protection and sustainable development. Moreover, despite their size and hitherto marginal role, Latin America's greens have been at the heart of co-operation among ecology parties globally. During the UNCED Rio Earth Summit in 1992, for example, the Brazilian PV hosted the first "Green Planetary Meeting" bringing together activists from all over the world to nurture co-operation. This met in 1993 in Mexico City and was a precursor to the "Global Green Network" of parties from around the world formed in 2001 in Australia. It is likely that green parties will grow in strength in relation to other political actors seeking environmental change, such as ENGOs, as green initiatives funded by the private sector grow, strengthening the role of parties in policy formation. Today, a significant number of green parties participate in democratic politics in Latin America and the Caribbean (see Table 4.1)

Table 4.1 Green parties in Latin America and the Caribbean*

Country	Name	Founded	Perentage of vote at last election, number of votes or legislative seats (year, election type)
Argentina	Acción Verde, Iniciativa Verde, Partido Verde (PV, Green Party) Partido Alternativa Verde (Alternative Green Party) Los Verdes–FPI (The Greens-Forum of Political Ecology)	2003	
Bolivia	Partido Verde (PV, Green Party)	2007	52.6%, 515,370 votes (2010, departmental/gubernatorial elections, Santa Cruz)
Brazil	Partido Verde (PV, Green Party)	1986	19,33%, 19,636,359 votes (2010, presidential election, first round); 3.0%, 5,047,797 votes (2010 election, Senate); 3.8%, 3,710,366 votes, 15 seats (2010 election, chamber of deputies); 37 seats (2010 election, state legislatures)
Chile	Partido Los Verdes Partido Ecologista Verde (PEV)	(1987–2001) 2002	5.5% of votes presidential election (1993, independent candidate) 0.1%, 3,818 votes (2009, elections, chamber of deputies); 1 seat (2008, municipal council elections)
Colombia	Partido Verde Oxígeno (PVO, Green Oxygen Party) Partido Verde (PV, Green Party)	1998–2005 2007 2010 2011	27.52%, 3,588,819 votes (2010 presidential election, second round); 4.77%, 531,293 votes, 5 seats (2010 parliamentary election, senate); 3.0%, 283,293 votes, 3 seats (2010 parliamentary election, chamber of deputies); 1,180,173 votes, 2 governors (2011 governors); 809,088 votes, 23 seats (2011 departmental assemblies); 707,688 votes, 49 mayors (2011 mayoral elections); 1,132,300 votes, 718 councillors (2011 municipal councils)
Costa Rica	Partido Verde Ecologista (PVE, Green Ecology Party, mainly Cartago) Partido del Sol (Santa Ana, San José)	2004	0.15%, 2,901 votes (2010, parliamentary election)
Dominican Republic	Partido Verde de la Unidad Democrática (PVUD, Green Party of Democratic Unity)	1994	0.02%, 520 votes (2010 parliamentary elections) 0.03%, 987 votes (2010 municipal elections)

Country	Name	Founded	Perentage of vote at last election, number of votes or legislative seats (year, election type)
Dominican Republic *continued*	Partido Socialista Verde (PASOVE, Green Socialist Party)	2009	0.20%, 6,595 votes (2010 parliamentary elections); 0.20%, 6,793 votes (2010 municipal elections)
Guatemala	Partido Los Verdes de Guatemala (PVG, The Greens)	1995	–
Mexico	Partido Verde Ecologista de México (PVEM, Green Ecology Party of Mexico)	1986	6.7%, 2,318,138, 4 district seats and 6.7%, 2,326,016, 17 party list seats, making a total of 21 seats (2009 parliamentary elections, chamber of deputies); 28.1%, 11,622,012 votes, 29 direct seats and 28.0%, 11,681,395 votes, 10 party list seats, making a total of 39 seats (2006 parliamentary elections, senate, in coalition with the PRI as the Alianza por México)
Nicaragua	Partido Verde Ecologista de Nicaragua (PVEN, Green Ecology Party of Nicaragua)	2003	
Peru	Partido Ecologista del Perú (PEP, Ecological Party of Peru)	1995	
	Partido Ecologista Alternativa Verde del Perú (PEAV, Green Alternative Ecology Party of Peru)	1997	
Puerto Rico	Puertorriqueños por Puerto Rico (PPR, Puerto Ricans for Puerto Rico)	2003	2.77%, 53,690 votes (2008 gubernatorial election); 2.39%, 44,126 votes (2008, resident commissioner election)
Uruguay	Partido Verde Eto-Ecologista (EE-PV, Animal Welfare-Ecological Green Party); split and separate parties formed:	1987	0.27%, 5,500 votes (1994, presidential election)
	Partido del Sol (Party of the Sun), now a grouping within Unión Cívica-Partido Nacional; and the Movimiento Ecologista Pacifista del Uruguay (MEPU)	1994	Partido del Sol: 0.13%, 2,258 votes (1994 presidential election)
	Partido Verde (PV)	2010	
Venezuela	Movimiento Ecológico de Venezuela (MOVEV, Venezuelan Ecological Movement)	2008	Claims 100,000 votes, 6 national assembly deputies within existing party coalitions (2010, parliamentary election)

* As of September 2012; some data is unavailable.

Source: Author.

The formation of green parties remains a recent development in the politics of most Latin American and Caribbean countries (see Boxes 4.1–4.7). In some countries, such as Brazil and Mexico, their development has been stable and grounded in social activism. In countries where a few dominant, traditional parties co-exist alongside a large number of smaller and provincial parties and electoral alliances, such as Chile, Uruguay and Argentina, it has been more difficult for green parties to take hold nationally. New parties either struggle to survive or are still being launched and these small parties are often concentrated in one region or city and extend their reach nationally only gradually.

The forms in which green parties developed can help to explain their different characteristics and how their positions vary, and a number of factors have contributed to their emergence:

Foreign and regional models. Green parties in Europe offered models for Latin America at a time when authoritarian regimes were beginning to crumble. In this period, political exiles from military regimes in countries such as Chile and Brazil spent time in Europe and were influenced by the political ideas and groups they encountered. In Brazil many of the environmentalists, artists, academics and anti-nuclear campaigners who helped to found the Partido Verde in 1986 were former leftwing activists who had been exiled, or who had studied in Europe, and had been in contact with European groups. The founder of Colombia's PVO, Ingrid Betancourt, was a dual Colombian–French national who had spent many years studying and living in Europe (see Box 4.3). In some cases, Europeans themselves influenced the creation of green parties. In Bolivia, for example, environmental activists have long been in contact with European greens. In 1994, the Poder Verde (Green Power) social group in Bolivia developed links with Les Verts in France and established relationships with the Federation of European Green Parties. The initial origins of the Partido Verde de Bolivia lay in a group of individuals who had been working together since a visit in 2004 to the country by the French green politician Alain Lipietz, culminating in the party's formal creation in 2007. Party formation in Latin America and the Caribbean has also been influenced by the activity and support of green parties from neighbouring states. The successes of the greens in Brazil has inspired smaller neighbouring parties such as those in Argentina and Chile. Mexico's PVEM has

Box 4.1   Potted history: Brazil's greens

Brazil's PV was created in 1986 by writers, ecologists and former political exiles and enjoyed early successes: in elections in 1986 in Rio de Janeiro the PV participated in an informal coalition with the PT and gained 8 per cent of votes for the governorship of Rio de Janeiro state, and São Paulo elected its first congressman on an environmental platform. The party gained momentum in the late 1980s from television footage of fires in the Amazon that alarmed the urban middle class. In the 1989 presidential elections, the PV ran as part of a leftwing alliance led by the PT but the green candidate won less than 0.2 per cent of the vote, thereafter supporting the PT's Luiz Inácio Lula da Silva. In 1990, the PV's first representative to the national legislature was elected in Rio state (Viola 1997). Brazil gained a high profile in environmental issues after the 1992 Earth Summit in Rio but, despite this, by the mid-1990s the PV's survival was still in doubt because of its limited electoral performance and for a long time its only representative in congress was Fernando Gabeira. While it failed to make headway nationally, it began to increase its representation in state assemblies and munici-palities and gained local offices. The environmental activist and PV co-founder Juca Ferreira, for example, served as a municipal environment secretary in Salvador for much of the 1990s and was president of Brazil's Associação Nacional de Órgãos Municipais de Meio Ambiente (ANAMMA, National Association of Municipal Environment Departments). It was the PV's relationship with the PT that shaped its subsequent role in politics and, from 2003 to 2005, the greens formed an important basis of support for the leftwing government of President Lula da Silva (2003–10). That relationship with the governing party has been a key characteristic of the PV and its candidate in the 2010 presidential elections, Marina Silva, had been a prominent PT member who had served as environment minister from 2003 to 2008. She resigned from the ruling party in 2008 and switched to the PV in 2009 after disagreeing with the PT's environmental policies towards the Amazon. In the 2010 presidential election, she gained 19.4 per cent of the first-round vote, surprising observers and forcing a runoff between José Serra of the centrist Partido da Social Democracia Brasileira (PSDB, Brazilian Social Democracy Party) and Dilma Rousseff of the PT, who became president in 2011. In 2013, the PV had 15 seats in the lower house of congress, 37 state legislators and about 1,200 municipal councillors.

also influenced the formation of green groups in Central America. Colombia's Betancourt was an influential supporter of a Nicaraguan initiative to establish a green party. In 2010, Guatemala's Verdes hosted a visit by Antanas Mockus, the green candidate in Colombia's elections of that year.

Party formation has sometimes gone hand in hand with involvement in regional groups such as the Federación de Partidos Verdes de las Américas (FPVA, Federation of Green Parties of the Americas). The FPVA was created in Mexico City in 1997 as a forum for like-minded parties and in 2012 its Latin American and Caribbean member parties came from Argentina, Brazil, Chile, Colombia, Guatemala, Mexico, Nicaragua, Peru, the Dominican Republic and Venezuela, with observers from Bolivia. The organization encourages the formation of green parties throughout the Americas and has been actively involved in setting some of these up. Nicaragua's PVEN coalesced out of talks between activists and the FPVA, which invited the Nicaraguan greens to set out their stall at a meeting in Peru in 2000, and thereafter to participate in the creation of the Global Greens in 2001 in Australia. The PVEN was launched in Managua in 2003 with the federation's support, and participated in elections in 2006 (see Box 4.7). Larger parties such as those from Brazil and Mexico have worked closely with the FPVA to influence the development of other green parties in the region. In 2003, for example, officials from Brazil's PV and the FPVA were present in Buenos Aires at the formation of the Partido Verde Argentina. Manuel Baquedano, the president of the Instituto de Ecología Política (IEP) in Chile, and the FPVA were formal witnesses of the Bolivian green party's inauguration in 2008.

Social movements. The main impetus for the creation of green parties in Latin America came from social movements concerned about the environment that had their origins in civil society mobilization against authoritarian rule (see Chapter 5). However, the transition from movement to party is a complex process and moving from demonstrations to formal party structures with democratic decision-making processes is difficult (see Rabelo 1998). In Brazil, the PV benefited from the new profile gained by the urban social movements that gave rise to the country's strongest party, the PT. An incipient environmental movement arose in the early 1970s in response to growing awareness of ecological damage caused by policies of rapid

Box 4.2 Potted history: Mexico's greens

In Mexico, the Partido Ecologista Mexicana (PEM, Mexican Ecologist Party) evolved out of the environmental movement that emerged in the 1970s (see Chapter 5). The PEM's origins lay in one of the country's first environmental groups created as a neighbourhood organization in Mexico City in 1979. This allied with other groups in the country in the early 1980s to form the Alianza Ecologista (Ecologist Alliance) some of whose members had concluded by 1987 that Mexico's environmental problems required political solutions. The greens contested local and congressional seats in the 1991 mid-term elections for the first time as an independent party and gained 330,799 votes, below the threshold that enabled them to gain legal recognition from electoral authorities. This compelled the party to change its name in 1993 to the Partido Verde Ecologista de México (PVEM, Green Ecologist Party of Mexico). Nonetheless, the government of President Carlos Salinas de Gortari (1988–94) responded to the growing profile of environmental issues and civil society mobilization with policy initiatives. The PVEM increased its vote in the 1994 elections, attracting the attention of larger parties. In the mid-term elections of 1997 it gained more than 1.1 million votes – increasing its share of the vote to 2.4 per cent from 1.4 per cent in 1994 and displacing the Partido del Trabajo (PT, Labour Party) as the country's fourth strongest political force. It also became the first green party in the Western hemisphere to hold a seat in an upper house of parliament, Mexico's senate, when the veteran politician Adolfo Aguilar Zínser won 1,180,804 votes. In elections in 1997 for the mayoralty of Mexico City and its assembly, the PVEM gained 6.9 per cent and 8.8 per cent of the votes respectively (see Fitz 1998). In the general election of 2000, it formed the Alianza por el Cambio (Alliance for Change) with the Partido Acción Nacional (PAN, National Action Party), and this carried the PAN candidate Vicente Fox Quesada to a presidential victory that put an end to 70 years of single-party rule by the PRI. The PVEM also won five seats in the senate. However, Fox's failure to award the PVEM cabinet seats and policy disagreements destroyed the alliance in 2001. In elections in 2003, the party gained 17 seats in the chamber of deputies and remained with five seats in the senate. Prior to the 2006 presidential elections, it nominated its own candidate but then formed a formal alliance with the PRI. In the 2006 legislative elections, the PVEM won 17 out of 500 seats in the chamber of deputies and 4 out of 128 Senators, and by 2012 held 21 chamber seats and six senate seats. In the 2012 elections, it revived its coalition agreement with the PRI and the joint PRI–PVEM coalition candidate, Enrique Peña Nieto, won with 38 per cent of votes. It currently has 22 seats in the lower house, seven senators and PVEM member Juan José Guerra serves as environment minister.

Box 4.3   Potted history: Colombia's greens

The Partido Verde Colombiano (PV, Colombian Green Party) is one of the best organized and most successful green parties in the region, but was not the first ecology party in the country and emerged with only loose links to the environmental movement. The country's first green party, the Partido Verde Oxígeno (PVO, Green Oxygen Party), was created in 1998 largely as an electoral vehicle for the former senator and presidential candidate Ingrid Betancourt, whose differences with her own Partido Liberal (Liberal Party) had left her politically isolated. The PVO gained two seats in the senate with more than 160,000 votes and a mayoralty, but the kidnapping of Betancourt in 2002, and subsequent political reforms, undermined support for the party. The Partido Verde (Green Party) originated in 2005 with the creation of the Partido Opción Centro (POC, Centrist Option Party) in Bogotá, which was created during a political reform process that made it easier to launch new parties. Limited success in the 2006 elections was followed by a move towards green themes with the renaming of the party as Partido Verde Opción Centro (PVOC, Green Centrist Option Party) in 2007 and participation in regional groups such as the FPVA. In the 2007 elections, the PVOC won 375 town councillors, 13 departmental deputies, 2 governorships and 27 mayoralties, and by 2009 was gaining the support of prominent national figures, not least Antanas Mockus, a former mayor of Bogotá and presidential candidate, which led to it relaunching itself as the Partido Verde in the run-up to the 2010 elections. In the 2010 legislative elections, Colombia's greens gained five seats in the senate and three in the chamber of deputies. Its presidential candidate, Mockus, took the conservative favourite Juan Manuel Santos to a second round in presidential elections later that year, gaining 3,588,819 votes (27.5 per cent) and establishing the greens as the country's second political force.

---

growth, a modest political liberalization by the military government, and the creation in 1973 of the Secretaria Especial do Meio Ambiente (SEMA, Special Environment Secretariat). From 1971 to 1976, environmentalism comprised fragmented activities by grassroots groups lacking mass support (see Viola 1997). ENGOs formed between 1974 and 1981, including several with national scope (see Mumme and Korzetz 1997; Viola 1997). With the restoration of competitive

Box 4.4 Potted history: Chile's greens

The growth of green parties in Chile has been unpredictable, with groupings emerging but then dissolving at various times. The Verdes supported opposition to Pinochet's military regime in the 1988 referendum and two green candidates ran in the 1989 elections, but early environmental policy achievements following the return to democracy can be attributed mainly to environmental factions within small leftwing parties of the centre-left Concertación coalition. Lack of electoral support in the 1989 vote, however, was the main reason for a subsequent merger between greens and the Partido Humanista, which also performed poorly in subsequent parliamentary elections and gained limited support in Chile's 1993 presidential elections. The Verdes again supported the humanist candidate in the 1999 presidential elections but lack of support and poor organization saw the party dissolve in 2001. In 2002, a successor party, the Partido Ecologista Verde de Chile (PEV) was formed, initially in three northern regions, and in 2008 this fought municipal elections, gaining one town councillor. The party contested the 2009 presidential elections alongside the humanists within the Nueva Mayoría para Chile (New Majority for Chile) electoral coalition that supported the independent candidate Marco Enríquez-Ominami, who came third in the first round with 1,405,124 votes (20.14 per cent).

Box 4.5 Potted history: Uruguay's greens

Green politics has been fractious in Uruguay, where the Partido Verde Eto-Ecologista (PVEE, Green Etho-Ecologist Party) was formed in 1987 and gained a national profile in the 1989 elections, gaining 11,000 votes. However, disputes over the right to use the name "green party" led to the creation in 1994 of the rival Partido del Sol, Ecologista, Federal y Pacifista (Party of the Sun: Ecologist, Federal and Pacifist), which weakened the PVEE. As a result, the PVEE fought elections in 1999 and 2004 as a grouping within the lists of the Christian-democratic Unión Cívica (Civic Union), which itself was absorbed by the conservative Partido Nacional (National Party) in 2008. The Partido del Sol, Ecologista supported the Partido Nacional presidential candidate Jorge Larrañaga in the 2009 elections. Since then, a new initiative to establish a green party in the country has begun to unfold.

elections in the 1980s a more political environmentalism developed and green groups began to organize in several states. The PV was created by environmentalists and other social movement activists, and its founding members such as Carlos Minc often co-ordinated their activities with the PT (see Box 4.1). Green social movements played a crucial role in advancing Brazil's environmental agenda in the early days of the PV, successfully lobbying for the inclusion of green themes in the 1988 constitution. The momentum this generated and the profile it gave Brazil's environmental movement provided impetus to the PV's subsequent development (Viola 1997).

In Mexico, new social movements began to emerge in the early 1980s, alongside conservation groups such as Pro Mariposa Monarca (1980), Pronatura (1981) and Biocenosis (1982) in an atmosphere of political reform and rising middle-class concern about the environment. Indigenous groups had also been mobilizing against resource concessions on their lands. President Miguel de la Madrid (1982–88) took office at a time when the PRI's legitimacy was coming under strain and promulgated a new environmental law in 1982. The PRI identified the environment as an issue outside the traditional left–right spectrum that it could benefit from as it faced down challenges from the emergent Partido Acción Nacional (PAN, National Action Party). As a result, it was the PRI itself that helped to fuel the political mobilization of ecology groups. Four organizations played a prominent subsequent role: the Movimiento Ecologista Mexicano (MEM, Mexican Ecologist Movement) formed in 1981; the Asociación Ecológica de Coyoacán, a middle-class neighbourhood of Mexico City, which was created in 1983; the Alianza Ecologista (Ecologist Alliance) formed in 1984 but with its origins in a Mexico City community group created in 1979; and the Grupo de los 100, established in 1985 among writers and artists denouncing pollution. Several environmental disasters enhanced growing public awareness of ecological issues and Mexico City's devastating 1985 earthquake fuelled mobilization through the creation of "green brigades" by ENGOs to help displaced people (see González Martínez 1992; Díez 2008). The earthquake gave impetus to the first national meeting of ecologists, and as the political climate changed pressure grew to create a green party, which resulted in 1986 in the formation of the Partido Verde Mexicano (PVM, Mexican Green Party) to fight the elections in 1988 (see Box 4.2).

Box 4.6 Potted history: Argentina's greens

It has been difficult for greens to make headway in Argentine politics, despite environmental consciousness within the country and a broad network of established organizations. The movement is divided politically and territorially, with several groups "in formation", and has applied much of its energy to contesting municipal seats. The Iniciativa Verde (IV, Green Initiative) party was formed in 2006 and fielded its first candidates in elections for the Buenos Aires city assembly in 2009. Its leaders include former politicians of groups like the social-liberal Afirmación para una República Igualitaria (ARI, Support for an Egalitarian Republic), such as Juan Manuel Velasco, who served as the Buenos Aires environment minister during the mayoralty of Jorge Telerman (2006–07), and the Iniciativa Verde continues to back Telerman. Iniciativa Verde maintains links with social movements in the country, and its leading figures include former directors of non-governmental organizations like Greenpeace (Juan Casavelos), and social or environmental activists such as Florencia Breyter. Three other nascent green parties have also emerged in recent years. The Los Verdes-FEP (Greens-Forum of Political Ecology), whose origins date back to 2001 and whose leader Juan Carlos Villalonga is also a prominent former Greenpeace activist, represents potentially the strongest green offering alongside Iniciativa Verde. A Partido Verde (PV) has also been established seeking to extend nationally the influence of the regional Movimiento Ecologista Verdes del Sur (the Green Ecologist Movement of the South). A last group, the Partido Alternativa Verde (Alternative Green Party), remains small and confined to the pages of Facebook but has found some representation in congress through the deputy Miguel Bonasso, who forms part of a leftwing coalition called Proyecto Sur (Southern Project).

In Chile during the mid-1980s ecologists began to participate in political activities, mainly through social movements and human rights associations. In 1987, activists came together as a political party under the name Los Verdes as part of the broader campaign against the Pinochet regime in the country's 1988 referendum (see Box 4.4). In Uruguay, the PVEE was formed in 1987 by existing ecology activists, such as the scientist Rodolfo Tálice, and gained initial prominence in elections in 1989 (see Box 4.5). In Bolivia, intellectuals and professionals came together in 1987 in the Poder Verde ecological movement calling for opposition to environmental destruction in the country. In 1992, Poder Verde agreed a pact with the centre-left Movimiento Bolivia Libre (MBL, Free Bolivia Movement), to incorporate environmental themes into its programme, and in 1995 benefited from an alliance with a small populist group holding the mayoralty of La Paz that enabled Poder Verde's representative to head the city's environmental office. Venezuela's MOVEV originated among social movement activists in 2005 before launching as a party in 2008, and was recognized by electoral authorities only in 2010. The absence of strong links with social movements can hamper a party's expansion, especially in smaller countries. Costa Rica's PVE, for example, was founded in Cartago in 2004 without a strong social movement base, which has confined its activity to the department.

Political reforms. The reform of laws and rules to establish or reinforce democratic politics has been an important feature of political development in Latin America since the late 1970s and was a factor in the emergence of green parties. In Colombia, political reform has been key to the development of one of the region's most successful green parties. In Venezuela, while MOVEV originated among social movement activists, the party's existence owes much to the divisions opened by the formation of the country's ruling Partido Socialista Unido de Venezuela (PSUV, United Socialist Party of Venezuela) from a number of existing parties. For a brief period, a sitting deputy of the then dominant Movimiento V República (MVR, 5th Republic Movement) represented MOVEV in the national assembly. Political liberalization generates new opportunities for environmental mobilization and policy development by enabling ecological themes to gain a place on policy agendas. Reform relaxes restrictions on organizations, stimulating the formation of new groups, and allows issues once proscribed to be discussed. Liberalization also stimulates state sponsorship of ENGOs, either directly or through support for their activities. Greater electoral competition prompts parties to address environmental issues and also leads to the creation of new green and indigenous parties. Easing obstacles to party registration and removing penalties that exist for poor performance in elections encourages the formation of new parties. In Ecuador, reforms that widened access to politics in the 1990s made it easier for new parties and alliances to

Box 4.7 Potted history: greens in Nicaragua, Costa Rica and the Dominican Republic

In Nicaragua, the origins of the small Partido Verde Ecologista de Nicaragua (PVEN, Green Ecologist Party of Nicaragua) lay in the new attention gained by environmental issues under the Sandinista revolutionary government in the 1980s, but it was not until after the restoration of competitive party politics in 1990 that the idea of a green party took hold. The PVEN was formed in 2003 in Managua, and participated with limited success in the 2006 elections in an alliance with the Movimiento de Renovación Sandinista (MRS, Sandinista Renovation Movement) on the MRS ticket as part of the Alianza Herty 2006, but since then its activity has been limited. Costa Rica's Partido del Sol was created in 1997 out of a neighbourhood organization in the city of Santa Ana formed to oppose the siting of a waste dump. At a local level, it has had considerable success, gaining municipal seats and advancing green policies in the Santa Ana canton. The country's Partido Verde Ecologista (PVE, Green Ecology Party) is, similarly, largely an affair confined to the city of Cartago, where in 2010 it won 2,901 votes in parliamentary elections and 5,319 votes in municipal elections, but failed to gain seats. Both parties operate in a system in which green issues have been extensively internalized by the leading political parties and actors. The social-democratic Partido Liberación Nacional (PLN, National Liberation Party) which held the presidency under Laura Chinchilla (2010–), has advocated an environmental agenda and the Partido Acción Ciudadana (PAC, Citizen's Action Party) is a vociferous champion of sustainable development (see Chapter 6). The Dominican Republic's Partido Socialista Verde (PASOVE, Green Socialist Party), established in 2009, and two parties legally recognized in 2011, Venezuela's Movimiento Ecológico de Venezuela (MOVEV, Venezuelan Ecological Movement) and Bolivia's Partido Verde, are the newest green parties in the region.

compete and led to the formation of indigenous parties. In Colombia and Venezuela, new constitutions allowed indigenous movements to participate in elections without forming parties. Bolivia was late to reform, only permitting indigenous movements and civil society groups to contest elections in 2004 (see Van Cott 2005). Reforms also gave a route for guerrillas to enter politics, and several founders or supporters of green parties, such as Fernando Gabeira and Alfredo

Syrkis in Brazil and Miguel Bonasso in Argentina, had once been armed activists in the 1970s or 1980s or members of the clandestine resistance to military rule, such as Juca Ferreira and Carlos Minc in Brazil. In Colombia, the Partido Verde originated in 2005 with the creation of the POC in Bogotá among a group of political activists including Carlos Ramón González, a former commander in the Movimiento 19 de Abril (M-19, 19th of April Movement) guerrilla organization.

Key characteristics

Green parties in Latin America and the Caribbean today are highly diverse, and can be compared according to a number of factors:

Size and impact. The greens in Mexico, Brazil and Colombia are major parties that have achieved a significant performance, but only in Brazil have they played a meaningful role in policymaking at a national level by gaining ministerial office. Greens have also grown increasingly influential in Colombia and gained cabinet representation under Mexico's new PRI president Enrique Peña Nieto (2012–) when PVEM member Juan José Guerra was appointed environment minister. Brazil's PV was represented in cabinet by the culture minister, Gilberto Gil, from 2003 to 2008 and Juca Ferreira from 2008 to 2010, and the PV's co-founder Carlos Minc served from 2008 to 2010 as environment minister. However, most green parties remain minor and nascent, and many may not even participate in elections, such as Guatemala's Los Verdes, which exists alongside a large number of small parties on the fringes of the political process. Many of these parties have made limited headway in systems often designed to reward large parties that complement a broader systemic ambition to achieve stability. Small green parties usually do not run on their own tickets but within alliances that back the stronger candidates of larger parties. They lack political experience and contacts and it has been common for a prominent figure with wider experience in politics to become associated with and take a commanding role in them. The origins of Colombia's green party, for example, lie in political reforms aimed at demobilizing the armed left and the creation in 2005 of the Partido Opción Centro in Bogotá, which shifted greenward. The POC's success in elections in 2007 caught the attention of key independents, not least Mockus and the career politician Enrique Peñalosa, both former mayors of Bogotá, and it rebranded itself as the Partido Verde in the run-up to 2010. Similarly, in Bolivia the leader of the newly established Partido Verde, Margoth Soria Saravia, is a prominent former deputy of the Unidad Democrática y Popular (UDP, Democratic and Popular Union), a ruling coalition that fell apart in the mid-1980s.

Funding. Political parties and candidates need money to run campaigns and convey proposals to voters, putting minor parties at a disadvantage. As a party grows, its funding needs increase rapidly. A key issue in Brazil following the strong performance of the PV candidate Marina Silva in the 2010 presidential elections became how the party restructured and financed itself in order to maintain its momentum in the 2014 polls. Mexico's PVEM demonstrates the scale of financing involved in running a green party. The party places information about its finances on its website (see below). This reveals that in 2009 it received 228 million pesos (then about $16 m) from the public purse for general party activities, and 75 million pesos for campaigning in the 2009 mid-term elections and other activities (see PVEM 2011). Campaign donations from sympathizers brought in 7 million pesos and, when combined with existing available funds, this gave it an election war chest of 149 million pesos. But who should foot the bill for the activities of political parties? All Latin American countries except Venezuela and Cuba provide direct and indirect forms of public financing to parties. In Mexico, public funds account for about four fifths of the resources allocated to political parties. While this makes it easier for green parties to survive, raising private funds can strengthen their links with society (see Griner and Zovatto 2005). How parties spend the funds at their disposal is another matter, with some seeking value and others being wasteful. Mexico's greens found a selling point in a country where the financial practices of politicians are constantly under scrutiny when they divided the amount parties received from public financing by the number of votes received in elections in 1997. Each vote received by the PVEM for national office accounted for about 10 pesos ($0.80) of public financing – the lowest for any party – while votes for other parties varied between 17 pesos per vote for the Partido de la Revolución Democrática (PRD, Party of the Democratic Revolution) and 85 pesos per vote for the Partido del Trabajo (PT, Labour Party) (see Fitz 1998).

The role of alliances. A key stratagem employed by most green parties to make progress at the polls and influence policymaking has been joining electoral alliances and entering coalitions. In most Latin American countries, alliances between parties are a characteristic feature of the political system. Since its inception, Brazil's PV has collaborated with more powerful parties, in particular the PT, and both have often campaigned on shared platforms. There have been intense discussions within the PV about what type of alliance to establish with the PT, and the PV has also worked with the centre-right PMDB. In some cases, alliances can be a way of getting around prohibitive laws on party registration. In Peru, for example, the failure in 1999 of the Alternativa Verde movement to register as a party did not stop it campaigning, and it allied with the Movimiento Solidaridad (Solidarity Movement), a registered party that then incorporated green principles in his platform. Chile has a strong tradition of coalition politics and greens have participated in elections as part of broad alliances. The Partido Ecologista del Perú participated in Peru's 2006 elections in an alliance with the Partido Fuerza Democrática. In Mexico, the PVEM helped to break the long monopoly of the PRI in the general election of 2000 by joining an alliance with the PAN and also won five seats in the senate. Parties may form only partial alliances that guarantee them the ability to fight some seats as shared candidates, greatly strengthening their ability to win, and to fight others competitively. In Mexico, for example, an electoral alliance between the PRI, PVEM and the Partido Nueva Alianza (PANAL, New Alliance Party) for the 2012 polls was initially formed on the basis that the PVEM and PANAL would support the PRI's presidential candidate but share out which of those directly elected congressional seats gained by plurality voting they would fight as part of the alliance. Alliances can be fragile, especially if one partner is much weaker than the other, or parties disagree about the best ways to protect the environment. The PRI–PVEM–PANAL alliance in 2012, for example, broke down just two months after its formation. Disputes over policy can also be divisive, prompting Brazil's former PT environment minister Marina Silva to quit the party in 2009 (see above). Small parties can wield disproportionate power within a coalition, depending on its nature and the characteristics of the party system (see Poguntke 2002).

Regionalism and localism. Some parties adopt a strongly regional focus, often because of their origins and strengths in a particular state or region. In Brazil, for example, the first activities by a group using the name "Partido Verde" were in the state of Paraná in 1982, four years before the establishment of a national party in Rio de Janeiro under that name. After the 1986 election, the new PV started organizing and spread to other regions (Rabelo 1998.) Nonetheless, until the mid-1990s, the PV remained a mostly Rio party and metropolitan areas – São Paulo, Rio de Janeiro, Belo Horizonte, Porto Alegre and Curitiba – still have most of the environmental groups. Environmentalism has expanded outside of the south in part because of international attention to the north and, in particular, the Amazon (see Hochstetler and Keck 2007). A regional focus can have implications for a party's programme and ideology. Despite their urban origins, Brazilian environmental groups have assumed a high profile in campaigns to protect specific ecosystems such as the Amazon, the Atlantic Forest and the Paraná watersheds (see Hochstetler and Keck 2007). In Mexico's 1997 mid-term elections, which represented a breakthrough for the greens, the PVEM scored well among voters in Mexico City. Support for the party was especially strong in some of the poorest areas where it worked to bring social services to urban communities (see Fitz 1998). Local government has been an important stronghold for green parties in political systems that are centralized and structured to reward nationalized parties. It is often at the city and municipal level that green parties have had most impact on policy outcomes. In Colombia, municipal power has been a key factor in the rise of the greens and former mayors of cities such as Bogotá and Medellín are leading figures in the party, which has secured many governorships and mayoralties. Although they may not extend their influence nationally, some green parties can dominate local agendas and enact policy innovations in such issues as waste disposal. Costa Rica's Partido del Sol, for example, is a well organized local party that claims many achievements in the district of Santa Ana.

Indigenous parties

In Latin America and the Caribbean parties formed by indigenous communities to advance their interests and distinctive world view incorporating ecological principles must form part of any discussion of political ecology (see Chapter 5). Parties representing indigenous people have emerged in a number of countries in the region and have had an important influence on politics. Indigenous and indigenous-based parties have included: in Ecuador, the Confederación de Nacionalidades Indígenas del Ecuador (CONAIE, Confederation of Indigenous Nationalities of Ecuador) and the Movimiento Unido Pluricultural Pachakutik (Pachakutik); in Bolivia, the Movimiento Indígena Pachakuti (MIP), Movimiento Indio Tupak Katari (MITKA), the Movimiento Revolucionario Tupaj Katari de Liberación (MRTKL), the Asamblea de la Soberanía del Pueblo (ASP), the Eje Pachakuti, and the Movimiento al Socialismo (MAS)/Instrumento Político para la Soberanía de los Pueblos (IPSP); in Colombia, the Autoridades Indígenas de Colombia (AICO) and the Movimiento Indígena Colombiano (MIC), the Alianza Social Indígena (ASI); in Venezuela, the Partido Unido Multiétnico de Amazonas (PUAMA); and in Peru, the Movimiento Indígena de la Amazonía Peruana (MIAP). Several countries in Latin America have established mechanisms to ensure representation of indigenous people and some, such as Bolivia, stipulate that political representation can be undertaken not only by parties but also by indigenous and civic associations, thereby removing regulatory obstacles to party formation (see Catón and Tuesta Soldevilla 2008). Some indigenous parties have achieved considerable political success. CONAIE formed part of the coalition that won Ecuador's 2002 presidential elections and two of its leaders were appointed to the cabinet. In Bolivia, Quechua and Aymara coca growers were prominent in the formation of the MAS that went on to win the 2005 and 2009 presidential elections.

Van Cott (2005) identified factors that influenced the decision to form an indigenous party and their subsequent performance that included: the density of an indigenous organization's network in a country; the movement's degree of unity; the age of the movement that spawned the party; and the size, dispersion and concentration of the indigenous population. Indigenous majorities exist in more than half of Bolivia's departments, a fifth of Peru's, about 14 per cent of Ecuador's provinces, three Amazonian departments in Colombia, and in Venezuela's state of Amazonas (see Van Cott 2005). Van Cott takes an approach to the study of indigenous parties within existing literature that considers, among other things, the organizational, cultural, constituency and policy links between social movements and parties, particularly left-libertarian or "new left" parties spawned by diverse coalitions, such as the Brazilian PT, which seek not only to change policies but also the form of politics by creating a more participatory, decentralized, egalitarian system.

Ideological base of green parties

Green parties in Latin America and the Caribbean share a commitment to sustainable development and equitable social policies that are put forward by similar parties elsewhere and by umbrella groups such as the Global Greens. Their platforms, programmes, manifestos and mission statements are easily accessible online (see websites). Beyond their ecological commitments, support for democracy and criticisms of development models (see Chapter 6), several features recur in their platforms:

Political centrism. Traditionally political debate in Latin America and the Caribbean has been shaped by disagreements influenced by social class. In many cases green parties have originated among urban social movements whose leadership has been in the hands of middle-class activists and scientific ecologists taking advantage of a political opening and the decline of class-based politics. Just as the objectives of social movements were often local or confined to a single theme, in many cases green positions did not fit neatly into established left–right divisions. This has positioned green parties on the centre in party politics, although they may espouse leftwing or centre-left positions on the economy and issues of social justice. Although they are diverse, green parties in Latin America and the Caribbean have also consciously sought to develop a critique of political processes dominated by centralized and authoritarian, hierarchical parties and characterized by polarized left–right positions. Some greens have argued that this has limited democratic development and prevented political progress on resolving many environmental and social problems.

In Colombia, for example, the country's first ecological party, the PVO, was created explicitly as an alternative to what its founders derided as a corrupt political elite within traditional conservative and liberal parties. The later growth of Colombia's main green party, the PV, reflected the development of viable centrism in a country plagued by deep divisions. In Bolivia, Poder Verde was created in 1987 calling for a political *alternative* able to halt environmental degradation. In a speech at its national congress in 1992, activist Diego Torres Peñaloza proposed a new "green politics" that "would bring forward an alternative to the old political answers" and get rid of "demagoguery, false promises, and unethical alliances" (Torres Peñaloza 1998). The leader of the Partido Verde formed later, Margoth Soria Saravia, is a political science professor who has been highly critical of the left–right divide in politics. In Mexico, during the 1990s, the PVEM sought to establish distance from traditional parties by tapping into public contempt for longstanding political fraud and one of the PVEM's main campaign slogans in 1997 was "Don't vote for a politician, vote for an ecologist" (see Fitz 1998). In Brazil, Marina Silva's impressive first-round vote in the 2010 presidential elections revealed support among voters frustrated with antagonism between the main forces in politics. Similarly, Venezuela's MOVEV states firmly that "we are not a party of the left: green ideology contains more important dimensions than leftwing socialism" (Movimiento Ecológico de Venezuela 2011). Chile's PEV states that it aims to offer citizens "an original option, different both to the traditional right and left and to social democracy" (Partido Ecologista Verde Chile 2011).

Antipathy towards "politics as normal" of this kind is well established in Latin America and the Caribbean as part of a tradition of "anti-politics" (see Loveman and Davies 1997).

Alternative politics. The reluctance of green parties to position themselves on a traditional left–right spectrum has been heavily influenced by ideas from Europe, especially by the "new left". In the 1970s, this term sought to distinguish the reformist positions of leftwing parties and movements from earlier, mainly Marxist organizations motivated by a rigid class-based understanding of society. Reformist parties adopting the new left position have aimed to capture the support of minorities marginalized for reasons that cannot obviously be explained by class, such as women and indigenous or black people.

In Brazil, for example, the nascent green party took positions closely associated with the new left. Its participation in the 1986 elections in Rio de Janeiro in an informal coalition with the PT pitched its leader Fernando Gabeira as a "red–green" PT/PV candidate for governor and, for the first time in Brazilian politics, the greens' platform put forward policies alongside its ecological commitments that represented radical socio-political ideas such as feminism, anti-racism, gay rights and drug legislation. A prominent strain in the platform of Brazil's PV since the mid-1990s has been the defence of indigenous people (see Chapters 5, 6). Nonetheless, support for Brazil's PV in recent years has come as much from the centre-right as the new left and in large cities such as São Paulo and Rio, the PV has supported PSDB candidates. Marina Silva has enhanced her appeal to alternative voters and has said she wants to be the "first African-Brazilian woman of poor origin" to become president (Reuters 2010). This commitment to alternative politics derives in part from the discourse of human rights that played a role in democratization within Latin America and the Caribbean. Most green parties in the region advocate strict adherence to universal human rights and respect for cultural diversity. Colombia's Partido Verde, for example, calls for the "elimination of all forms of sexual or gender discrimination" and recognition of and respect for "difference and plurality" (Partido Verde Colombia 2011a, 2011b, 2011c). Human diversity is sometimes linked to biodiversity as an essential component of life, and often assumes the existence of ecological rights (see Partido Verde de Bolivia 2011).

Ecology. Issues of ecology help to explain the origins of the social movements that gave rise to green parties in Latin America and the Caribbean, but have not always dominated their programmes. For example, among the seven objectives of Costa Rica's Partido del Sol, only two are solely aimed at the environment – the promotion of sustainable development and reforestation – while others address such issues as arts policy and public security (Partido del Sol Costa Rica 2011). In Brazil, it was not for two years after the formation of the PV that the ecological focus of the greens ignited national debate. One reason for the greens' limited focus on environmental issues is that parties are often formed around locally specific issues, and this can pose difficulties when they need to take a national approach. A way of getting round this is for a party to portray environmental problems as the origin of *all* social problems, as does Argentina's Partido Verde. There may also be political risks for a party that concentrates its programme solely on ecology. In Brazil's 2010 presidential elections, for example, environmental issues were not among the most important for voters and, despite Marina Silva's popularity, the environment was in some instances used as a weapon to criticize her. She was accused by some opponents of being a "One note samba", an accusation that suggested she did not have a programme that took into account other issues such as public safety, social security or foreign policy. Some green parties such as Mexico's PVEM have even been criticized by groups such as Greenpeace for their apparent *lack of* interest in ecological issues. A point of departure on discussions of ecology among several parties is the anthropomorphic personification of nature as a life-giving and nurturing "Mother Earth" (see Box 1.5). This idea is found both in urban-based parties within countries in which it does not exist in traditional indigenous mythology, such as the Partido del Sol in Uruguay, as well as in those such as the Andean states where it is central to indigenous cosmology. Urban ecology has become a visible area of debate and in several cities greens have created new environmental institutions and pioneered innovative projects (see Hochstetler and Keck 2007). The Puertorriqueños por Puerto Rico party calls for a "new urbanism" aimed at creating a better quality of life for all (Puertorriqueños por Puerto Rico 2011).

Economic equality and sustainable development. Green parties such as the PV in Brazil have tended to assume "red–green" positions that combine a socialist or social-democratic vision of greater equality with environmental protection. At the "Green Horizons" meeting in Mexico City in 1997, the new Latin American members of the FPVA approved a declaration on "Democracy, Social Justice, and the Environment" that criticized globalization and neoliberal policies. The origin of green economic positions often lies in a critique of industrialism and capitalism as the principal sources of environmental degradation (see Partido Verde Argentina 2011). While some parties such as Argentina's Partido Verde commit to the achievement of a vision of socialism that is close to traditional Marxist positions, others such as Chile's PEV express a vaguer commitment to "social justice" that reflects social-democratic positions. In Puerto Rico, the PPR advocates a mixed economy to generate local capital while protecting the environment (Puertorriqueños por Puerto Rico 2011). Nicaragua's Verde Ecologista party places emphasis on co-operative economic institutions (Verde Ecologista Nicaragua 2007). The dominant position of almost all these parties is a desire to achieve sustainable development (see Chapter 6). Sustainable development, or "ecodesarrollo" (eco-development) is the first article of Venezuela's MOVEV, one of the few green parties in the region to identify over-consumption as a problem (MOVEV 2011).

Localism. Localism is a prominent theme in the platforms of green parties. In Uruguay, for example, the Partido del Sol, Ecologista, Federal y Pacifista commits itself to seeking political decentralization of the country in opposition to the centralizing dominance of Montevideo (Portillo 1998). Argentina's Partido Verde argues that popular power resides in municipal and neighbourhood associations and not in parliament, where they are only represented (Partido Verde Argentina 2011). This focus on the local sometimes supports the promotion of participative democracy (see, for example, Partido Ecologista Verde Chile 2011; Partido Verde Ecologista Costa Rica 2011). Brazil's PV advocates participative democracy through national, regional or local referendums, and extensive policies to educate citizens in democratic and ecological values (Partido Verde Brazil 2011). A commitment to localism may be a reflection of a party's local concentration. Costa Rica's Partido del Sol advocates change aimed largely at the canton of Santa Ana where it is active (Partido del Sol Costa Rica 2011).

Constraints on political ecology

The emergence of green politics poses important questions about the relationship between environmentalism and democracy such as how, for example, the green movement in countries such as Chile was able to assume a non-class position that was not threatening to the authoritarian regime, giving it more freedom to organize. The Chilean case lends support to the argument that environmental concerns in developing countries can be addressed more effectively under economically stable democratic regimes than authoritarian ones (see Silva 1996). Nonetheless, as we have seen, environmental policy in Chile since the reestablishment of democracy has been limited by a consensus within the political elite subordinating environmental concerns to the traditional policy paradigm (see Chapter 2). Incomplete consolidation coupled with the constraints of economic development has limited the extent to which environmental parties can influence politics, complicating the organizational, institutional and ideological obstacles faced by greens when they try to mobilize in systems dominated by class-based parties (see Mumme and Korzetz 1997). Other political factors continue to constrain the growth of green parties, not least the development by mainstream parties of their own green platforms. Significant divisions have sometimes developed within and between green parties, and in some countries several ecology parties have competed for representation. Peru demonstrates how political reforms enabling multiparty politics can sometimes be a double-edged sword for a small green movement. At various times two groupings have competed for public attention, the Partido Verde del Perú and the Partido Ecologista Alternativa Verde del Perú (Green Alternative Ecologist Party of Peru). An issue that has often divided environmentalists has been over whether to form a political party in the first place. In Brazil, by 1986, environmentalists were engaging in fierce debates about the future of their movement and some activists felt that a green party could be an obstacle to the environmental movement (see Viola 1997). In Mexico, within a few years of the creation of the Partido Ecologista Mexicana (PEM) critics were accusing the green party of serving PRI interests.

The merits or demerits of party formation can be clearer when considered alongside the general level of environmental awareness in a country. In some cases, the high profile of environmental issues themselves can limit the growth of political environmentalism. Costa Rica's Partido Verde Ecologista (PVE Green Ecological Party) has struggled to establish its presence in a country where environmental awareness is high and the mainstream parties have all developed green agendas (see below). Moreover, having a party may not be essential to advance the cause: even in the absence of a party or electoral success environmentalists can still influence policy. In Brazil, by running in the first round of presidential elections in 2010, Marina Silva, the PV candidate, provided the main impetus for the ambitious targets for reductions in greenhouse gas emissions that the government presented before the 2009 UN Climate Change Conference in Copenhagen.

Leaders of Argentina's Iniciativa Verde continue to dwell upon the trade-off between creating a strong, independent political party and trying to monopolize the green vote, or nurturing the environmental agendas of established parties and working to establish green deputies among other parties (see ComAmbiental 2011).

Although the 1980s saw the creation of green parties and some had limited success, many candidates had their platforms co-opted by mainstream parties. However, dominant parties often give green themes low priority as they seek to shape national platforms premised on economic growth. While conservative parties generally oppose environmental agendas, the left has paid significant attention to the environment not least because greens are their electoral rivals, concern for the environment is often strongest among the left's core constituencies such as the poor, and the issue has the potential to garner universal support. A large number of grassroots organizations that take an interest in the environment are politically on the left (see Kaimowitz 1996; Hochstetler and Keck 2007). For example, there is a strong environmental current within the Partido Socialista de Chile (PS, Chilean Socialist Party). Early environmental policymaking within Chile's ruling Concertación coalition in 1990 was conducted largely by environmental factions within two centre-left parties, the PS and the Partido Por la Democracia (PPD, Party for Democracy). In Paraguay, the small social-democratic Partido Revolucionario Febrerista (PRF, Revolutionary Febrerist Party) is a good example of a mainstream party that promotes a green agenda.

However, the left's commitment to the environment is weakened by its own divisions on this issue and it tends to subordinate environmental concerns to developmental agendas. Some activists on the left consider the environment to be a superficial issue imported from rich northern countries. Parties such as the PRD in Mexico, the Frente Farabundo Martí para la Liberación Nacional (FMLN, Farabundo Martí National Liberation Front) in El Salvador, and the Frente Sandinista de Liberación Nacional (FSLN, Sandinista National Liberation Front) in Nicaragua have given green issues low priority, and support for environmental causes is often confined to their middle-class supporters rather than among poorer constituencies. Trades unions sometimes resist environmental regulation in the belief that this will limit job creation. Where leftwing leaders have come to power in Latin America, they have frequently given development projects precedence over environmental regulation and stressed that the need to raise living standards for the poor is their first priority (see Kaimowitz 1996). In Brazil, for example, a number of decisions by the Rousseff administration have been portrayed by greens and environmental groups as representing a policy shift away from environmental protection in favour of economic development (see Hurwitz 2012).

In newly liberalized political systems, a number of formal and informal limitations on political expression and mobilization handicap efforts by environmental groups to mobilize support:

- *Regulations and thresholds*. Political parties have to obey regulations that affect their behaviour and performance which are included in constitutions, statute laws, electoral codes and even executive decrees (see Catón and Tuesta Soldevilla 2008). All the countries in the region except Argentina and Brazil, for example, require parties to win a minimum share of votes at parliamentary elections. These rules are intended to prevent many small parties from clogging up the democratic process and can work to exclude small parties, hindering the emergence of green or ecologically oriented parties. A key issue in the development of green parties has been the level at which thresholds for parties to register have been set. In Latin America there is evidence that stricter requirements to form a party can help the consolidation of democratic institutions (Birnir 2008; see above). Although Latin American thresholds are not highly restrictive, the most well-established green parties in Mexico and Brazil have nonetheless both fallen foul of registration procedures. In Chile, the PEV was formed in 2002 initially in three northern regions, but its limited size precluded it from fielding a candidate in presidential elections.

- *Seat allocation formulas*. Formulas for allocating seats – the ratio of votes to seats for each party – can work alongside thresholds to constrain small parties. Where a formula awards seats to parties winning small proportions of the vote, this should promote the formation of new parties and improve their electoral performance, but where a formula favours larger parties this is likely to inhibit them. In Latin America the d'Hondt formula is often used for allocating seats, and this tends to favour larger parties (see Van Cott 2005). The number of seats in a district also has an impact on the number of parties in a political system, and those with more seats help smaller parties. Psychologically, districts with fewer seats discourage citizens from "wasting" their votes on smaller parties that are unlikely to win

(Taagepera and Shugart 1989). The number of seats in a district may be particularly important in explaining the formation and viability of indigenous parties. In Colombia, when the number of seats allocated to districts was increased, this led to the creation of ethnic parties that made electoral gains, prior to which few minorities had gained representation (see Van Cott 2005). In some countries, reserved seats and quotas have enhanced access to the political system for indigenous groups.

- *Voting systems.* Proportional representation is more likely to encourage new and minority parties than majoritarian systems because it lowers obstacles to them entering the system and increases choice for voters. Majoritarian systems often reproduce two-party dominance and make it hard for citizens to form new parties. PR is used throughout Latin America, usually in mixed systems in which half of the legislature's lower chamber is elected in a single-member district (see Van Cott 2005). However, voting systems have in practice tended to constrain the activity of greens and minor parties (see above). Rules on who is eligible to vote can also have an impact on their fortunes. In countries such as Bolivia, for example, support for the greens, and indigenous groups that may support a green agenda, is likely to be highest in rural and highland areas, where the obstacles to voter registration are greater.

- *Decentralization.* Levels of decentralization vary throughout Latin America and the Caribbean but most countries hold direct municipal or regional elections (see Chapter 1). Devolution of power to sub-national authorities has created conditions more favourable to the rise of green political groups. Decentralization and the creation of new electoral districts can also encourage the formation of indigenous parties. New parties will be more successful in decentralized countries because the costs involved in forming a party are lower, a smaller organization is needed to undertake a campaign, and they need fewer signatures to register. Parties that win local elections often develop their powerbase as a source of support for elections in other districts and at higher levels (see Dalton, Flanagan and Beck 1984). In Argentina, decentralization was an important aspect of democratization and the development of municipal political networks was a factor in the emergence of a national green movement.

- *Political violence.* In Latin America the candidates of minor parties and environmental activists can be at risk of violence and intimidation. In Brazil, for example, the murder of the rubber tappers' leader Chico Mendes in 1988 aroused worldwide attention to the risks faced by environmental activists (see Hochstetler and Keck 2007; Rabelo 1998). In 2011, in the Amazonian state of Pará, at least eight environmental activists were murdered by gunmen. In Mexico, during campaigning for the 1997 mid-term elections, two PVEM members were murdered in the states of Guerrero and Mexico respectively. Disputes over logging and mining have been linked to several killings in recent years. In 2011, an environmental campaigner Javier Torres Cruz was murdered by gunmen in Guerrero, Mexico (Fitz 1998). In 2009, the Inter-American Court of Human Rights (IACHR) ruled that the Honduran government shared responsibility for the murder in 1995 of an environmental activist who had accused timber companies of illegal logging. In El Salvador, in 2009, an activist campaigning against a mining project owned by the Canadian Pacific Rim Mining Corporation was murdered. Even in relatively safe countries such as Costa Rica, environmentalists have been targeted. In June 2013, Jairo Mora, an activist campaigning to protect endangered sea turtles, considered a delicacy in some parts of the world, was found dead in a suspected killing by smugglers.

Two principal criticisms of green parties often made further highlight difficulties they face inserting themselves in the traditional political landscape: lack of coherence and continuity; and personalism.

Green parties are often accused by their critics of being less ideologically coherent on non-ecological issues than mainstream parties and they can struggle to establish a credible policy offering in some areas. Brazil's PV, for example, has at times been accused by opponents of being an ideologically loose gathering of regional groups and political aspirants more focused on securing official jobs than on following a long-term programme. The PV's own debates over policy and ideological differences within the party have complicated its relations with other parties (see above). PV activists have, at the same time, sometimes favoured candidates more likely to secure electoral success over those with clear ideological positions. A source of apparent incoherence can be the wide range of positions that green parties and the individuals within them take on political and economic issues. These may ignore controversies involving natural resource use that are considered "off limits" because of their importance to the wider economy. For example, mining has become the engine of growth in Peru with an estimated $50 bn of investment in the sector likely by 2020. In 2011, mobilization by groups opposing the impact of large mining projects on their communities became the principal political issue in the country. In 2011, however, the Partido Ecologista del Perú made no mention in its programme of mining or the disputes that the sector generates in the country (Partido Ecologista del Perú 2011). Similarly, Colombia's Partido Verde has ignored the issue of free trade and made no statements about this when the US president approved a bilateral free trade agreement with the country in 2011 even though critics said the deal would be bad for the environment.

Some green parties combine economic positions that are associated with the left with social positions associated with the right. On some social issues, Mexico's PVEM for example, has taken a stance on the right of the political spectrum. In 2008, for example, the PVEM supported introduction of the death penalty for murderers and kidnappers in the country, which since 2006 has been racked by serious violence. PVEM candidates have also been embroiled in disputes over their apparent hostility towards lesbian and gay rights. The PVEM has based its positions on an anti-corruption platform, although it was itself embroiled in at least one high-profile corruption scandal in 2004.

Personalism and corporatism has also been evident among some green parties. Levels of internal democracy vary within green parties which, being small, are sometimes dominated by skilful politicians who can monopolize party resources. In Brazil's PV, key positions have tended to remain in the hands of a few individuals linked to the mobilization of the 1970s and 1980s. In Colombia, the PV has been dominated by career politicians with experience outside the environmental movement that limits the mobility of internal candidates with activist backgrounds. As a result, the party has been riven by disputes. In Mexico, since its initial registration in 1991 the PVEM has been dominated by one family. Jorge González Torres, its first president and a former member of the PRI, was succeeded to the presidency of the party by his son, Jorge Emilio González Martínez, a senator. The party has faced accusations of nepotism, breaches of electoral law and corruption (see bbc.co.uk 2004).

Conclusion

The formation of green parties in Latin America and the Caribbean may seem as natural a development in politics as that of what we might consider to be the mainstream groups on the right and left that tend to dominate politics in the region. Yet green parties have faced a unique set of political circumstances that can make it much harder to survive upon the shifting sands of democratic politics (see Hochstetler and Keck 2007). They are often small and hampered by their local origins, lack of funds and the rules of political systems that were designed to ensure stability between two or three large political parties after many years of authoritarian rule. Their ideas and programmes can be taken by larger, mainstream parties, and their politicians can grow frustrated with the limited opportunities to bring about change that they provide and so move on to more fertile political pastures. The incomplete consolidation of democracy in some Latin American countries coupled with the constraints of economic development limits the degree to which environmental parties can influence politics. In some countries, green activists may also face the risk of intimidation and violence from powerful vested interests seeking to resist criticism of their environmental record or any effort to regulate their activities. When studied by the conventional political science indicators of party activity, with a few exceptions the greens undoubtedly seem to be largely marginal actors. Yet, the growing profile of environmental issues in Latin America and the Caribbean and some of the stark choices posed by the inescapable tension between rapid development and environmental protection, can offer greens unprecedented political opportunities to garner the support that mainstream parties cannot. The rise of green parties, therefore, offers lessons about the structural constraints that can be found in democratic systems but also about what is possible in politics. In that sense, green parties can provide scholars with valuable clues about the characteristics and condition of the political process more generally.

Recommended reading

Hochstetler, Kathryn and Margaret E Keck. 2007. *Greening Brazil: Environmental Activism in State and Society*. Durham, NC: Duke University Press.

Mainwaring, Scott and Timothy Scully (eds). 1995. *Building Democratic Institutions: Party Systems in Latin America*. Stanford, CA: Stanford University Press.

O'Donnell, Guillermo, Joseph S Tulchin and Augusto Varas (eds) with Adam Stubits. 2008. *New Voices in the Study of Democracy in Latin America*. Washington, DC: Woodrow Wilson International Center for Scholars.

Simonian, Lane. 1995. *Defending the Land of the Jaguar: A History of Conservation in Mexico*. Austin: University of Texas Press.

Van Cott, Donna Lee. 2005. *From Movements to Parties in Latin America: The Evolution of Ethnic Politics*. Cambridge: Cambridge University Press.

Useful websites

Federación de Partidos Verdes de las Américas (FPVA, Federation of Green Parties of the Americas): http://fpva.org.mx/

Global Greens: www.globalgreens.org/

Parties

Argentina: Iniciativa Verde: www.iniciativaverde.org.ar/

    Los Verdes-FEP: www.losverdes-fep.org/sitio/index.php, http://losverdes. org.ar

    Partido Alternativa Verde http://es-es.facebook.com/alternativaverde

    Partido Verde: www.partidoverde.org.ar/

Bolivia: Partido Verde www.partidoverdebolivia.org/

Brazil: Partido Verde http://pv.org.br/

Chile: Partido Ecologista Verde (PEV) www.ecologistaverde.cl/ www. partidoecologista.cl/

Colombia: Partido Verde www.partidoverde.org.co/

Costa Rica: Partido Verde Ecologista (PVE) www.partidoverdeecologista. webs.com/

    Partido del Sol: www.partidodelsol.com/index.php?option=com_contac t&view=contact&id=1&Itemid=68

Dominican Republic: Partido Verde de la Unidad Democrática www. udusa.org/

Guatemala: Partido Los Verdes de Guatemala: http://es-es.facebook.com/ pages/Partido-Los-Verdes-de-Guatemala/110447888993776

Mexico: Partido Verde Ecologista de México (PVEM) www.partidoverde. org.mx/pvem/

Peru: Partido Verde del Peru (PVP) http://wayback.archive-it. org/212/20050927214602/www.unii.net/unii/allparuna/peruverde. html (archived)

    Partido Ecologista del Perú (PEP, Ecological Party of Peru): www. partidoecologista.com/

Puerto Rico: Puertorriqueños por Puerto Rico (PPR) www.porpuertorico.com/

Uruguay: Partido Verde http://pv-uruguay.blogspot.com/

Movimiento Ecologista y Pacifista del Uruguay http://es-es.facebook.com/pages/Movimiento-Ecologista-y-Pacifista-del-Uruguay/113500575380935

Venezuela: Movimiento Ecológico de Venezuela (MEV) www.movimientoecologicovzla.es.tl/

||||||||||||||||||||||||||||||||||||||||||||||||||||||||||||||||||||||||||||||||||||||||||||||||||||||||||||||||||||||||||||||||

CHAPTER FIVE

Actors – social movements and NGOs

ENVIRONMENTAL ACTIVISM in Latin America and the Caribbean has taken place largely outside the formal realms of politics among citizens brought together or led by a large number of diverse social groups both well organized and highly informal. Some of these have become permanent features of the landscape, working professionally to lobby policymakers and corporations about environmental issues. Others may emerge over single issues in one part of a country, mobilize support, and later disappear. Indigenous movements with social and environmental aims have arisen and now exert a powerful political and cultural influence. At times, all these groups and movements have gained recognition and support from well funded non-governmental organizations (NGOs), both domestic and international, which have offered them the technical expertise and practical assistance they need to challenge governments and corporate interests. The shifting mosaic of environmental activism and the many networks and alliances that comprise it has been studied through the notion of civil society, which has grown in importance in Latin American and Caribbean politics, providing the basis of new theoretical understandings of democratization based on autonomous social organizations (see Alvarez, Dagnino and Escobar 1998). An emphasis on civil society became a key characteristic of the study of democracy in the region in the 1990s although there has been considerable disagreement about what it comprises (see O'Donnell et al. 2008). This chapter examines social movements campaigning on environmental issues and NGOs that are considered integral to the idea of civil society. It looks at their emergence, characteristics and the strategies open to them in their efforts to bring about change.

Civil society

In the last few decades, Latin America and the Caribbean has experienced new levels of mobilization outside the formal institutions of politics as social movements have become a focus of activity. These were once commonly portrayed as "new" social movements to the extent that they rejected conventional political institutions such as parties and legislatures for more diverse tactics and forms of organization. In several countries these movements played a key role in popular mobilization against military dictatorships and, with the re-establishment of democracy, they have often contributed to a shift to the left. Civil society has also been treated increasingly as an international concept because of alliances between foreign NGOs and social groups, and scholars often talk of the emergence of a "global civil society". Indigenous groups in Mexico and Brazil, for example, have been very successful in using new communications media to nurture transnational solidarities. Transnational lobbying was also at the heart of the success of environmental activism at Vieques Island, Puerto Rico, which drew attention to environmental damage caused by the US navy.

A key characteristic of civil society is diversity and social movements today range from environmental groups and organizations of indigenous people to human rights organizations and feminists. Many take advantage of information and communications technologies to undertake collective initiatives. The Zapatistas in Mexico, for example, generated international solidarity through the use of the internet and email (see Akinwumi 2006). An important shared objective of many of these groups has been to challenge the impact of rapid economic development, and environmental protection has become a prominent aspect of this.

Some authors point out that civil society can also be a terrain of struggle in which there arise undemocratic relationships of power and types of exclusion (see Alvarez, Dagnino and Escobar 1998; Foweraker, Landman and Harvey 2003). Civil society can host "uncivil" anti-democratic elements such as paramilitary organizations. In Mexico and Guatemala, for example, it might be said to include drug-traffickers and their networks that work against democracy and environmental protection. In Guatemala, for example, environmentalists say parts of the rainforest are being cleared illegally by impoverished settlers working for powerful drug cartels (see Carroll 2011). Civil society is also the realm of business and producer interests which can often have an overbearing influence on regulatory policy (see Chapter 2; Clapp 2003). The study of global environmental policymaking has focused heavily on the role of states in agreeing treaties, but in an era of globalization powerful non-state interests such as business and transnational corporations play an important role in policy formation (see Box 5.1).

However, although civil society played a significant role in democratization, its political role has since become more complex and some scholars have suggested that it is now more limited in its ability to influence politics (see Foweraker 2001). Grassroots movements have to become more organized in order to negotiate with the state and to connect with domestic and foreign NGOs, resulting in increasing institutionalization and diminishing autonomy. Some social movements and NGOs turned towards the state for funds to survive, which sometimes meant co-option and reduced their ability to influence policy (see Chapter 2). In turn, the state has increasingly tried to structure relationships within civil society. In Bolivia, for example, the Federación de Juntas Vecinales (Fejuve, Federation of Neighbourhood Councils) of El Alto near La Paz led opposition to the privatization of gas reserves in 2003. Abel Mamari, one of its leaders, was then appointed to head a new water ministry in 2006. Ecuador's indigenous movement (see below) and the organizations of unemployed workers in Argentina (*piqueteros*) both challenged the state until it tamed them without giving in to their demands (see Wolff 2007). In the 1990s, therefore, the limitations of social movements in Latin America and the Caribbean became apparent and scholars began to reassess their capacity to provide alternative mechanisms of representation (see Dangl 2010). A key theme of debate has been their relationships with political parties, which have often sought to control social movements because they are a source of competition (see Chapter 4). Some scholars have argued that civil society cannot be a substitute for an institutionalized party system because associations

Box 5.1 Business in environmental policymaking

The involvement of business lobbies in global environmental politics is rising as transnational corporations engage directly in public debates about issues such as waste disposal, energy and deforestation. Discussions on multilateral environmental agreements (MEAs) in which transnational corporations and industry groups have lobbied governments and the media, for example, have included the Cartagena Protocol on biosafety and the Stockholm Convention on organic pollutants. Multilateral agencies also increasingly emphasize the role that private investment plays in the development of a "green economy" through the commercialization of clean technology. At the Rio+20 summit in 2012, for example, the Inter-American Development Bank's Multilateral Investment Fund, in partnership with the clean energy market research firm Bloomberg New Energy Finance, launched a new index evaluating the ability of Latin American and Caribbean economies to attract capital for low-carbon energy sources (see MIF/Bloomberg 2012). In an effort to understand the nature of industry lobbying, analyses of the role of transnational businesses have examined differing influences on their behaviour, such as culture or economic factors. Clapp (2003) has argued that economic considerations were key explanatory factors for understanding industry's stance in the Cartagena and Stockholm agreements, and that the positions taken by industry players did not divide along regional or country lines. Clapp says that in both cases industry groups presented a unified front in the talks. Key to their positions on environmental treaties are factors that influence the *profitability* of the agricultural chemical and seed industries, which include the status of intellectual property (IP) protection on products and the level of scientific understanding of an issue. Many industry groups were represented in the negotiations for the Cartagena Protocol on Biosafety, with some corporations such as Monsanto, DuPont and Syngenta sending their own representatives alongside those of business organizations such as the Biotech Industry Organization (BIO). Despite a large variety of industries involved they adopted similar positions opposing strict rules to limit the production and trade in genetically engineered seeds and crops. During the talks, the diverse range of industry players evolved rapidly towards a common position and they were able to present a unified voice by creating the so-called Global Industry Coalition (GIC), chaired by BioteCanada, to co-ordinate lobbying.

organized around specific demands do not enjoy permanent channels of access to the state. However, it has also been suggested that social movements may be at an *advantage* over parties in areas such as the environment because they can identify problems, suggest solutions and mobilize without the need for a formal political infrastructure. Green parties in Latin America, such as the PV in Brazil and PVEM in Mexico, have often had a complex relationship with social movements, able to mobilize diverse sectors of society through them yet sometimes unable to forge stable relationships with them. Attention has focused in particular on the role social movements have played in the ascent of a new generation of leftwing leaders across Latin America and the Caribbean (see Petras and Veltmeyer 2005). There is no doubt that civil society represented through social movements has demonstrated significant mobilizing power greater in many instances than green parties (see Box 5.2).

Pressure from civil society and organized social movements has made environmental awareness an important part of the language of governance in Latin America and the Caribbean. Politicians often premise policymaking on the pledge that initiatives will not cause pollution or damage livelihoods, and governments have grown more sensitive to protests. At Isla de Vieques, an island municipality of Puerto Rico, for example, well-organized protests by the local community over the environmental impact of the US Navy's use of the island as a bombing and weapons-testing range led to the navy's departure in 2003. Governments are also more willing to enforce strict regulations to ensure that corporations extracting natural resources do not harm the environment. In 2009, for example, the Mexican government shut down a mine in the state of Chiapas operated by the Canadian company Blackfire, alleging a string of environmental problems (Montgomery 2009).

The emergence of social movements

Social movements have generated a theoretical literature because they do not easily fit the traditional understanding of protest in terms of factors such as class or ideology (see Slater 1985a; Tarrow 1994). In the 1990s, they were often distinguished by their novelty, given the decline of older forms of representation such as unions, and the phrase "new social movements" came into vogue although there were

Box 5.2 Green grassroots: civil society mobilizes

A snapshot of popular mobilization against large development projects likely to have environmental consequences reveals extensive social movement activity throughout Latin America and the Caribbean. In April 2012, Bolivia's president Evo Morales rescinded a contract to build a road through the Amazon rainforest that provoked protests in 2011. He had already suspended a section of the planned highway which was to pass through an indigenous reserve known as TIPNIS. Work was halted after a protest march by indigenous tribes. Counter demonstrations by other communities in favour of the highway were also held. In Brazil the struggle over construction of the Belo Monte dam complex on a tributary of the Amazon river in Pará state has become an iconic issue defining the tension between environmental protection and economic growth (see Diamond 2010). In 2011, a judge barred work that would interfere with the flow of the Xingu river, ruling in favour of a group that argued the dam would affect fish stocks and harm livelihoods. Campaigners later occupied the Belo Monte construction site. The Amazon is the scene of numerous other struggles over issues such as deforestation, biodiversity loss and mining. Gold-mining and the continuing use of mercury for extraction has sparked recurrent protests (see Sponsel 2011). In Peru there are more than 200 active conflicts underway over mining projects that opponents claim have potentially negative environmental consequences (see Jiménez, Huante and Rincón 2006). In November 2011, for example, the US mining company Newmont halted construction on a huge open-cast gold mine in northern Peru after violent clashes at the site. In July 2012, at least three people were killed in clashes between police and demonstrators in the town of Celendín. In May 2012, the Peruvian government declared a state of emergency in Espinar, near Cusco, following a week of violent protests at a copper mine. In Central America, an increase in mining has been accompanied by a proliferation of socio-environmental conflicts. The Observatory of Mining Conflicts in Latin America says conflicts in the sub-region and in Mexico intensified during the first decade of the 2000s. In Argentina, in February 2012, the Canadian mining company Osisko suspended a gold-mining project in La Rioja after protests. In Guatemala, in May 2012, the government declared a state of siege in Santa Cruz Barillas following clashes over the death of a community leader who had opposed the construction of a hydroelectric dam. Mayan villagers supported by social groups have filed human rights lawsuits in Ontario, Canada, against HudBay Minerals related to violence in 2009 at a mining project it formerly owned in eastern Guatemala. In Chile, in May 2012, residents blocked access to a large meat-processing plant owned by Agrosuper and widespread protests obstructed plans to build the giant HidroAysén dam in Patagonia.

debates about what is in fact new about them (see Stahler-Sholk, Vanden and Kuecker 2007). The emergence of social movements has been explained in many ways: as an autonomous expression of interests; as a reflection of the growing use of the language of rights; or as a "structural" manifestation of the crisis of the state (see Foweraker, Landman and Harvey 2003). Chalmers, Martin and Piester (1997) argued that the shift of decision-making activity away from the state had restructured popular representation into networks better suited to influencing public policy in a globalized and decentralized era. Slater (1985b) developed an influential characterization of new social movements as the reflection of new forms of struggle in late capitalist society. New social movement theory argues that the meanings invested in struggles are not economic but social and cultural, and movements have often mobilized around identity and cultural differences. Latin America greatly enriched the study of social movements by adding many comparative analyses. Literature has often focused on the notion that the expansion of civil society movements strengthens democracy through:

- *representation*: civil society offers representation outside ineffective institutions;

- *pluralism*: a healthy democracy is built on widespread participation;

- *attitudes*: social movements help to foster democratic attitudes.

The context within which social movements emerged is important for understanding them. The economic crisis of the 1980s and ensuing neoliberal reforms had a significant impact on marginalized groups. For indigenous groups in the Amazon, for example, crisis often meant an intensification of extractive activities such as logging and oil drilling and a willingness by the state to overlook the environmental impact. At the same time, Latin American states were undergoing democratization leading to greater inclusiveness and freedom to organize. This context of diminishing economic opportunities alongside the strengthening of rights to participate shaped social movement activities (Roper, Perreault and Wilson 2003). Key social movements characteristics include the following:

Rejection of traditional political structures. Social movements operate outside institutionalized channels and challenge traditional definitions of citizenship, democracy and participation; traditional forms of rule by dominant classes and political interests; and traditional hierarchies. They seek autonomy from conventional political institutions and aspire to participatory decision-making (see Stahler-Sholk, Vanden and Kuecker 2007). They often realize their goals through negotiation, and co-operation between groups may be the only way to ensure basic rights in weak rural communities in countries such as Honduras (see Phillips 2011). But social movements can still destabilize governments and generate instability. They have awkward relationships with leftwing parties such as Brazil's PT and Mexico's Partido de la Revolución Democrática (PRD, Party of the Democratic Revolution) while forcing policy leftwards in countries lacking a strong left such as Argentina.

Formation of transnational networks. The evolution of social movements has been determined by the emergence of a global civil society, and they often forge transnational links (Brysk 2000). The activities of NGOs are among the most important international factors commonly influencing environmental awareness and policy shifts in Latin America and the Caribbean (Torres 1997). The most prominent transnational social movement of recent decades is the so-called "anti-globalization" movement – a large collection of diverse groups across the world that emerged during the 1990s opposing neoliberal reform. Indigenous organizations have been particularly prominent in forging transnational solidarity groups (Keck and Sikkink 1998; Roper, Perreault and Wilson 2003). Alliances among civil society organizations, international NGOs and academic institutions have both influenced development policy and nurtured alternative perspectives on governance (Baud, de Castro and Hogenboom 2011). In international relations, the concept of "issue networks" has been used to characterize relations among non-state actors as well as political relations not bound by traditional ideas about national sovereignty. International issue networks form between organizations that share values as well as information and services in a non-hierarchical manner (see Rodrigues 2000). The effectiveness of international networks in defending the environment of Brazilian Amazonia, for example, has been examined by Rodrigues (2000) in terms of networks of environmentally concerned actors that mobilize to promote local action ("environmental protection issue networks", EPINs). These networks include individuals or groups within governments, churches, trades unions, intellectuals, scientific and policy communities and the media (Sikkink 1993; Keck and Sikkink 1998). International issue networks employ various strategies such as lobbying campaigns and promotional activities to influence decision-making. A common transnational approach among domestic NGOs has been called the "boomerang" strategy whereby they bypass their own state and seek international allies directly to apply pressure on a government from outside (see Hochstetler 2002). Environmental campaigns in Latin America have often been transnational, reflecting alliances between national organizations across frontiers and the cross-border nature of many environmental disputes (see Chapter 3). The La Plata River basin in South America, for example, has been the focus of transnational mobilization, and the use of the boomerang strategy against development on the waterway, most recently during a dispute between Argentina and Uruguay over the construction of a paper mill, demonstrated the capacity of large projects to unite opposition across borders (see Box 5.3).

Cultural discourses. Study of new social movements has often focused on identity and cultural politics (see Chapter 6). These organizations have sometimes articulated a form of solidarity linked to identities such as ethnicity or gender. The fluidity of identity construction offers a tool for pursuing a wide range of goals. Many indigenous leaders, for example, have couched their goals in terms of environmental protection and human rights then forged alliances with other organizations (see Roper, Perreault and Wilson 2003). In Peru, in 1999, representatives of 1,200 communities came together to form the Confederación Nacional de Comunidades del Perú Afectadas por la Minería (CONACAMI, National Confederation of Communities Affected by Mining). However, at its second national congress, in

Box 5.3 The Uruguay River dispute and transnational activism

In 2010, Argentina and Uruguay resolved a dispute over the construction of pulp mills on the Uruguay River which forms their shared border and is protected by a treaty. The dispute began in 2003 when Uruguay's government permitted the Spanish company ENCE to build a pulp mill in Fray Bentos. A Finnish company, Botnia, then announced its intention to build another pulp mill in the area and gained authorization to do so in 2005. Argentinians in Entre Ríos claimed that the ENCE mill would pollute the river and protested against it, but in 2006 ENCE cancelled its project for commercial reasons. Under President Néstor Kirchner (2003–07), Argentina's government argued that Uruguay had violated the bilateral river treaty by failing to consult with Buenos Aires before authorizing the mills. It said they would damage aquatic life and water quality, and referred the matter to the International Court of Justice (ICJ) in The Hague. Uruguayan authorities argued that the treaty did not require that permission be obtained and insisted the $1.2 bn Botnia enterprise would use the latest technology and would not pollute the environment. Botnia argued the mill would have a positive impact on water quality. An initial ICJ ruling that the project could go ahead was followed by World Bank approval. The decision by Uruguay's president, Tabaré Vázquez (2005–09), to allow the Finnish mill to begin its operations in 2007 provoked angry protests by Argentine demonstrators and strained relations between the two countries. Protests against the project united Argentine, Uruguayan and transnational activists and groups involved in opposition to the mill included REDES-Friends of the Earth Uruguay, Guayubira of Uruguay and Argentina's Fundación Centro de Derechos Humanos y Ambiente (CEDHA, Centre for Human Rights and Environment). There is an established history of transnational mobilization by environmental groups in the La Plata River basin where active NGOs have often employed the "boomerang strategy" (see Hochstetler 2002). In the 1990s, for example, a coalition of about 300 ENGOs and other groups called Rios Vivos (Living Rivers) mobilized to block the Hidrovía project, which involves construction of a transnational water highway along the river system. The coalition went outside the domestic politics of Argentina, Bolivia, Brazil, Paraguay and Uruguay to seek the support of northern NGOs. It pressured the Inter-American Development Bank (IDB) to withdraw support for Hidrovía in 1997, although states in the region are proceeding.

2003, delegates voted to reconstitute CONACAMI as an indigenous confederation that would centre its demands on defending indigenous rights. CONACAMI has expanded in the Andean region through the Co-ordenadora Andina de Organizaciones Indígenas (CAOI, Andean Co-ordinator of Indigenous Organizations), an umbrella organization that it helped establish in 2006. The development of these cultural positions has helped environmental discourses to move from the arena of popular activism to national political institutions (Baud, de Castro and Hogenboom 2011; see Edelman 2008). Analysis of social movements should, therefore, explore how different expressions of identity interact with each other and the broader political economy (see Alvarez, Dagnino, and Escobar 1998). NGOs themselves have been understood as cultural actors because they shape how people understand the world and their identity (see Wapner 2002).

Neoliberalism and globalization. Globalization has often been associated with social movement mobilization because the pressure to become integrated into global markets affects diverse social sectors. Popular mobilization in Latin America and the Caribbean can often be understood as a response to the impact of global economic forces because rural populations experience neoliberalism in terms of decreasing access to land or environmental destruction (see Deere and Royce 2009; Deere and León 2001). There is a large literature about social movements that oppose or resist globalization and consumerism and its ecological consequences (see, for example, Starr 2000). In Latin America there are many examples of social movements that have been formed to express opposition to inequality and social exclusion that their supporters associate with development policies, such as the Brazilian Movimento dos Trabalhadores Sem Terra (MST, Landless Workers' Movement) created in 1985 and now the region's largest social movement (see Box 5.4). These movements often argue that prevailing economic conditions polarize society and damage the environment (see Akinwumi 2006). Ignatow (2005) argues that globalization produces a hybrid, multicultural form of politics highly relevant to contemporary environmentalism, which is a product not only of industrialization and ecological degradation, but also of cultural modernization.

Environmental movements in Latin America and the Caribbean

During the 1970s, incipient environmental mobilization at the grassroots level was occurring in just three Latin American countries – Brazil, Mexico and Venezuela – but by the 1980s mobilization was extending across the region (Viola 1997). The profile of environmental movements has grown as part of the democratization process, often in a relationship with indigenous movements, although the ideas of these two groups do not always coincide. Environmental movements gained momentum in the 1980s from the growth of international NGOs and campaign groups such as Greenpeace. However, Latin America has not merely imported the environmental concerns of the developed world but has given rise to many local initiatives, some of which have gone global. In an examination of the evolution of the movement in Brazil, for example, Hochstetler and Keck (2007) contested what they call the "transnational narrative" – by which environmentalism supposedly arrived in the 1980s as a result of the international uproar over Amazon deforestation. Argentina's Ecoclubs initiative for teenagers and young people has expanded to 30 countries in Latin America, Europe and Africa.

The environmental movements in Mexico, Brazil and Chile emerged in different ways: first, from within a corporatist political tradition in which the state played a key role in spurring environmental mobilization; second, as part of the broader emergence of social movements independent of the state that gradually became institutionalized; and, lastly, in an uneasy accommodation with authoritarianism, permissible by virtue of the non-class nature of conservationism, and thereafter with the main forces in a new democratic state.

Mexico. In Mexico, political reforms that began in 1977 coincided with rising public concern over deteriorating environmental conditions, especially in Mexico City. The administration of President Miguel de la Madrid (1982–88) saw the environment as a new issue that could help the governing, corporatist Partido Revolucionario Institucional (PRI, Institutional Revolutionary Party) and so actively mobilized environmental groups. This gave momentum to the organizational efforts of environmentalists and national umbrella associations emerged from 1982 to 1984. In 1985, for example, the Federación Conservacionista

Mexicana (FCM, Mexican Conservationist Federation) was formed to present a collective voice to policymakers. By the end of the 1980s, there were more than 100 such groups in the country (Mumme and Korzetz 1997). The state supported this mobilization with institutional and legal reforms that created a new infrastructure for environmental policymaking (see Chapters 1, 2). When the process of neoliberal economic reform began in the mid-1980s there was significant growth in the number of independent social movements as well as a growth in political opposition to the PRI. For many Mexican environmentalists, the economic and political crisis of the 1980s, and the authoritarian state's response, was synonymous with the failure of development strategy. A new generation of scholars and activists also began to emphasize principles of sustainability and new grassroots organizations began to incorporate these ideas in publications, training and support for peasant organizations and community projects (see Carruthers 1996)

Brazil. Hochstetler and Keck (2007) identify three waves of environmentalism from 1972 to 1992 according to periods of military dictatorship, democratization and globalization. As early as the 1970s, the city of Cubatão had become a focus for environmentalists because of severe air pollution caused by rapid industrial growth. An incipient environmental movement emerged in the early 1970s in response to modest political liberalization by the military government. In this climate a number of non-political ENGOs were formed and social networks, new publications and activism grew (Viola 1997). As Brazil underwent the transition to democracy, the construction of large dams became an important focus for a more militant activism resulting in the formation of one of the first transnational environmental movements (see McCormick 2007). A more political environmentalism emerged and organizations began to participate in politics, mainly at a state level. By the mid-1980s, Brazil's environmental movement was undergoing institutionalization and developing a more professional approach. NGOs proliferated, and by 1992 an estimated 1,300 environmental activist groups that had operated for more than one year were in existence (Viola 1997; Mumme and Korzetz 1997). Environmentalism expanded from the south across the country and international attention and funding stimulated the development of the movement in the Amazon. Amazonian environmentalism differed

Box 5.4 The MST and the environment

Highly unequal land tenure in Brazil combined with the rapid growth of agro-industry producing for export and backed by state policies has given rise to Latin America's largest social movement, the Movimento dos Trabalhadores Sem Terra (MST). The number of landless people is estimated at between 3.3 million and 6.1 million families, yet Brazil's unproductive farmland comprises more than a quarter of national territory. According to De Almeida and Sanchez (2000), the emergence of the MST reflects three processes:

- a strongly conservative capitalist modernization that dominated Brazilian agriculture in the 1960s and 1970s and was responsible for intensifying conflicts over land;
- the pastoral activity of Christians aligned with liberation theology reflected in urban church base communities (see Chapter 6);
- the experience of peasant leagues before the military takeover of 1964. As Brazil's regime began to falter, peasants began to organize land invasions, inaugurating the MST.

There has been considerable debate about the nature of the MST's proposals. The left argues that these are economic, aiming to provide a livelihood for millions of poor Brazilians, and also political, aiming to gain them democratic and citizenship rights (see Miguel Carter 2010). The right claims MST proposals for land reform in a globalized economy are out of date and its confrontational stance harmful to democracy. The MST's demands for more equitable land distribution draw attention to the relationship between a specific model of development and visions of how land should be used in the most sustainable way through small-scale farming and a commitment to agro-ecology (see Chapter 6). In Brazil, comparisons of the large agri-business model often advanced by powerful US multinational corporations and that of local smallholders have often pointed out the significant differences in approach to issues of sustainability. Brazil's modernized agricultural economy has turned it into a leading exporter of major food commodities, while millions of Brazilians still suffer from poverty and hunger (see Segall-Corrêa et al. 2007). A powerful agrarian elite and agribusiness sector has used its influence to prevent agrarian reform. State policies have protected large landholders through, for example, lax enforcement of environmental laws. The MST's analysis of the relationship between the dominant form of agricultural production in Brazil, and the issue of landlessness, led it after the mid-1990s to reappraise its policies and promote agro-ecology and food sovereignty. In 1997, it created BioNatur, its first co-operative for organic seeds, and within a decade this had become the largest producer of organic seeds in Latin America. The MST has also supported the development of other Brazilian popular movements including those representing groups affected by the environmental impact of large projects such as dams. (Main sources: De Almeida and Sanchez 2000; Miguel Carter 2010; Branford and Rocha 2002)

from the urban. environmentalism of southern Brazil and received disproportionate levels of support from international ENGOs, scientific bodies and multilateral agencies. Brazil's environmental movement also engaged with other social movements, trades unions and NGOs, shaping a form of environmentalism that has been more politicized and to the left than in many other countries, sometimes referred as "socio-environmentalism" (see Chapter 6). Socio-environmentalism illustrates how social movements can employ environmentalism and identity politics to forge alliances and gain support for their own agendas. The landless movement in Brazil offers a good example of a social movement's relationship with environmentalism (see Box 5.4).

Chile. Chile's environmental movement is one of the oldest in Latin America and can trace its origins to 1963 with the foundation by ecologists of the Comité Nacional Pro Defensa de la Flora y Fauna (CODEFF, Committee for the Defence of Flora and Fauna). The Stockholm Conference in 1972 and the creation of UNEP gave impetus to Chile's environmental movement, and in 1974, shortly after the military coup, ecologists formed the Instituto de Ecología (Ecology Institute), an NGO that lobbied the military to create a legal and administrative framework to address Chile's environmental problems. The Centro de Investigación y Planificación para el Medio Ambiente (CIPMA, Centre for Environmental Investigation and Planning), the Grupo de Investigaciones Agrarias (GIA), the Centro de Estudios y Tecnología (CET), El Canelo de Nos, and the Instituto de Ecología Política (IEP) were all formed in the early 1980s and went beyond conservationism to link concern about the environment with issues of development and social justice. CIPMA played an important role in building consensus among different groups and setting the political agenda (see Silva 1996). Growing international attention to green issues and the growth of Chile's movement obliged the military regime to recognize environmental themes in the 1980 constitution. In 1983, CIPMA organized Chile's first scientific congress on the environment. The military regime responded by creating a Comisión Nacional de Ecología (National Commission for Ecology) in 1984 to establish a national environmental policy and the government took a prominent role in negotiations to establish the ozone layer convention of 1985 and CFC Convention of 1987. With the return of democracy in 1990 environmentalism gained an institutional presence on policy committees established by the new centre-left coalition (Silva 1996).

In some countries, the development of environmental social movements has been rapid. In Costa Rica, for example, environmentalism was almost absent in the early 1970s, with a small number of local activist groups facing considerable official indifference (see Boza 1993). However, by the late 1990s, there were several hundred environmental groups active in the country, which, today has a dynamic environment ministry, bipartisan political support for conservation at a high level and a model system of protected areas (see Wallace 1992; Gámez et al. 1993; Jakobeit 1996; Figueres 2002).

Membership in environmental groups in Latin America and the Caribbean today almost certainly exceeds that of green political parties (see Chapter 4) and the movement has become more influential in politics (Meyer et al. 1997; Dalton et al. 2003). A study by Dalton (2005) found that environmental groups represent one of the most common forms of political group membership on a global scale, and membership levels are increasing. Reasons for this rapid evolution include the following:

Socio-economic development. Modernization theory is often used to explain the emergence of the environmental movement in advanced industrial societies, suggesting that affluent societies possess the national infrastructure needed to mobilize large groups; a relatively large number of citizens possess characteristics more conducive to civil society mobilization; and communication structures and levels of education, urbanization and social mobility make mobilization more likely. Latin American countries exhibit a correlation, albeit weak, between the UN Human Development Index (HDI) and the strength of the environmental movement (see Viola 1997). However, while problems caused by industrialization and over-consumption, such as pollution, create strong incentives for environmental action in the industrialized world, this may not always hold true in countries that are struggling to develop (see Caldwell 1990). Environmental problems in the developing world may be caused by *insufficient* levels of development.

Political opportunity structures and democratic institutions. Another area of theory in the social movement literature maintains that "political opportunity structures" influence the potential of movements to mobilize, which is enhanced by democracy (see, for example, Osa and Corduneanu-Huci 2003; Meyer 2004). The political opportunities offered by democratic structures are important for environmental movements because their proposals usually have to overcome the opposition of economic interests that are better institutionalized and funded, and enjoy greater political access. Studies suggest environmental group membership tends to be higher in more democratic nations (see Dalton 2005).

Cultural theories. Another explanation of environmental activism is ideological. Between the 1972 Stockholm and 1992 Rio Conferences, there were significant changes in attitudes and political discourse in Latin America regarding the environment, with growing awareness of the negative long-term consequences of environmental degradation. State institutions and actors, social groups and ideas from abroad also influenced how new policies were shaped (Torres 1997). Inglehart (1995) suggests that in industrial societies as the economic needs of citizens are met a growing proportion turn their attention to "post-material" issues about the quality of life, including environmental protection. A new consciousness may also develop that suggests nature is somehow out of balance (see Pi-Sunyer and Thomas 2011). Innovative initiatives aimed at changing attitudes towards the environment that often arose in the developed world – from the promotion of green spaces to reductions in working time, slow food, and eco-villages – have all been pursued in Latin America and the Caribbean (see Dawson 2010; Andrews and Urbanska 2010; de Graaf 2010).

These potential explanations for why people join environment movements link a country's level of development with citizen activism. Environmentalists in less developed nations face greater obstacles in mobilizing public support because they often lack the necessary

179

infrastructure and confront undemocratic circumstances (see Dalton 2005).

Profiles and classification

Key issues facing the environmental movement are its heterogeneity, disagreements among groups over values, expectations and demands, and a lack of consensus about policy priorities. Some groups argue that economic globalization and social inequality are the main causes of environmental degradation. The term "environmental justice" – which brings together broader issues of global injustice and local concerns about the environment – has grown in use as a way of addressing ideas that link inequality and environmental degradation in Latin America and the Caribbean (see Chapter 6; see Carruthers 2008b). In 2005, García-Guadilla developed a typology that identified four main types of environmental NGOs and social movements operating in Latin America:

- *Global ecologists*. Large, formal, institutionalized organizations that prioritize global policies (for example, the Fórum Brasileiro de ONGs e Movimentos Sociais para o Meio Ambiente e o Desenvolvimento, FBOMS, Brazilian Forum of NGOs and Social Movements for the Environment and Development, see below);

- *Southern ecologists*. Environmental social movements that prioritize ecological issues – biodiversity conservation and climate change – over socio-economic concerns (for example, the Latin American branches of Friends of the Earth and Greenpeace). They can be institutionalized, attract international funding and influence official agendas.

- *Political environmentalists*. Anti-system group that includes environmental organizations and NGOs that lobby against globalization, free trade and privatization (for example, CONACAMI). They focus more on the socio-political aspects of sustainable development than on its ecological dimensions, and often reject the official agenda adopted at the Earth Summit in Rio in 1992. They derive power from networking and mass mobilization, have a low level of institutionalization and have difficulty obtaining funding.

- *Social environmentalists*. This group emphasizes social equity and participatory democracy as prerequisites for sustainable development and focus on the local and regional levels, but also act at a global level through informal networks that mobilize at summits (for example, the MST). They aim for social justice, greater equality and democratic access to basic services such as water, housing, food, land, health, sanitation, employment and education.

Environmental social movements are intrinsically multi-sectoral, fostering linkages between a large and diverse number of indigenous, peasant, public health, labour, student and urban popular groups. Kaimowitz (1996) identified several important constituents of the movement:

Urban middle class

Middle-class environmental organizations have emerged throughout Latin American and Caribbean cities and towns. In Brazil, the middle class was a key constituency of the green movement as it developed in the prosperous south-east and, in particular, the cities of São Paulo and Rio de Janeiro. In Chile, middle-class environmentalists played a major role in bringing national attention to the destruction of native forests. In Venezuela, middle-class activists have waged many successful environmental campaigns, such as pioneering opposition to the Trans-Amazon Rally in 1987. Middle-class interest in the environment tends to centre on urban pollution, well-publicized symbols of the destruction of nature, such as Amazon deforestation, extinction risks facing iconic species, and the struggles of indigenous people. Successful environmental campaigns have often reflected collaboration between marginalized sectors and the urban middle-class with resources to devote to campaigning. The middle class has had a strong influence in Latin America's political parties and has often been behind their adoption of green platforms.

Groups motivated by material interests

A green business lobby comprising companies and farmers who sell green products has emerged in the region and is growing. More companies and smallholder groups are taking advantage of new opportunities offered by the markets for eco-tourism, organic food, recyclable containers and products from sustainably managed forests. They have a vested interest in the growth of environmental awareness and many have incorporated ecological messages or symbols into their advertising. The "green industry" that has probably had the most influence on politics is tourism in countries such as Costa Rica, where it is a major foreign exchange earner.

Tourism clearly profits from Costa Rica's international reputation as a country that protects its environment, and so the sector supports policies that foster this image. Recycling has also been an important source of income for the poor in the large cities of Latin America and the Caribbean (see Pacheco 1996). In Brazil, as environmental policy increasingly employs economic mechanisms (see Chapter 2), bankers are becoming involved in efforts to protect the Amazon rainforest (see Box 5.5). Producers and communities suffering losses as a result of pollution and natural resource depletion include petty extractors, such as rubber tappers and fishermen. Honduran fishermen, for example, have opposed the clearing of wetlands for shrimp farming because they claim this endangers fish stocks and restricts their access to coastal areas (see Stanley 1996). Haitian peasants have mobilized over soil erosion because it reduces even further the yield on their small plots (Arthur 1996). In Argentina, the Wichí people campaigned against the activities of cattle ranchers who they said created dustbowl conditions in the Chaco region that threatens their survival (see Rankin 1996).

The social justice movement

The strengthening of neoliberal currents, declining confidence in political parties, and the disappearance of the socialist bloc in the early 1990s weakened the Latin American left. Environmental concerns offer the left an opportunity to construct new forms of support and alliances. This makes it possible to link ecological concerns with the struggle for social justice as a way of making green issues relevant to the bulk of the population (see Chapter 6). The inclusion of environmental issues in the agenda of social justice movements is essential to developing mass constituencies for major policy reforms related to the environment but also wider issues such as land use. There is a strong environmental current within the Brazilian PT and to a lesser extent the Chilean Socialist Party, for example. Similarly, organizations of small-scale farmers throughout Latin America see the emergence of environmental concerns as an opportunity to strengthen the case for preserving diversified production systems. By stressing their role as stewards of their environment, they have found a way to gain the support of the urban middle classes and overseas aid agencies (Kaimowitz 1996). By combining notions of social justice with environmental sustainability, activism can draw upon the concept of

Box 5.5 Bankers battle for the forest

Although international capital is often blamed for much of the environmental damage caused to Latin America and the Caribbean, private banks are likely to be essential to solving problems such as deforestation. Countries around the world have already signed up to the UN's Reduced Emissions from Deforestation and Degradation programme, or REDD, under which forest owners are, in effect, paid not to cut down trees (see Chapter 6). For REDD to work, large sums of money are needed: to hit 2020 targets, UNEP estimates that between $17 bn and $30 bn a year is required. Governments alone cannot provide this kind of money and it is unlikely that the problem can be addressed without the private sector – so market mechanisms will be key to REDD's success. The aim is for private sector investors to fund REDD projects which will generate carbon credits that can then be sold on the open market. Banks will play a key role in this process as financial intermediaries, providing cash flow (liquidity), managing risk and putting together loan capital ("structured finance"). They will help raise the capital needed to fund REDD projects, probably by making an upfront payment and taking a share of funds generated by carbon credits. Implementing such initiatives has to confront the problem of the absence of a stable market for forestry credits, and without a regulated market investors will not be prepared to risk the level of capital needed to make REDD work. This explains why only a few banks, including Bank of America Merrill Lynch (BoA), BNP Paribas and Macquarie, are actively involved in REDD and it could be years before confidence in carbon markets attracts sufficient funds. Other potential mechanisms by which banks can raise capital for REDD reduce the centrality of carbon credits, which means they can be launched more quickly. These include forestry bonds, whereby banks issue bonds to raise funds that are then lent to governments to help preserve forests.

environmental rights – individual and collective rights that pertain to the minimum biological requirements necessary for survival – in struggles over resources. Struggles with an environmental dimension often take the form of efforts by marginalized groups to assert their rights, which has given rise to the concept of "environmental justice". Carruthers (2008a) has examined mobilization behind the concept of "environmental justice" in Latin America and the Caribbean and how social movements manage the relationship between environmental issues and human rights. Social justice environmentalism also has political aims, seeking empowerment for marginalized and weak sectors of society and demanding accountability to ensure institutions and organizations that created environmental problems are held to account for their actions (see Chapter 6; Johnston 2011a). Latin America has also been at the forefront of the international "anti-globalization" movement that has emerged from social and popular organizations across the world opposing the impact of free-trade policies. One of the stated aims of the Zapatista rebellion in Mexico in 1994, for example, was to oppose NAFTA on the grounds that this would harm indigenous communities. During the 1990s, a global solidarity network developed in support of the Zapatistas among civil society groups and the networks that emerged were important precursors of the anti-globalization movement.

Environmental NGOs (ENGOs)

NGOs are private organizations funded either by voluntary contributions through membership, donations from larger organizations or are self-financing (Foweraker, Landman and Harvey 2003). They have played a crucial role in shaping attitudes towards the environment and pushing issues up policy agendas (Torres 1997). NGOs often transcend traditional political and class boundaries by incorporating participants from diverse backgrounds and relying on a diversity of benefactors. They tend to be pragmatic and more inclined to co-operate with government than to oppose it, and, by linking ecological and economic concerns in Latin America and the Caribbean, they have attracted participants who were previously not interested in ecological issues (see Price 1994). NGOs range from small single-issue groups that organize at a local level to international organizations with resources and clout (see Roper, Perreault and Wilson 2003). Laura Macdonald (1997) identified several approaches to understanding their role in civil society: "neo-conservative" positions see NGOs as private-sector actors capable of mobilizing society without state intervention; "liberal-pluralist positions" suggest that NGOs provide a focus for individual political participation and counterbalance the power of authoritarian states; "post-Marxist" perspectives build on Gramsci's argument that state power is maintained not just through formal political institutions but also through those of civil society and so attribute to NGOs a role in promoting democracy (see Gramsci 1971). NGOs themselves often emphasize their democratic role, although the main justification of most NGO projects continues to be their contribution to economic development.

In Latin America and the Caribbean early ENGOs originated as conservation groups. In the Dominican Republic, for example, the country's first ENGO, the Sociedad Dominicana de Orquidiología (Dominican Orchidology Society), was founded in 1966. Brazil's first major ENGO, formed by the environmentalist José Lutzenberger in 1971, protested against tree cutting in Porto Alegre (see Hochstetler and Keck 2007). Until the late 1980s, Chile had only two environmental NGOs – the Comité Nacional Pro Defensa de la Flora y Fauna (CODEFF), a conservation group founded in the late 1960s, and the Instituto de Ecología Política in Chile, set up in 1974, but with democratization in the 1990s many new ENGOs appeared (see Bradley 2006). In the 1960s and early 1970s, Latin American and Caribbean NGOs began to focus on grassroots development and were heavily influenced by debates that originated in Marxism and liberation theology. In the late 1970s, more pragmatic ENGOs began to emerge, and in the 1980s their numbers grew rapidly as a result of democratization, in opposition to neoliberal reform, and out of growing frustration with weak environmental policies. In this period, multilateral agencies also increasingly began to view NGOs as an effective way of supporting change (see Foweraker, Landman and Harvey 2003). Some NGOs, such as Brazil's SOS Mata Atlântica, established large, professional organizational structures bringing together environmentalists, scientists, business figures and journalists, and by the early 1990s the group claimed over 6,000 paying members (Hochstetler and Keck 2007). The number of NGOs operating in the region has varied over time, but in 2004 Radcliffe suggested that about 25,000 were at work.

ENGOs have been studied according to several typologies and research has differentiated between those that work for change within governance institutions and those that adopt a more confrontational stance (see Alcock 2008; Young 1999; Grant 2000; Betsill and Corell 2001; Betsill 2006; Winston 2002; Pulver 2004; and Richards and Heard 2005). Groups with an ecological perspective are more likely to resort to direct action and confrontational strategies while those with a conservation perspective tend to work within the existing institutional framework (Rohrschneider and Dalton 2002). McCormick (2004) divided the US ENGO community into three groups: pragmatic reformers, deep ecologists and radicals (see also Rosenbaum 2003; Clapp and Dauvergne 2005).

Several themes emerge in efforts to determine the impact of NGOs in Latin America. First, they have sometimes been depicted as the reflection of an international consensus on neoliberal reform championed by the industrialized countries by providing services that the state has withdrawn from, fuelling a debate about whether they can, in fact, be counted as part of civil society at all (see Radcliffe 2004; Macdonald 1997). NGOs still receive considerable funding from the state – which channels international grants to them. Governments in Nicaragua and Costa Rica, for example, have at times tried to limit the autonomy of NGOs and popular movements. In Mexico, NGOs emerged after the 1985 earthquake and acquired an independent presence before the state sought to co-opt them through funding and the creation of an official body for NGOs. In Brazil, by contrast, the state did not seek to co-opt NGOs and they preserved a grassroots perspective known as *basismo*. Second, NGOs are often accountable to international donors, and there is always the risk that these may influence their agendas to the detriment of local needs. In Central America, for example, the US government channelled aid to US-based NGOs as part of its counterinsurgency strategy.

The impact of external funding of NGOs in Latin America has been the subject of debate. A reduction in external funding following the transition to democracy forced many NGOs to turn towards newly democratic states at a time when these were aiming to increase their legitimacy through social activities, blurring their original separation from government. In Chile, for example, during the Pinochet regime, NGOs offered a niche for opposition researchers and activists that enabled them to maintain distance from the authoritarian state (see Lambrou 1997). After the restoration of democratic government, some ENGO professionals then joined the government. Today, ENGOs in Latin America and the Caribbean receive substantial levels of funding from foreign organizations and individual entrepreneurs (see Bradley 2006). It has been argued that aid to NGOs reinforces the status quo because, as they become dependent on external funding, they lose sight of their original goals (see Brown, Brown and Desposato 2007).

International NGOs first collaborated with conservationists in Latin America before linking up with local NGOs, often for pragmatic and not ideological reasons. The US National Wildlife Federation (NWF), for example, is often seen as having a conservative membership, yet formed a strategic alliance with Brazil's National Council of Rubber Tappers which was leftwing (Torres 1997). Costa Rica was a pioneer of interaction with international ENGOs in the late 1980s when economic difficulties limited the funds available for environmental protection (see, for example, Silva 1999). Its domestic ENGOs have often comprised individuals who trained abroad and benefited from links with researchers and international NGO personnel (see Torres 1997).

Brazil has been a high priority of international NGOs because of the perceived link between deforestation, climate change, and ozone depletion and because of destruction of the rainforest during the 1980s. In Mexico, trade integration, proximity to the US and the environmental problems shared by both countries increased the interest of US ENGOs in the country. NAFTA played an important role in the development of NGOs on both sides of the border (see Box 5.6; Chapter 3).

A large number of ENGOs based in the US and Europe such as Friends of the Earth, the World Wildlife Fund and Greenpeace International, now fund affiliates in the region. The International Union for Conservation of Nature has been highly influential, and religious organizations such as the Catholic charity Cafod also undertake environmental policy initiatives in the region. Transnational environmental activism in Latin America and the Caribbean has been influenced by factors such as a country's size, degree of openness and political system; its vulnerability to pressure through, for example, the ability of groups to influence the conditions placed on external financing; its sensitivity to foreign criticism; and the access environmental groups gain to the policymaking process. Costa Rica, for example, was willing to accept NGO demands on protected areas while disregarding foreign complaints about the practices of local cattle ranchers and banana planters (Torres 1997). However, despite the key role of transnational links in the development of Latin American environmentalism, international NGOs may in some circumstances have heightened opposition to the green agenda among groups that resent foreign involvement in local affairs or seek protectionism, such

Box 5.6 NGOs and NAFTA

Negotiations on a North American free trade deal galvanized US and Canadian NGOs but only a few Mexican groups organized. In the late 1980s, Mexican groups were on the decline after a period of growth, and their focus on the forthcoming Earth Summit in Rio in 1991 further limited their attention to NAFTA. As a result, the concerns of US environmentalists played a disproportionately influential role in the discussion of environmental issues within the NAFTA framework. Nonetheless, these US groups were in contact with their Mexican counterparts and were informed by them. A Mexican umbrella group, the Unión de Grupos Ambientalistas (UGAM, Union of Environmentalist Groups), had a limited influence on negotiators compared to that of US NGOs. The Red Mexicana de Acción frente al Libre Comercio (RMALC, Mexican Action Network on Free Trade) brought together environmentalists opposed to the treaty and had some success in organizing opposition to it but was focused primarily on labour and socio-economic issues. US NGOs incorporated the rhetoric of free trade by arguing against what they claimed was unfair competition from products entering from a country with low environmental standards, suggesting NAFTA would weaken US standards and voiced concern about the potential overexploitation of Mexican natural resources (see Tosun 2009); while Mexican NGOs paid little attention to concerns about the traffic of US toxic wastes into Mexico and exports from the US of banned insecticides. US NGOs gained leverage because congressional approval of NAFTA was required and they were able to lobby extensively and had access to an open media and the courts. Mindful of the influence of US NGOs, the Mexican government undertook one of its first foreign lobbying campaigns within the US to respond to their concerns. According to Torres (1997), the contrasts between ENGOs within both countries left a legacy of mistrust after the NAFTA debate. One lesson is that the ENGOs in both countries found it difficult to detach themselves from national loyalties and agendas. (Main source: Torres 1997)

as trades unions. An important division among local NGOs continues to be between those that refuse any foreign support and those willing to accept it.

Characteristics and role

The role of local NGOs in Latin America and the Caribbean has been shaped by the development of the institutional structures in which they can play a policymaking role. Local ENGOs grew throughout the region in the 1980s, taking advantage of widening access to policymaking and growing international attention to green issues. Initially, they only found sympathy for their demands in weak environmental affairs departments within sectoral ministries, but as these evolved into ministries focusing exclusively on environmental matters the access of ENGOs grew correspondingly. ENGOs also began to participate at different levels of governance in countries such as Brazil, Costa Rica and Mexico in municipal councils, commissions and working groups. Where legislative bodies established ecological commissions these sometimes collaborated with ENGOs. For example, the Brazilian so-called "green congressional bloc" promoted the inclusion of several environmental provisions in the 1988 constitution (see Chapter 2). Local ENGOs can provide important public services, especially environmental education, research and the management of reserves, but face key challenges:

Funding. Latin American and Caribbean ENGOs are limited in their ability to self-fund, and external funding from international NGOs and development agencies or universities is the main reason why their numbers grew in the 1980s and 1990s. Local NGOs are in general too small to benefit from MDB loans although aid is sometimes provided by private foundations. Financial uncertainty shapes the objectives of many NGOs, which often bundle objectives to widen the net of potential funders, blurring their focus. Local conditions also shape funding profiles. A study in Venezuela and Mexico in the early 1990s, for example, showed that many Venezuelan NGOs relied solely on national funding through private donations, corporate sponsorship and private membership whereas few of the Mexican ones did, opting instead for financial backing from North American and European environmental and charitable organizations (see Price 1994). Where NGOs are dependent on public money, they are sometimes referred to as quangos, quasi-NGOs. Latin American entrepreneurs are showing interest as benefactors of local ENGOs and there is growing private sector willingness to finance environmental initiatives in larger economies such as Brazil and Mexico.

Rivalry. The aims, geographical coverage and practices of NGOs often overlap, leading to competition for funding and access to policy-makers. In Brazil, for example, legalizing shantytowns has been seen by homelessness campaigners as an important objective but has been opposed by ecologists (see Simms and Reid 2006). However, most NGO organizers recognize that building links is an essential part of their work and as environmental groups have multiplied, so have the bodies seeking to co-ordinate them. NGO umbrella groups have developed in a number of countries to monitor activities and to channel resources. In Brazil, the FBOMS was created in 1990 to facilitate the partici-pation of civil society in the 1992 Rio Earth Summit (see above). Since 2006 this has co-ordinated consultations at intergovernmental events with bodies such as the Northern Alliance for Sustainability (ANPED) and the UN Non-Governmental Liaison Service (UN-NGLS). FBOMS, together with the Vitae Civilis Institute for the Environment, Development and Peace, organized two Latin American consultations on international environmental governance in São Paulo in 2007 and in Curitiba, Brazil, supported by UNEP, Brazil's environment ministry and ANPED. These initiatives do not always endure and divisions between groups are common.

Professionalization. In countries where ENGOs grew rapidly, such as Mexico and Brazil, organizations with a more professional approach began to institutionalize in the late 1980s (Viola 1997). Efforts to strengthen the institutional structure of local ENGOs has been an important focus of international NGOs (Torres 1997). Profession-alization changes the focus of ENGOs, with pragmatism substituting idealism and replacing a rhetorical identification with radical democracy with hierarchies committed to efficiency (see Viola 1997). This process has informed a debate about whether environmental movements should still be conceived as social movements or as scientific or policy interest groups in an institutionalized terrain (see Diani and Rambaldo 2007; Jordan and Maloney 1997). However, when civil society representatives collaborate with scientific researchers it can blur the distinction between grassroots voluntary organi-zations and professionalized interest groups (see McCormick 2007). Collaborations of this kind are often a response to the poor design of participatory mechanisms (see McCormick 2007). The influence of NGOs on policy has varied considerably across Latin America and the Caribbean but in many cases they have shaped new legislation, influenced environmental planning and pressed governments to sign multilateral agreements. ENGOs have had a significant influence on Brazilian policy towards the Amazon and, in addition to lobbying for changes to well-publicized megaprojects such as the Carajas mining project, they successfully opposed other proposals, such as the siting of the São Paulo International Airport. ENGOs have had a central role in arranging the debt-for-nature swaps, and Mexican and Costa Rican ENGOs have successfully opposed road projects and large tourist projects.

The indigenous movement

About 50 million people within 800 linguistic groups maintain indigenous lifestyles in Latin America which are often communitarian and rural (see World Bank 2012). Most indigenous communities live in peasantized, agricultural areas such as Mesoamerica and the Andes and all of them exhibit high levels of poverty and inequality (see Hall and Patrinos 2005; World Bank 2005). Indigenous groups have been mobilizing to demand recognition of land rights since the nineteenth century, but since the 1970s a more politically self-conscious movement has emerged across Latin America and forged international links. Rising indigenous consciousness has pushed issues such as cultural diversity and autonomy up the political agenda. The erosion of class-based socialist ideas following the end of the Cold War and the impact of neoliberalism have acted as catalysts for the resurgence of indigenous movements. Drawing on legacies of past agrarian struggles, indigenous groups in the 1980s and 1990s benefited from an international climate in which governments were encouraged to recognize minority rights, and this has been reinforced by the emergence since the 1970s of an *international* indigenous movement originating in Church and UN human rights initiatives. In 1992 and 1993, these trends came together in large, high-profile events such as the Earth Summit in Rio; commemorations to mark the 500th anniversary of the arrival of Columbus in the Americas; the award of the Nobel Peace prize to the Guatemalan Mayan activist Rigoberta Menchú; and the naming by the UN of 1993 as the "Year of Indigenous Peoples". The Earth Summit included indigenous delegations and explored the role of indigenous ecological knowledge in the quest for sustainable development. After 1992, the UN called for an international "Decade of the World's Indigenous People" (1995–2004) and worked to complete the declaration on the Rights of Indigenous People, which was adopted in 2007. Most multilateral agencies have formulated policies in support of indigenous people. In some countries indigenous movements have become a powerful political force and mobilizations in Ecuador (2008) and Bolivia (2009) have led to constitutions that recognize the "plurinational" character of these states and, in Bolivia, establish autonomy for indigenous peoples.

In recent years indigenous people have played a prominent role in environmental protests, articulating common responses to the unsustainable extraction of natural resources and putting forward new perspectives on development. As a result, indigenous organizations have shown a capacity to forge regional organizations and, in 2009, at the IV Continental Summit of Indigenous Peoples and Nationalities of Abya-Yala, held in Puno, Peru, 5,000 delegates gathered from across the Americas and called for a broad alliance with non-indigenous groups on an anti-capitalist platform (see NACLA 2010). Indigenous protests with an environmental dimension are linked to the rapid growth of mining, hydrocarbon extraction and agro-industry, and the construction of large infrastructure projects, often under leftwing leaders. In Brazil, for example, President Lula Da Silva and his successor Dilma Rousseff supported large hydroelectric projects that will flood large areas of rainforest. In Peru, indigenous communities from the Andes and Amazon have combined to resist efforts to expand mining and in Ecuador they have confronted President Rafael Correa's development strategy privileging mining and oil. In Bolivia, indigenous movements have openly confronted Evo Morales, the country's first indigenous president, over a broad range of issues.

Indigenous mobilization took place in the context of a region wide transition to democracy, which opened space for new organizations to mobilize, and against the background of neoliberal economic reforms that threatened collective property rights (see Chapter 4; Van Cott 2005). At the same time, domestic and international NGOs became interested in the concerns of indigenous peoples and helped new organizations to expand (Brysk 2000; Keck and Sikkink 1998). Given this context, a prominent explanation for indigenous mobilization has been the demand for citizenship rights and political inclusion. There has also been rapid demographic growth among some indigenous communities in Latin America and the Caribbean in recent decades (see McSweeney and Arps 2005). Since the 1970s, many indigenous organizations have framed demands on the basis of their ethnic distinctiveness and have often argued that autonomy is essential if they are to overcome centuries of discrimination that they attribute to racism (see bbc.co.uk 2006; Gilly 2008).

Yashar (2005) considered a range of potential explanations for the rise of indigenous movements in Latin America: primordialist arguments, which understand the emergence of indigenous protest as a natural expression of deeply rooted ethnic identities; instrumentalist analyses, which position the causes of ethnic mobilization in broader arguments about, for example, modernization or political change; structural explanations, which highlight the poor material conditions endured by indigenous people; post-structural arguments, which stress the contexts in which identities are constructed and reconstructed; and arguments informed by theories of globalization, which suggest that economic integration, the growth of civil society and the development of international norms and cultures all contributed to indigenous collective action (see also Wolff 2007). An important characteristic of the indigenous movement in Latin America has been local alliances with the left and transnational links with foreign human rights, environmental and gender movements. Evidence from the Andean countries has revealed a marked tendency of indigenous organizations to form alliances with leftwing parties (see Van Cott 2005).

Indigenous movements combine material and cultural demands as part of a broader opposition to economic and political exclusion (Foweraker, Landman and Harvey 2003). They have often provided a unifying focus for other organizations and non-indigenous groups, particularly those on the left, around shared goals. Today they are motivated by four main issues:

Self-determination and autonomy. Since the 1970s, indigenous organizations have often framed demands in terms of self-determination based upon legal recognition of their culturally distinct decision-making institutions and, in practical terms, this has often been articulated through demands for local autonomy, enhanced political participation and protection for their cultures. In Mexico, autonomy has been central to the demands of the national indigenous movement since the Zapatista uprising in 1994 (see Mattiace 2003). Although the main objectives of indigenous proposals for autonomy are to improve living conditions or protect resources such as forests, they often seek to redefine their relation to the nation state and articulate a new concept of citizenship, often based on a strong commitment to environmental stewardship (see Hernández Castillo and Furio 2006). Environmental innovations such as eco-tourism are offering some indigenous groups the opportunity to strengthen their autonomy (see Chernela 2011).

Territorial rights and control over natural resources. A second aim of indigenous mobilization, related to demands for autonomy, is for control of land and resources (see Mander and Tauli-Corpuz 2006). In Brazil, in 2013, for example, the government sent soldiers to a farm in Mato Grosso do Sul where the Terena indigenous group were involved in a violent dispute over property owned by a local politician which they say lies on their ancestral land. In the 1970s and 1980s, land tensions increased throughout Latin America and pressure on the land grew further with neoliberal reforms (see Howard 1998; Harvey 1998). The state and political parties linked to business interests have often been complicit in this process, seeking to exploit untapped resources or profiting from the privatization of those located in indigenous territories (see Hernández Castillo and Furio 2006). In the struggle over land, ethnic and environmental issues have become increasingly intertwined. In Peru, for example, Greene (2006) has argued that "eco-ethnic" alliances now shape the terms of debate between the state, the international community and the indigenous movement. In Mexico, an emergent indigenous agro-ecological movement has set a goal of recovering land not just in terms of its territorial aspects but also the ways in which it is used (see Altieri and Toledo 2011). Disputes over the environment were also germane to clashes between indigenous people and the Mexican government in Chiapas (see Box 5.7). Nonetheless, there are also disagreements within the Zapatista movement itself about the environment (see Simon 1997). In struggles for territorial rights, many indigenous leaders have used the transnational environmental movement as a strategic ally, and this movement has often embraced indigenous people as symbols of sustainability (see Yashar 2005). Multilateral organizations have also recognized the relationship between indigenous land claims

Box 5.7 The Chiapas struggle and the environment

The Chiapas rebellion highlighted the benefits to the environment of indigenous claims even if these were not explicitly based on ecological arguments. Zapatistas claimed that the policy of the Mexican federal government and state government in the conflict area has been shaped by interest in exploiting its oil reserves with no regard for fragile ecosystems. The government, by contrast, has portrayed the Zapatistas as a threat to environmentally sensitive areas of the Lacandón rainforest. O'Brien (1998) identified an environmental agenda in the debate about the Zapatista rebellion by linking the uprising to the broader social impact of land use and deforestation caused by the growth of commercial logging, the market in land, oil exploration and road construction. She suggested that the emergence of the Zapatistas was linked to the agrarian politics that precipitated during the 1960s the migration of thousands of campesinos into the jungle. O'Brien argued that while the Zapatistas have given little explicit attention to ecological issues, because the underlying causes of deforestation are related to the causes of the rebellion achieving their goals will benefit rainforest conservation. The rebellion took place in a region where there is considerable competition over natural resources involving complex alliances that has generated major environmental disputes over logging, hydroelectric power and "biopiracy" (see Weinberg 2003). Mexico's government has planned major development in the region linked to the Plan Puebla-Panama, a series of interoceanic rail and highway links, industrial zones and free-trade enclaves extending to the Panama Canal. Attempts at commercial bioprospecting in Chiapas have also provoked indigenous protests (see Belejack 2002).

and how land is used in countries such as Peru (see GEF/UNDP/SGP 2010; Fiona Wilson 2003). However, once indigenous peoples secure lands the problems do not disappear. In Bolivia, some lands have been granted by the state as multiethnic territories to be managed collectively leading to conflict between ethnic groups over control of timber resources (see Roper, Perreault and Wilson 2003). Nor does the recognition of ethnic territories end the encroachment of corporate interests on to indigenous lands (see Gedicks 2001).

Political reform. Indigenous organizations have often entered politics in pursuit of constitutional and legislative reforms that address their demands for greater participation (see Chapter 4). In countries across the region in the 1990s constitutional reforms often resulted in the political incorporation of excluded groups such as indigenous people. Constitutional reforms have increased indigenous participation in policy processes, although critics suggest that in countries such as Brazil this remains limited (see Carvalho 2000).

Indigenous rights. The struggle for *collective* rights has been an important explanation for mobilization and pressure for change has resulted in constitutional provisions and new laws codifying these and accompanied by new agrarian and forestry laws. Bolivia's 1996 agrarian reform law, for example, guaranteed the rights of indigenous peoples to community lands of origin and recognized indigenous territory as collective property (see Roper 2003).

The emergence of the indigenous movement has had important implications for politics in Latin America:

- *The state*. Indigenous mobilization represents more than just a demand for greater inclusion and often amounts to an effort to redefine *statehood* (see Kay 2004). Official recognition of indigenous identity in law has implications for governance and the characteristics of democracy, implying the need for policies that meet the needs of excluded groups. It can strengthen arguments often put forward by environmentalists that these groups are better stewards of nature, and can also enhance the relative power of social movements in politics. In Mexico, for example, the Chiapas rebellion generated a debate about the institutional limitations of liberal democracy based upon party competition if it is not accompanied by economic redistribution.

- *Multiculturalism and national identity*. Multicultural rights or official recognition of indigenous cultures and languages have been enshrined in law throughout Latin America since the 1980s. However, indigenous mobilization poses dilemmas for national identity by raising questions about the past understanding of nationhood and advancing a manifesto for multiculturalism. What is sometimes referred to as "indigeneity" – self-identification as indigenous – can also pose problems for international agencies if it occurs outside the policy definitions they apply (see Assies, van der Haar and Hoekema 2000; Horton 2006).

- *Individual versus collective rights*. Indigenous mobilization in Latin America has generated debates about the relationship between individual and collective or social rights. Policies of multiculturalism can generate a conflict between the recognition of group rights and of universal individual human rights (see Eckstein and Wickham-Crowley 2003; Sieder 2002; Warren and Jackson 2002).

- *Relations with formal politics, other social movements and NGOs.* Indigenous organizations have forged significant relationships with three types of non-governmental organization: ENGOs; those addressing humanitarian and socioeconomic development concerns; and those involved in the provision of credit (see Roper, Perreault and Wilson 2003). Links with ENGOs have grown since the mid-1980s, particularly in areas where indigenous groups are engaged in disputes over territorial and resource rights. Nonetheless, these relationships have not been without problems. NGO motives for engaging with indigenous communities may be influenced by their own institutional needs in order to attract funds. Indigenous groups are often torn between a desire to pursue their development agendas autonomously and the need for technical and financial assistance from non-indigenous NGOs, leading to internal conflicts. Using indigenous culture as a way of promoting alternative development strategies can also politicize it and make sustainable development initiatives contentious (Patrick Wilson 2003). Where projects have strengthened local dependency on the market, this can lead to competition and conflict within and between indigenous communities.

Strategies open to social movements

Environmental groups use a variety of conventional and unconventional methods to gain resources, allies and influence. Research on social movements in industrial societies has distinguished between fundamental opposition and protest and pragmatic attempts at reform within the political system:

- *Fundamentalism.* Some scholars argue that social movements' distinctive aims require them to confront the political establishment using unconventional and direct political action such as protest (see Lipsky 1968; McAdam, Tarrow and Tilly 2001). These put the spotlight on environmental causes that would otherwise be ignored and help to put greens at the vanguard of calls for a more participatory democracy. The participatory style of environmental groups may encourage expressive types of activity and nurture a critique that challenges dominant norms and champions alternative values (see Dalton, Recchia and Rohrschneider 2003). Yet, given the power of producer interests, ENGOs adopting protest actions may be less successful in changing policy than those using conventional lobbying or voting.

- *Pragmatism.* Other scholars have suggested that, because governments design and implement policy, it is necessary to engage in conventional lobbying activities to influence it. There are many examples in Europe and the US of environmental groups working in conventional ways with legislators and lobbying (see Dalton 1994; Dalton, Recchia and Rohrschneider 2003).

The choice between fundamentalism and pragmatism is more problematic in democracies that are being consolidated where environmental problems may be more severe and where tolerance of dissent can be more limited. Some scholars suggest that pragmatism can take precedence over ideological considerations in these societies (see, for example, Tarrow 1994). Given that social movements in regions such as Latin America are often motivated by an imperative to survive, this reinforces pressure to use conventional methods to gain resources, allies and influence, and limits anti-establishment approaches (Dalton, Recchia and Rohrschneider 2003). Social movements are also increasingly identified with the development and deployment of "green" and "clean" technologies, such as renewable energy, which are at the heart of notions of ecological modernization (see Toke 2011). As a result, they are now being seen as participants in a process to reform production and not just as lobbying organizations (see, for example, Mol 2000).

Studies of environmental movements globally show that they employ a broad repertoire of tactics which vary over time but found that the most frequent forms of behaviour are contacts with the media and efforts to mobilize public opinion (see Dalton, Recchia and Rohrschneider 2003). Most environmental groups routinely employ conventional approaches, such as informal meetings with civil servants or government ministers, and often form alliances. While there are good reasons to hypothesize that unconventional and confrontational actions are more likely to occur in the developing world, evidence suggests that this is not the case; indeed, groups in Latin America are less likely than their counterparts in the developed world to engage in challenging tactics such as protests or direct action: 22 per cent of European groups often employ challenging tactics compared with only 11 per cent in Latin America (Dalton, Recchia and Rohrschneider 2003). Democratic politics and decentralization in Latin America and the Caribbean have fostered ties between state actors and pragmatic environmental coalitions, especially in the context of reform-oriented local governance that minimizes traditional patterns of co-option and clientelism (see Lemos and Looye 2003). This means that while the relationship between state agencies charged with managing natural resources and environmental groups is sometimes conflictive, it is usually co-operative. There are several potential explanations for how movements behave:

- *Resource mobilization*. Resource mobilization theory argues that the behaviour of social movements will be dependent on organizational resources, so resource levels differentially affect their activity (see McCarthy and Zald 1977). Having a paid staff, for example, prioritizes organizational maintenance over confrontation, meaning that resource-rich or professional organizations might tend to undertake low-risk, conventional activities while poorly funded groups relying on volunteers might engage in protest-based tactics. This suggests that ENGOs with small budgets and staffs may be more likely to undertake confrontational activities, yet data indicates that protest is more common among groups with larger staffs and budgets (see Dalton, Recchia and Rohrschneider 2003).

- *Ideology*. Ideology shapes how organizations understand environmental problems and respond to them, making some types of activity more likely than others. Environmental groups emphasize their ideological distinctiveness and independence from larger networks and their positions may as a result isolate them, making it more likely they will engage in unconventional activity such as civil disobedience and demonstrations. A distinction is sometimes made between *ecologist* and *conservation* groups (see Dalton, Recchia and Rohrschneider 2003; Dalton, 1994). Ecologist groups are more likely to focus on environmental problems whose solutions call for changes in societal and political relations and so are more likely to use protest and mobilization; conservation groups focus on wildlife and preservation issues that they pursue without challenging dominant norms.

- *Political opportunity structures*. Political opportunity structure theories (see above) which place an emphasis on the institutional context in which social movements exist suggest a movement will choose the most effective way of exerting influence depending on the circumstances. Several factors influence the choice of activity such as levels of democratic development, access to allies within government, and a country's level of development.

On the ground, social movements in Latin America and the Caribbean exhibit a broad and diverse range of tactics. There are examples of both direct action and mass protest, and of conventional, reformist actions as well as the use of strategic tools such as spatial politics, identity and even revolutionary activity:

Mass mobilization. Where mass mobilization has been employed in environmental disputes, indigenous communities have often been at the heart of activity. Bolivia, Ecuador and Colombia have been the scene of recurrent protests led by indigenous groups, often over resource use (see Box 5.8; Murillo 2010). Land invasions have also been a common form of mass protest in rural areas, but have also occurred in cities in countries such as Guatemala (see Murphy 2004). Given these mobilizations and conflicts, international NGOs and multilateral agencies have given attention to environmental dispute resolution processes (see World Bank 2010; Partners for Democratic Change 2009).

Reformist activism. While social movements using mass protest have demonstrated their capacity to bring down governments in countries such as Bolivia and Ecuador, they still need to influence policy in more routine ways (see Stahler-Sholk, Vanden and Kuecker 2007). Collaboration leading to reform has been an effective policy tool, especially where leftwing governments have a natural affinity with popular sectors. Latin American and Caribbean governments have rarely reformed environmental rules without pressure from their own citizens, often in an alliance with international groups (see Kaimowitz 1996). Environmentalists have a range of conventional tools such as lobbying legislatures and bureaucracies, providing policymakers with information and expertise, and employing the media. Some green organizations use litigation to protect the environment (see Chapter 2) and there are many examples of activism that adopts a pragmatic approach to changing behaviour. In Puerto Rico, for example, grassroots campaigns have played a key role in changing energy policies (see Meyn 1996). In Cuba, an organic farming lobby has influenced policy development (see Rosset 1996). The indigenous Shuar of Ecuador have even resorted to shareholder activism (see Box 5.9).

Box 5.8 Indigenous protest in Bolivia

Bolivia's indigenous movement has used a wide range of tactics to advance its claims – from confrontations with state authorities, alliance building and conventional political mobilization to cultural assertion. In the early 1980s, there was a resurgence of Bolivian indigenous organization in both the Andean highlands and the Amazonian lowlands. The lowland movement gained prominence with the 1990 "March for Dignity and Territory" from the Beni department to La Paz protesting against commercial logging and advancing land claims (see Roper 2003). By framing the debate in terms of indigenous rights, leaders attracted the support of highland indigenous communities allowing the creation of a broad coalition that also took in non-indigenous civil society groups. In response, President Jaime Paz Zamora (1989–93) decreed the creation of indigenous territories, including the Territorio Indígena y Parque Nacional Isiboro Sécure (TIPNIS, Isiboro Sécure Indigenous Territory and National Park), and gave community institutions legal standing. A similar march to La Paz took place in 2011 by TIPNIS protesters demonstrating against government plans for a road through their land that they claimed would cause environmental and social chaos (see Phillips and Cabitza 2011). President Evo Morales – an Aymara whose election in 2005 represented a major political achievement for the country's indigenous movement – was forced to suspend construction work after police clashes with TIPNIS protesters. In a different form of activity, the work of an influential Aymara NGO known as the Taller de Historia Oral Andina (THOA, Andean Oral History Workshop) has also contributed to the articulation of an indigenous identity that challenges dominant norms. THOA's work has supported efforts to re-establish the role of the *ayllu* – the basic political and social unit of the Quechua and Aymara cultures – as a model of community governance (see Stephenson 2002).

Spatial politics. An important aspect of mobilization on environmental issues is captured by the notion of "spatial politics" which seeks to understand the influence on activism of factors such as local level processes (see Chapter 2; Perreault 2003). Spatial politics has, for example, been at the heart of mass mobilizations in urban areas by indigenous organizations in Ecuador and Colombia. Spatial limitations constrain the ability of local social movements to understand and negotiate laws, weaken them vis-à-vis powerful actors such as

---

Box 5.9 Indigenous groups target the boardroom

Brand image and company social responsibility policies offer activists new opportunities to place corporations under pressure. In 2004, a representative of the indigenous Shuar people of Ecuador addressed the annual shareholder meeting of the oil company Burlington Resources in Texas to call on it to halt exploration in areas of Ecuador's Amazon rainforest. McAteer and Pulver (2009) have examined the case as an example of ways in which corporate shareholders now play a role in transnational advocacy networks. They identify mechanisms by which activists in transnational networks can exert pressure by using the corporate arena itself in what is known as leverage politics, by which the parent-subsidiary structure of multinational corporations means that the parent corporation can exert decisive leverage on a subsidiary. Shareholder advocacy has become a common form of leverage politics in the US and has resulted in the creation of shareholder transnational advocacy networks involving local communities and social movements, international NGOs, the media and corporate shareholders. Campaigns use shareholder tactics to persuade investor groups that environmental damage poses financial, competitive, reputational or legal risks to a company and its shareholders. A network of this kind employed shareholder mechanisms to target US-based companies implicated in disputes over oil exploration in the Ecuadorian Amazon between 2002 and 2007 on behalf of local communities. The strategy pushed Burlington into a dialogue and forced policy change by which it published an indigenous rights policy and made a commitment that it would not proceed with its Ecuadorean concessions by force.

---

municipal elites and corporate interests and fuel divisions within and between organizations (see Roper 2003). Social movements can overcome spatial constraints by forging relationships with actors at different levels – local, regional, national and transnational – who have different degrees of access to institutional, financial and political support, a political strategy that is sometimes called "jumping scales". In Latin America, indigenous organizations have often been able to gain political influence and legitimacy for their claims vis-à-vis the state by jumping scales through strategic links with transnational networks (Brysk 2000).

Revolutionary or guerrilla activity. The pursuit of revolution was an important feature of politics on the left in Latin America and the Caribbean from the 1960s until the 1980s. Some of the progressive themes advanced by revolutionary groups, such as social justice, have been taken up by social movements. The Chiapas rebellion in Mexico in 1994 represented a fusion of revolutionary demands with the organizational dynamics of new social movements. It raised questions about whether the objective of seizing state power through armed action remains valid (see Stahler-Sholk, Vanden and Kuecker 2007). Guerrilla movements often try to win the support of local communities, and the relationship can sometimes yield benefits for both (see Barmeyer 2003; Harvey 1998). Other indigenous communities have resorted to armed action over resources. The Mapuche in Chile, for example, have at times sabotaged the equipment of logging companies in their long campaign for control over ancestral lands, an activity sometimes described as "ecotage". In turn, state security discourses have identified some environmental or animal activists as terrorists (see Welsh 2007).

Conclusion

Social movements and NGOs have been key actors in the evolution of environmental politics in Latin America and the Caribbean, and can be studied within theoretical literature that has taken as its focus the notion of civil society. Environmental social organizations are intrinsically multi-sectoral, often bringing together a large and diverse number of indigenous, peasant, public health, labour, student and urban popular groups. Indigenous groups draw heavily upon longstanding links with particular localities, a history of marginalization and cosmologies that tend to advocate sustainable forms of resource use, yet have also provided an important focus for non-indigenous mobilization. The heterogeneity of environmental and indigenous groups can be a strength, particularly if it enables organizations to mobilize a broad constituency of support and on that basis attract international attention. But it can also represent a weakness, providing a source of disagreements among groups over values and demands and hence a lack of consensus on policy. NGOs form alliances with many environmental and indigenous groups, transcending established political and class boundaries, and tend to be more pragmatic and prepared to co-operate with the state to achieve environmental aims. Although there are many prominent international ENGOs working in Latin America and the Caribbean, many groups in the region emerged autonomously, often from within the conservation movement. Nonetheless, the role played by international NGOs, and the international funding available to Latin American NGOs, mean that transnational factors and influences are often prominent in the study of these organizations and the alliances they form in the region. Environmental and indigenous social movements use a large variety of conventional and unconventional methods to gain support and influence policymaking, from mass mobilization in protests and marches that may confront state authorities directly to shareholder activism that puts pressure on the boards of corporations, and their tactics are constantly evolving.

Recommended reading

Brown, David S, Christopher Brown and Scott W Desposato. 2007. "Promoting and Preventing Political Change through Internationally Funded NGO Activity", *Latin American Research Review*, Vol. 42, No. 1, pp. 126–38.

Dalton, Russell J, Steve Recchia and Robert Rohrschneider. 2003. "The Environmental Movement and the Modes of Political Action", *Comparative Political Studies*, Vol. 36, No. 7 (September), pp. 743–71.

Dangl, Benjamin. 2010. *Dancing With Dynamite: Social Movements and States in Latin America*. Oakland, CA: AK Press.

Deere, Carmen Diana and Frederick S Royce (eds). 2009. *Rural Social Movements in Latin America: Organizing for Sustainable Livelihoods*. Gainsville: University of Florida Press.

Roper, J Montgomery, Thomas Perreault and Patrick C Wilson. 2003. "Introduction", *Latin American Perspectives*, Vol. 30, No. 1 (January), pp. 5–22.

Stahler-Sholk, Richard, Harry E Vanden and Glen David Kuecker. 2007. "Introduction; Globalizing Resistance: The New Politics of Social Movements in Latin America", *Latin American Perspectives*, Vol. 34, No. 2, *Globalizing Resistance: The New Politics of Social Movements in Latin America* (March), pp. 5–16.

Torres, Blanca. 1997. "Transnational Environmental NGOs: Linkages and Impact on Policy", in Gordon J MacDonald, Daniel L Nielson and Marc A Stern (eds), *Latin American Environmental Policy in International Perspective*. Boulder, CO: Westview Press.

Useful websites

Acción Ecológica, Ecuador: www.accionecologica.org/

Amigos de la Tierra (Friends of the Earth) Colombia: www.censat.org/

Comité Nacional Pro Defensa de la Flora y Fauna, Chile: www.codeff.cl/

El Green Times online magazine, Guatemala: http://elgreentimes.com/

Fórum Brasileiro de ONGs e Movimentos Sociais para o Meio Ambiente e o Desenvolvimento (FBOMS, Brazilian Forum of NGOs and Social Movements for the Environment and Development): www.fboms.org. br

Fundación Ambiente y Recursos Naturales (FARN, Environment and Natural Resources Foundation), Argentina: www.farn.org.ar/

Fundación Centro de Derechos Humanos y Ambiente (CEDHA, Center for Human Rights and Environment), Argentina: http://wp.cedha. net/?lang=en

Fundación Sinchi Saha eco-tourism initiative, Ecuador: www.sinchisacha. org

Instituto de Ecología Política (Chile): www.iepe.org/2011/fundacion-iep/

IEP's online magazine *Revista Ecología Política*: www.ecologiapolitica.iepe. org/index.php

Instituto do Homem e Meio Ambiente da Amazônia (Imazon, Institute for the People and Environment of Amazonia): www.imazon.org.br/

Instituto O Direito por Um Planeta Verde (Law for a Green Planet Institute), Brazil: www.planetaverde.org/

Puerto Rico Biosafety Project's bilingual blog: http://bioseguridad. blogspot.com/

Red Argentina de Abogados para la Defensa del Ambiente (RADA, Argentine Network of Environmental Defence Lawyers): www. oikosredambiental.org/

Zapatista websites

Chiapas Media Project: www.chiapasmediaproject.org/

CIEPAC: www.ciepac.org/bulletins/

Enlace Civil: www.enlacecivil.org.mx/index.htm

Frente Zapatista de Liberación Nacional: http://spin.com.mx/~floresu/ FZLN/home.html

CHAPTER SIX

Green ideology

IDEAS ARE AT THE VERY HEART OF POLITICS, proposing norms for the distribution and use of power, and political ideas are of great importance to the environment and have played a key role in shaping the natural landscape of Latin America and the Caribbean. Ideas have driven deforestation of the region, for example, underpinning the developmental nationalism that was premised on a longstanding Iberian desire to conquer nature and tame the wilderness (see Volume 1). In 1940, Brazil's then president Getulio Vargas (1930–45) expressed this position: "To conquer the land, tame the waters, and subjugate the jungle, these have been our tasks. And in this centuries-old battle, we have won victory upon victory" (Franko 1999: 45). This conviction has only strengthened in recent generations and large-scale clearing of tropical forests began in the 1960s, with three-quarters of the deforestation in the Brazilian Amazon taking place in the 20 years prior to the Rio Earth Summit in 1992 (Ryan 1991). Similarly, notions about the city and its role in progress have been at the core of the Latin American and Caribbean understanding of modernity. Generations of migrants from rural areas have looked down upon those back on the land as provincial, and many conservationists have been urban elites. Since the 1970s, ideologies of environmentalism have gained ground throughout the region, whose natural environment has also generated considerable anxiety in the developed world. More recently, attention has turned to the ideas and traditions of indigenous people throughout the region and how these might contribute to efforts to protect the environment and use natural resources responsibly. This focus has been sharpened by the emergence of a dominant official emphasis by governments and multilateral bodies on the need for "sustainable development", a reformist notion that appears to resolve the tension existing between environmental protection and economic development. This chapter introduces some of the main ideological themes that have influenced political development in Latin America and the Caribbean – from those promoted on the left and right that take class as their underlying motif to those advanced by nationalist and indigenous movements that stress identity – and examines how the environment fits into these.

Political ideas

A dualism runs through environmental philosophy deriving from a belief that human attitudes towards the natural world are responsible for ecological crisis legitimizing the exploitation of nature for the benefit of humans. The belief that ethical principles exist solely in the interest of humankind is known as anthropocentrism, and this attributes an instrumental value to nature by suggesting that it deserves moral consideration only to the extent that it is related to human well-being. Anthropocentrism derives from Enlightenment ideas and the triumph of scientific notions about mankind's mastery of nature. It has been challenged by "ecocentric" stances in environmental philosophy, which argue that other forms of life also have ethical value (see Carter 2007). In Latin America and the Caribbean one reflection of this dualism is the way new ideas such as environmentalism, as well as ancient beliefs about nature in indigenous societies, coexist with the dominant framework of economic developmentalism. Indeed, the region is a laboratory in which this coexistence of ideas and the broader notion of "sustainable development" can be examined.

The study of political ideas is bedevilled by many variables, and it is helpful to identify key strands in political thought in order to examine how these might accommodate ecological positions. Latin America and the Caribbean has, overall, been mainly an importer of ideas, ideology and social theory, and the Western heritage of its elites and the ties that have developed between its republics and the international capitalist economy have shaped the ways in which political thought has developed. Most of the main ideologies of the last 150 years were generated by the impact of the industrial revolution on northern European societies then superimposed upon the Iberian tradition (see Volume 1). Industrialization occurred much later in Latin America without similar changes in social structure and modernity itself was often conceived of as a European or US phenomenon. Modernization theories modelled on experiences elsewhere have long made assumptions about the nature of Latin American and Caribbean development. Yet in recent times this perspective has been questioned by a growing conviction that it is impossible, in the short term, for industrialization and the large-scale modernization of agriculture to bring about a structural transformation of developing economies (see Blokland 1995; Saith 1985). Green thinkers have sometimes argued that because environmental ethicists tend to think of nature and culture as distinct spheres of moral concern and focus mainly on the "non-natural" environments (cities) where much industrialization takes place, this has produced an anti-urban bias in political ecology (see Light 2001). Mindful of assumptions made on the basis of imported notions, some environmentalists warn against "eco-colonialism" in the realm of ideas. At the same time, while tracing their origins to Europe and the US, many of the ideas permeating Latin American political thought have gained a distinctively local quality, shaped by the region's own legacies and divisions. Hochstetler and Keck (2007), for example, argue that environmentalism in Brazil is in large measure a domestic construct – a product of political projects, social struggles and scientific arguments within Brazil itself.

The character of political ideas in Latin America and the Caribbean has been shaped by several formative local themes such as centralism, liberalism, positivism and corporatism. Political culture in the region has been influenced by two broad sources of struggle: the conflict between left and right based on a loose understanding of politics as a competition between socio-economic classes; and social contestation based on identities that provide inherent or imagined sources of difference between groups. Both have important implications for the development of environmental ideas in the region.

Left versus right

The clash between leftwing and rightwing ideas has had an important influence upon Latin America's political evolution, and an important development since the end of the Cold War has been the effort by competitive parties to develop a centrist politics that challenges the rigidity of the former left–right spectrum (see Chapter 4). In recent years the left has shifted towards social-democratic positions and the right towards greater acceptance of democratic pluralism, and there has been a convergence of ideas in the mainstream "centre", particularly in countries that have achieved stable growth such as Chile. This decline in the force of traditional left–right poles has been a key factor in the development of environmentalism, offering the prospect of a politics that transcends past divisions that can confront non-class issues once considered marginal. It is valuable to explore where the environment fits into the main ideas on the right and left.

The right (conservatism). Although the centre-left has made significant gains in Latin America and the Caribbean in recent years, the right remains a potent force in politics and has regrouped in some countries (see Domínguez, Lievesley and Ludlam 2011). Early conservatives built upon an existing critique of liberalism deriving from disagreements about morality and the nature of mankind, challenging the anthropocentric liberal vision that man was an autonomous and rational being who must control his own destiny. Conservatives saw men as imperfect beings who needed spiritual guidance to live good lives, and attacked individualism for its dangerous egotism. Traditionalism has also been a core theme in conservative thought, but a conservative dilemma was the desire to preserve traditional society while accepting that traditional values can stand in the way of economic progress. Corporatist ideas also influenced the right as it began to respond to arguments based on the theme of class conflict. Christian democracy grew rapidly in some countries in the Cold War atmosphere by being able to attract support from both left and right. In 1947, the Organización Demócrata Cristiana de América (ODCA, Christian Democrat Organization of America), an international association of political parties and groups adhering to Christian humanist and democratic ideology, was founded. It has focused on six themes, from a commitment to humanism, founded on the need to confront a materialistic and individualistic way of life, to a commitment to the environment, based on respect for a religiously inspired view of the natural order of creation. In the 1960s and 1970s, civilian conservative forces generally co-operated with military regimes, revealing much about conservative attitudes towards democracy (see Arceneaux 2001). Even today, the right is often assessed from the position of fear of a re-emergence of support for unconstitutional politics. In general, however, the restoration of democracy in the 1980s was accompanied by a new commitment to party pluralism and the creation of new conservative parties. A hallmark of the right in Latin America since the 1980s has been the neoliberal critique of the state's economic role, and throughout the region conservative parties played a prominent role in promoting market-oriented reforms that often led to environmental degradation (see Volume 1). Nonetheless, conservatives today speak less about order while continuing to value concepts such as the "common good". Traditional conservative ideas sometimes coincide with green principles: both share a suspicion of Enlightenment ideas of progress while cherishing nostalgic visions of a pre-modern age. However, conservatives have grown suspicious of ecological arguments and in recent years influential conservative positions – often originating in the US – have been associated with scepticism about the notion of global warming (see Box 6.1).

The left (socialism and Marxism). Leftwing thought in Latin America and the Caribbean has taken many forms but agrarian radicalism and anarcho-syndicalism – a radical and militant trade unionism that fought to improve peasant and working-class conditions – were precursors of socialist and communist movements in the twentieth century as export economies expanded. Marxist philosophy and its concern with redistribution has been highly influential in the region because of the persistence of inequality, but in general Marxist ideas have found it hard to adapt to Latin American conditions. A traditional emphasis on industrialism helps to explain one of the left's principal failures: its reluctance to come to terms with the peasant question. Many communists were urban activists, reinforcing the role of the city as a source of political ideas in modern Latin America. Some leftwing thinkers recognized these weaknesses, such as the writer

Box 6.1 Environmental scepticism on the right

In the 1990s, environmentalism evolved into a global movement that challenged the precepts of capitalism as it spread across the world through policies of privatization and free trade. This prompted many conservatives to substitute for the "red scare" of Soviet communism something akin to a "green scare". Environmentalists argued that global problems such as loss of biodiversity and climate change indicated that the lifestyles and industrial practices of modern societies were not sustainable. US conservatives led the response, arguing that environmentalism was a growing threat to social and economic progress. A study of 141 English-language environmentally sceptical books published between 1972 and 2005 found that over 92 per cent of these, most published in the US since 1992, are linked to conservative think tanks (see Jacques, Dunlap and Freeman 2008). The right has had some success portraying environmentalism as a threat to US values and interests, justifying the creation of an institutionalized anti-environmental movement funded by wealthy foundations and corporations. Their main weapon is "environmental scepticism" – questioning the seriousness of environmental problems and the validity of environmental science. Neoliberal and new right ideas are also generally hostile to ecologism because it restrains pure free market activities and property rights. They promote counter-claims that question the problematic state of environmental quality and need for regulations. The influence of conservative think tanks on environmental policy has been extensive and their efforts to replace regulation with free market solutions have often been accepted without detailed scrutiny of the underlying ideological agenda. (Main sources: Jacques, Dunlap and Freeman. 2008; Beder 2001)

José Carlos Mariátegui (1894–1930), who founded a socialist party in Peru in 1929. In recent times, Mariátegui's ideas have been reassessed in countries such as Ecuador and Bolivia, providing a Marxist justification for the claims to indigenous autonomy (see Becker 2008). The Cuban Revolution (1959) overturned accepted notions about the stages a society had to go through before revolution became possible, revived interest in Marxist theory and influenced the rise of an intellectual "new left" globally which has been an important source of environmentalist positions (see Chapters 4, 5). The collapse of the socialist bloc from 1989 to 1991 called into question the viability of socialism, and neoliberalism became a dominant orthodoxy, partly because the left was devoid of alternatives. By the mid-1990s, a range of different tendencies could be identified within the Latin American left: a minority fundamentalist position committed to Marxist–Leninist orthodoxy; class-based populism that encouraged confrontation yet was unable to garner mass support; a radical democratic project that combines the struggle against capitalism with those against patriarchy, ethnic discrimination and environmental destruction, and has been influential within the Partido dos Trabalhadores (PT, Workers' Party) in Brazil and the Mexican Zapatistas; and social democracy, that aspired within a democratic framework to transform the left into a viable governing alternative using state power as an instrument for reform. Many of the leftwing leaders and parties that have assumed power in Latin America and the Caribbean in recent years have pursued social-democratic policies. Democratization has had an important ideological impact on the left and an important strain in leftwing thought in Latin America today is the idea of extending democracy beyond the notion of electoral inclusion through voting to a much more participative idea of governance ("participatory democracy") often implicit in the idea of decentralization (see Chapter 1). Another vision of direct democracy of this kind is "deliberative democracy", which has been an important focus of ecological thought (see Zwart 2003). Deliberative democracy, also known as discursive democracy, adopts elements of both consensus decision-making and majority rule in an effort to go beyond a simple aggregation of votes. It has provoked lively debate within the environmental movement about the conditions necessary for it to be achieved (see Hobson 2009; Gupte and Bartlett 2007). Complementing a greater commitment to democracy has been the left's embrace of pluralism, which found expression in new alliances and coalitions. The growth of social movements has been an important focus of leftwing ideas (see Chapter 5), and the thesis that social movements are the precursors of a new type of participatory democracy has been influential. Some thinkers have sought an ideological mechanism to justify stronger links between the left and social organizations, in particular indigenous movements. A prominent Latin American thinker whose work has been inspired by the new pluralism of the left and social movements is the Argentine Enrique Dussel, who became identified with debates at the World Social Forum. Today, the Latin American left is highly heterogeneous and a distinguishing characteristic of it is policy diversity.

Environmental justice and eco-socialism. Green positions do not obey the framework of ideological debate provided by traditional issues of class (see Box 6.2). However, many environmentalists place themselves on the left because they relate to its positions on the market economy, democratization, decentralization and social justice (see Carter 2007). The question of class is relevant to sustainability, and the relationship between organized labour and environmentalism has been the focus of debate. Norton (2003) has examined this issue in cases where the labour movement has collaborated with environmental groups and argues that the evidence suggests that class does not have a significant bearing on co-operation but that, nonetheless, it circumscribes social actors' abilities to shape, and respond to, environmental and economic change. In Latin America the relationship between the environment and class is more nuanced than in Europe, with evidence suggesting that in sub-regions such as Central America the causes of environmental degradation often have their origins in social relations (see Painter and Durham 1995). When it comes to land use, for example, the conditions faced by the poor, on the one hand, combined with the granting of land on concessionary rates to powerful individuals and corporations, on the other, create disincentives to conservation. This is because resource use can be understood in technical material terms – as a response to the conditions of the physical environment – but also in terms of *access*: who controls a resource and the institutional arrangements by which that control is exercised. Moreover, the competition for resources between classes has international dynamics. In Central America, for example, US strategic interests have formed an important context in which agricultural and commercial relations have been shaped.

In Latin America there have often been strong links between the left and ecology parties, and similar views on social justice, democratization and equality have encouraged both to explore the potential of rainbow alliances and "red–green" coalitions. Overlapping but nonetheless distinctive strains of thought have emerged in efforts to reconcile positions.

Box 6.2   Core themes of ecologism

Ecologism advances a vision of a sustainable society based on four main principles established in 1983 by the German greens:

Ecological responsibility. Development must be self-sufficient and safeguard the environment for future generations.

Grassroots democracy and decentralization. The pursuit of sustainability has implications for democratic governance because it must consider the needs of future generations (see above, and Beckman 2008). Ecologists presume active citizen participation in governance and greater localism through decentralization (see Carter 2007; Chapter 1). Decentralized political communities are smaller and might be better stewards of the land. The practical model of "bioregionalism" has been put forward by Sale (1980) that envisages humane and reciprocal solidaristic communities that are self-reliant and know the land (see Pepper 1993).

Social justice. Greater equality both between and within countries is seen as good for the environment because injustice contributes to environmental degradation (see Carter 2007).

Non-violence. Greens oppose any use of violence, war, armies and weapons of mass destruction, although some believe that violent acts towards property may be legitimate forms of protest in some circumstances. In Chile, for example, environmentalists have sometimes been reluctant to condemn the Mapuche indigenous people for sabotage.

A report by Meadows et al., published in 1972, modelled the consequences of a rapidly rising world population on finite resources, and also established an influential thesis within ecologism that finite resources place limits on future industrial growth while suggesting that ecological problems cannot be treated in isolation. Critics argue that economic growth through the operation of markets and free trade ultimately improves environmental quality (see Lomborg 2001).

Environmental justice

The concept of human rights has become the most important theme in Latin American jurisprudence in terms of highlighting environmental degradation and seeking the enforcement of regulations. Given the way in which courts have often interpreted constitutional provisions based on universal rights in favour of environmental protection (see Chapter 1), struggles with an environmental component often take the form of efforts by marginalized groups to assert their human rights. Since the early 1990s, there have been important developments in environmental protection from a human rights approach in domestic courts given the widespread recognition of the right to a healthy environment in the region's constitutions (see Fabra and Arnal 2002; Chapter 2). An important development in the sphere of rights was the Protocol of San Salvador (1999), providing protection for a range of "second-generation" economic, social and cultural rights. Its provisions cover such areas as the rights to work, health, food and education. Some prominent green thinkers have argued that climate change should be interpreted predominantly as a threat to human rights, particularly the right to a healthy environment (see Caney 2008; UNHRC 2008; ICHRP 2008; OHCHR 2009). Environmental rights are considered to be those individual and collective rights that pertain to the minimum biological requirements necessary for survival, as well as rights that sustain life in the long term (see Johnston 2011a). These rights are often affected by our efforts to manage and use resources, which can generate conflicts and abuses.

A concept that has been of clear relevance in Latin America and the Caribbean is that of environmental justice, which emerged in the US as an extension of the civil rights movement in which it equated with social inequality, often based on race or ethnicity (see Carruthers 2008b; Adamson, Evans and Stein 2002; Agyeman, Bullard and Evans 2003; Martinez-Alier 2002; Westra and Lawson 2001). The environmental justice movement built on the discourse of rights in the 1990s as democratization gathered pace. The concept of environmental justice has been understood in different ways, but what all definitions share is a concern for equity – equal rights to participate in environmental policymaking and to benefit from the distribution of environmental goods (see Box 6.3; Kütting 2004). In recent decades, several Latin American and Caribbean countries have embraced concepts of environmental justice, in some cases by establishing specialized tribunals – for example, the Tribunal Ambiental Administrativo in Costa Rica (see UNEP 2012a). The concept is of clear relevance in a region where poor and indigenous people and minorities such as Afro-Latinos face major environmental and social inequalities because of both poverty and race (see Carruthers 2008b).

> **Box 6.3** Environmental justice
>
> Schlosberg (2004) has examined different meanings given to environmental justice and argues that understanding this solely in terms of distributive justice is insufficient. Justice itself has many meanings and concentrating merely on distribution cannot encompass the broad and diverse demands made by the global environmental justice movement, which include the recognition of cultural identity and full participatory democratic rights. Rather than seek to understand environmental justice solely as a theoretical concept, Schlosberg looks at how it is defined in practice by social groups within the highly diverse "environmental justice movement". Schlosberg argues that the justice these demand is in fact threefold: equity in the distribution of environmental risk; recognition of diversity; and participation in the political processes that create and manage environmental policy. Carruthers (2007) examined the effort to apply the language, tools or assumptions of the US concept of environmental justice in Latin America both as a discourse of popular mobilization and as a set of principles for analysis, interpretation and policy. He suggests that although there are problems applying this in countries such as Mexico, local and regional organizations and advocacy networks have successfully employed the language, images and direct-action strategies of other environmental justice campaigns and this notion offers a potent opportunity for transnational advocacy. In a second work, Carruthers (2008a) brings together scholarship on a broad range of social conflicts in urban and rural contexts in which environmental justice is understood in practice in a variety of ways that associate it with other forms of inequality – from racial injustice and disputes over land and water to issues of fairness in trade and the politics of waste management in countries such as Mexico. Carruthers argues that claims for justice are embedded in different forms of popular environmentalism in Latin America and the Caribbean, and that their use of language, principles, tactics and questions offer new ways of understanding the region's social and environmental challenges.

In developed nations – where ecologism is often driven by the ways in which modernization and development have alienated citizens from nature – environmentalism tends to emphasize conservation and quality of life issues, whereas in Latin America and the Caribbean, where environmentalism is motivated by the dependence on nature of peoples for their survival and where many environmental disputes are as much about *access* to resources – clean water, fertile land, forest resources – as about saving them, the struggle to protect nature has often been linked to the struggle for economic and social justice (see Faber 1993; Roberts and Thanos 2003; Carruthers 2008b). This marriage between the language of social justice and environmentalism often fuses imported notions with local, indigenous ideas or experiences to give rise to what has broadly been called "socio-environmentalism". Linking environmental and social issues offers a political resource by allowing established movements on the left to attract broader support than from a purely class focus. The inclusion of environmental issues in the agenda of social justice movements may be one of the only ways today of developing mass constituencies for major policy reforms (see Kaimowitz 1996). Political parties have learned the value of these links and there is a strong environmental current within the Brazilian PT and Partido Socialista de Chile (PSCh, Chilean Socialist Party). Socio-environmentalism has mainly political aims:

1. *Improved social conditions*. Debates about the impact of globalization on Latin America and the Caribbean are increasingly framed by themes of equality and participation. A desire for greater equality is often expressed as opposition to free-market policies which either exacerbate poverty or promote economic growth that damages the environment. In Latin America these debates are often reflected in the politics of competing land uses between advocates of environmental values and champions of extractive industries (see Zebich-Knos 2008; Wolford 2008). The politics of control of resources varies widely and local conditions shape the character of struggles for environmental justice (see Wickstrom 2008). Bolivia has experienced recurrent struggles over control of resources (see Perreault 2008; Box 5.2).

2. *Environmental protection*. Industrial development in Latin America has distributed the burdens of environmental degradation unevenly, generating a sense of injustice. Leaders have long advocated developmentalism and powerful public and private interests have pursued rapid growth, meaning that development was relatively unregulated until recently and has had little regard for environmental well-being. As a result, social justice and environmental health concerns come together in the popular response to industrial hazards (Carruthers 2008b). In Mexico, this is very evident in the border zone where issues

of industrial waste and labour mobilization for better conditions characterize development (see Díez and Rodriguez 2008).

3. *Empowerment and accountability*. Concerns about political inequality and demands for greater participation and improved citizenship rights are central themes of environmental justice in Latin America. Communities affected by environmental degradation often argue that they have been deliberately excluded from the policy decisions that cause environmental harm (Carruthers 2008b). They also often seek to ensure that the institutions and organizations that created ecological problems acknowledge their culpability (see Johnston 2011a).

The notions of "ecological citizenship" or "environmental citizenship" are sometimes deployed in discussions about environmental justice. These have generated debate among green thinkers and have been interpreted either as a way of emphasizing the existing rights of citizens to enjoy an environment free from degradation and to participate in bringing that about, or as offering a normative standard for how citizens should conduct their lives in order to reduce their environmental impact, defining their rights and duties in the effort to achieve sustainability (see Dobson and Bell 2006). Citizenship is a valuable concept because, on the one hand, it stresses the importance of the relationship between ecologism and the possibility for greater democratic participation, and, on the other, it envisages a new, global political community that tests ideas of nationhood (see Dobson and Bell 2006; Latta 2007a, 2007b; Sáiz 2005; Christoff 1996; Wolf, Brown and Conway 2009).

In recent years, the issue of climate change has provided another focus for demands for environmental justice, sometimes called "climate justice", especially among developing countries such as Bolivia (see Athanasiou and Baer 2002; Angus 2009; Building Bridges Collective 2010). The concept of climate justice challenges existing concepts of justice and democracy because of the far-reaching implications of climate change (see Beckman and Page 2008).

A distinctively Latin American environmental justice framework has emerged that takes many localized forms and fuses local environmental and health concerns with the language and the tactics of mobilization on social issues (see Johnston 2011a). Brazil hosted Latin America's first international conference on environmental justice in 2001 and is home to the Brazilian Network of Environmental Justice, created in 2002 (Roberts and Thanos 2003). The network comprises about 80 social, environmental, union and academic organizations and debates environmental injustices. Elsewhere in the region other networks and groups have debated injustices in mining, oil, agriculture and development in Peru, Nicaragua and Ecuador (see Carruthers 2008b).

Eco-socialism

Environmental awareness in Latin America has grown alongside both the "pink tide" that has brought leftwing leaders with a more assertive social agenda to power throughout the region, and the rise of the indigenous movement which is often associated with ideas about sustainable development (see below). It would be surprising if there had not been attempts in the region to build bridges between socialism and ecologism, and a second discernible strain of thinking that links social and environmental concerns is eco-socialism (see Pepper 1993). Several political experiments have aimed to marry environmental and socialist ideas, beginning with what has been called the "revolutionary ecology" of Nicaragua's Sandinista government in the 1980s. This employed revolutionary rhetoric to fuse principles of equity and social justice with more traditional environmental notions of conservation (see Faber 2002). More recently, eco-socialist ideas have been attributed to the leaders and activities of socialist movements or parties that place a strong emphasis on environmental issues, such as Evo Morales in Bolivia, Rafael Correa in Ecuador and Hugo Chávez in Venezuela. Morales has described himself as an eco-socialist, and was prominent in struggles associated with the environmental justice movement such as the so-called "Water Wars" in Cochabamba against the privatization of the city's municipal water supplies in 1999–2000. Ecological challenges are also at the heart of what has been called "socialism of the twenty-first century" delineated by thinkers associated with Chávez in Venezuela. Chávez articulated a vision sometimes described as "eco-socialism of the twenty-first century" that combines *sui generis* ideas about Latin America being a pioneer of a revived global socialism with ecological themes (see Box 6.4).

The notion of eco-socialism begins from the position that ecological destruction is an inherent aspect of capitalism by which decisions about what to produce, how to organize production and how to distribute commodities are determined neither by social need nor ecological sustainability but by profitability. As growth is the key to raising

> **Box 6.4** Twenty-first century eco-socialism
>
> García-Guadilla (2009) traces use of the term "twenty-first century eco-socialism" to 2007 and its use by various intellectuals close to Chávez at a time in which the Venezuelan president was campaigning to incorporate socialist ideals in the constitution, and argues that it represents an effort to simplify the country's environmental crisis by blaming capitalism for all its ills. The notion suggests that all the country's environmental conflicts and problems will be resolved through the transition from capitalism to socialism and the construction of a new revolutionary consciousness. In May 2007, a round table was held at the headquarters of the Venezuelan state oil monopoly PDVSA to explore this notion, entitled "Ecosocialismo del Siglo XXI", sponsored by the energy and environment ministries. A key Venezuelan proponent of the idea was Francisco Javier Velasco, who argued in 2007 that this could be situated within both socialist and anarchist critiques of capitalism such as those of Marx, Engels, Lenin, Rosa Luxemburg, Gramsci and Bakunin, all of whom developed ideas about man's relationship with nature. In order to end the forms of domination that exist between humans, and between them and nature, it was necessary to adopt a "social ecology" perspective that combined revolutionary theories of the twentieth and twenty-first century with environmental concerns. This position derives from a catastrophic vision of capitalism that blames it for all social and environmental ills that create conditions in which it is increasingly difficult to live (García-Guadilla 2009).

profits, such a system continually seeks to expand production and consumption – resulting in ever greater environmental degradation (see also Dore 1996a). Such a perspective implies that efforts at reforming capitalism by superimposing upon it an agenda of environmental protection are futile. A prominent eco-socialist who makes this argument is the Belgian Marxist and agronomist Daniel Tanuro, who has argued in *L'impossible capitalisme vert* (2010) that attempts to resolve the climate crisis using market mechanisms such as carbon trading and eco-taxes, which fail to challenge the profit motive and capital accumulation, cannot succeed.

Eco-socialism suggests that a radical transformation in the relationship between society and the environment must be based on a conscious critique of the traditional paradigm underlying natural resource use and dominant property relations. The ecology movement has made this more possible by raising consciousness about the consequences of environmental destruction and advancing a green critique of capitalism. Nonetheless, green thinkers have argued that property theory has been a blind spot in environmental political thought and that ecocentric theorists have neglected the task of developing an alternative theory of property (see Breen 2001).

Nonetheless, key struggles mounted by eco-socialists in Latin America and the Caribbean have been over property relations, namely the privatization of strategic natural resource sectors, such as water provision, and foreign activity in the commercial extraction of natural resources. The positions they take on these issues often draw upon existing discourses of anti-imperialism or hostility to foreign capital that derive from dependency theory (see Chapter 3). More radical statements of eco-socialist arguments coincide with such notions as "eco-imperialism" and "eco-dependency" (see Dore 1996a).

Eco-socialist discourses have practical political value by strengthening the ability of leftwing leaders to associate the domestic control of natural resources, energy and food production with environmental protection and national sovereignty. This enables these leaders to eschew the involvement of multinational corporations in their economies, portray these as having played an environmentally destructive role, and thereby extend domestic state control. It also explains why Morales and the MAS make common cause with indigenous organizations in Bolivia, which provide a cross-cutting appeal and urgency to politics (see Albro 2005). In Venezuela under Chávez, socialist positions prioritizing national sovereignty came together with environmental policies aiming to end mono-crop production and the use of chemical inputs in agriculture through reforms aimed at achieving national control of resources or self-sufficiency in food production (see Box 6.5).

The Via Campesina transnational social movement and the Brazilian Movimento dos Trabalhadores Sem Terra (MST) are examples of how these ideas allow protests against globalization to be combined with attempts to establish alternative rural livelihoods aimed at self-sufficiency in food production. Environmental rights are at the heart of the concept of "food sovereignty", which stresses that peoples have the "right to produce [their] own food in [their] own territory" in ways that enhance the local environment and cultural

Box 6.5 Agro-ecology and food sovereignty

In late 2007, and throughout most of 2008, Latin American countries endured the impact of soaring world food prices (see Rosset 2009). This was caused by a complex range of factors that include domination of world food supplies by large transnational corporations; deregulation of international trade in foodstuffs; the privatization of grain markets; and speculation on commodity markets. Fluctuating food prices have a dramatic impact in Latin American and Caribbean countries such as Haiti which are dependent on the global economy and are not self-sufficient in food production. At the root of a dependency on food imports is the behaviour of the transnational corporations that dominate global food production and constantly undermine government price controls and food supply policies. In 2007, for example, Mexicans protested against a sudden doubling of tortilla prices which government officials and industry spokesmen blamed on global market factors. However, hoarding and price speculation by private grain-trading corporations such as Cargill, a beneficiary of the privatization of grain reserves in Mexico, played a major role in the increase (Rosset 2009). In that year, Venezuelans also faced milk shortages which President Hugo Chávez blamed on the transnational dairy giants Nestlé and Parmalat. In Bolivia, President Morales had to ban temporarily exports of cooking oil, chicken, beef, wheat, corn and rice as the private sector hoarded and exported foodstuffs. These cases help to explain a commitment in many states in Latin America and the Caribbean to achieving "food sovereignty" whereby domestic production allows them to end their vulnerability to price fluctuations beyond their control. In recent years, governments in Venezuela, Bolivia, Argentina, Cuba, Ecuador, Nicaragua, Honduras and elsewhere in Latin America and the Caribbean, as well as international NGOs such as Via Campesina (see Chapter 5), have advocated much stricter regulation of the food commodity markets. Such policies imply, for example, the renationalization of national grain reserves and export controls to stop the exportation of food needed locally. The constitutions of Venezuela, Bolivia and Ecuador all now contain food sovereignty clauses. The issue has sparked renewed debate about agrarian reform that aims to stimulate the recovery of national food-producing capacity in the peasant and family farm sectors. Growing attention is being paid to the role agro-ecology can play in food production, again led by Venezuela through laws to regulate production (see Broughton 2011). These are premised on the principles that farmers should have control of their land and product, that the country should produce its own food, and that chemical fertilizers and pesticides should not be employed. Via Campesina, the international NGO that originated in Latin America, has been a proponent of food sovereignty and in 2008 stated that its achievement requires the establishment of agriculture systems that do not include patented life-forms, pesticides, genetically modified organisms, agro-fuels – or the presence of multinational corporations (see Desmarais 2009a, 2009b).

values (Desmarais 2009b). Food sovereignty can be contrasted with the notion of food security, which means that every person must have the certainty of having enough to eat every day but which does not prescribe the conditions of production, distribution or consumption (Rosset 2009). Food sovereignty can only be viable after a significant programme of redistributive land reform and where this is subsequently reversed, as happened in Nicaragua after the end of the revolution in 1990, it can result in malnutrition (see Selwyn 2011; Linkogle 1998).

However, despite the potential of eco-socialism as a source of ideas that can unite two of the most important strains in progressive thought in Latin America and the Caribbean, there are fault lines in the relationship between socialism and ecologism:

Faultlines: development and limits to growth. Ecologists do not accept the commitment to unrestrained economic development that is at the heart of socialist ideas and derives from the industrialism that socialist theory shares with capitalism. Ecologists argue that socialism is a materialist and anthropocentric philosophy that, at root, strives for human domination of nature (see Carter 2007). They often point to the record of ecological degradation of socialist systems such as Cuba (see Díaz-Briquets and Pérez-López 2000). Marxists depict the concept of a "steady state economy" – challenging the vision of permanent growth with the notion of finite resources in mind – as in conflict with their vision of equality built upon material abundance. Eco-socialists respond by conceding that growth must take account of ecological limits, or blame environmental degradation on capitalism, not industrialism (see Carter 2007). The Marxist philosopher Terry

Eagleton (2012) has argued that there is a strong, if concealed, relationship between Marxist theory and environmentalist objectives. Nonetheless, the priority that the left gives to economic growth remains the main fault line in the relationship between socialism and ecologism. Leftwing parties such as the Partido de la Revolución Democrática (PRD, Party of the Democratic Revolution) in Mexico, the Frente Farabundo Martí para la Liberación Nacional (FMLN, Farabundo Martí National Liberation Front) in El Salvador, and the Frente Sandinista de Liberación Nacional (FSLN, Sandinista National Liberation Front) in Nicaragua show little substantive interest in green issues (see Chapter 4). Indeed, core constituents of these parties, such as trades unions, are often afraid that environmental regulations will limit job opportunities. The tensions between developmentalism inspired by socialist ideas and environmental degradation have been very evident under leftwing governments in Brazil, Bolivia, Ecuador and Peru. In Ecuador, for example, President Correa came under pressure in 2012 from both sides of a debate about the expansion of a Chinese copper mining concession in the highlands which his government has supported. In Bolivia, Morales has operated under considerable pressure to satisfy the country's economic needs through extractive industries that damage the environment – gas drilling, mining and forestry – while struggling to maintain a position that advocates protection of the environment from what he depicts as rapacious foreign interests (see Box 6.6).

In Venezuela, critics of Chávez argued both that he failed to end the neoliberal model and that environmental protections he sanctioned failed to resolve pressing ecological problems (see García-Guadilla 2009). Venezuelan environmental organizations such as Amigransa, Grupo Ecológico Mujer y Ambiente (GEMA, Woman and Environment Ecology Group) and the Asociación Venezolana para la Conservación de Áreas Naturales (ACOANA, Venezuelan Association for the Conservation of Natural Areas) were critical of Chávez's commitment to large infrastructure projects under his "Bolivarian" vision (see below). Venezuela is a party to the ambitious Iniciativa para la Integración de la Infraestructura Regional Suramericana (IIRSA, Initiative for the Integration of the Regional Infrastructure of South America). Many environmentalists argue that these projects, and Chávez's record on the environment, called into question his commitment to eco-socialism (see García-Guadilla 2009).

Box 6.6 The left, extraction and the environment in Bolivia

The government of Evo Morales in Bolivia has encountered significant opposition to its efforts to spur the development of extractive industries (Farthing 2009). For example, a protest by villagers in the Nor Lipez province in Bolivia's south-western department of Potosí in April 2010 against mining activities was timed to coincide with the opening of the World People's Conference on Climate Change and the Rights of Mother Earth, hosted by Morales himself (see Weinberg 2010b). The protest aimed to draw attention to the government's support for environmentally destructive industries – just as Morales was asserting Bolivia as a leading international force against climate change. There have been many similar protests over resources. In 2008, tensions created by a secessionist movement in eastern Bolivia demanding control of hydrocarbon resources from the national government culminated in a massacre of indigenous government supporters. Bolivia highlights the dilemmas that exist at the heart of the left's support for extractive development. The country boasts considerable natural resources yet is also one of Latin America's poorest. It has two of the world's largest silver mines, half of world's lithium reserves, the largest potential iron ore mine and the second largest proven gas reserves in South America. Since the election of Morales, in 2006, there has been huge political pressure to satisfy economic needs through extractive industries such as natural gas, mining and forestry that pose significant environmental risks. Continued extraction is also supported by the political demands from government supporters in powerful social movements that have long insisted that Bolivia's vast natural resources should benefit the country rather than foreigners. These social movements usually outweigh Bolivia's environmental movement, which comprises largely middle-class NGOs as well as local indigenous groups (see NACLA 2009).

Faultlines: the state. Eco-socialists have contributed to a reassessment of the role of the state by environmental thinkers while emphasizing a decentralist and non-bureaucratic vision of it that has much in common with the utopian socialists, early leftwing thinkers who imagined ideal societies (see Carter 2007). García-Guadilla (2009) argues that the notion of "twenty-first century eco-socialism" in Venezuela, for example, revives nineteenth-century romantic ideas that emphasized social forms such as the "commune". She says this suggests that the main exponents of eco-socialism within the Chávez administration were not familiar with the concrete impact of the extractive development of key resources such as oil that is required to achieve such a visionary society. One of these Venezuelan thinkers, Francisco Javier Velasco, argued in 2007 that eco-socialism could also be situated within anarchist critiques of capitalism such as those of Bakunin who, alongside later Marxists, often dwelled on man's relationship with nature (see García-Guadilla 2009). Another Venezuelan proponent of "twenty-first century eco-socialism", Néstor Francia (2007), envisaged a change of consciousness in order to overcome anthropocentrism based on society regaining an ancestral vision of nature. This utopian vision assumes implicitly that the simple elimination of capitalism will automatically result in a sustainable society (see Velasco 2007). Chávez himself articulated a vision of social transformation based on local participative democracy in which environmental problems are resolved by local communal organizations. Another position on the ecological left that does not have such a positive vision of the state's potential for resolving environmental problems also draws upon anarchist traditions (see Smith 2007; Morris 1996). Certain forms of anarchism regard nature as the source of individual liberty and often combine a conservation ethos with a critique of environmentally damaging "civilization" (see Bookchin 1982, 1986, 1990). A common eco-anarchist theme is how technology is destroying our way of life, and eco-anarchists sometimes employ sabotage. Many variants exist, such as eco-communalism that promotes a utopian notion of small, co-operative communities. More extreme eco-anarchist positions have informed such phenomena as "eco-terrorism", which first appeared in England during the 1970s and spread to the US in the 1980s (see Welsh 2007). A highly successful "red–green" alliance in Brazil that reflects the convergence of ecological and socialist mobilization brings together the PV and the PT. Nonetheless, this and similar alliances are not necessarily eco-socialist – they align environmental and socialist objectives programmatically and originate in the shared aims of social movements. An attempt to fuse environmental and labour ideologies that does not derive directly from the left's Marxist tradition has been called "green syndicalism", or syndical ecology, which finds common cause in themes shared by anarcho-syndicalism (revolutionary unionism) and radical ecology (see Shantz 2002; Purchase

1994, 1997; Kaufmann and Ditz 1992; Shantz and Adam 1999). These envisage a synergy between worker and ecologist that originates in the location of workers in the industrial workplace at the point of production, where ecological damage takes place. Green syndicalists, therefore, reject the premises of the traditional left that issues such as ecology are external to questions of production.

Identity politics

Identities provide inherent or imagined sources of difference between social groups and have been a key source of political struggle in Latin American and the Caribbean. The region's history as one conquered and colonized by European settlers who coexisted with large indigenous and imported slave populations has always made questions of personal and group identity prominent in political and social thought. Activity motivated by identification with a national idea, ethnicity and race, or gender has become an important theme in the study of politics, partly as a result of the challenges posed by the collapse of the socialist bloc to traditional class-based arguments (see above), and of globalization, which tests loyalties to historical entities such as the nation state. Democratization fostered a new pluralism, and ethnicity and gender themes represent key examples of new directions in politics associated with the emergence of social movements (see Chapter 5). Identity can be a valuable resource in the construction of political projects, and often provides the motivation for collective action (see Roper 2003). "Post-material" identities such as ethnicity and gender are often used by groups both to challenge and benefit from the state. Theories of cultural analysis in the work of the social thinker Gramsci are helpful in illustrating the role of political discourse in resistance (see Lucero 2003). Representation, by which certain kinds of political subjects and communities are identified and institutionalized, helps to shape relationships of power. Ideas deriving from a sense of identification with a nation, ethnicity, race or gender can unite or divide societies, although they may not offer a coherent strategy for governance, and have also informed environmental debates (see, for example, Rubin 2004; Grisaffi 2010). Steinberg (2003) has argued from a study of the development of environmental policy in Costa Rica and Bolivia that the translation of green ideas from one society to another occurs by means of "conceptual bundling" – sometimes called "value connection" – with pre-existing domestic discourses such as nationalism, ethnic identity and religion (see below; Rochon 1998). Several sources of identity have been prominent in Latin American and Caribbean history:

Nationalism. Scholars have debated the character and content of nationalism extensively and there is general agreement that this appeared in Latin America in an early form at the time of Independence and that, in the ethnically diverse republics of the region, the creation of the state preceded a generalized acceptance of the existence of the "nation". This meant that awareness of a national consciousness or identity was usually an elite affair long before it became a mass characteristic. As a result, one objective of the new states governed by elites became the *creation* of nations, and a key theme in nationalist thought in Latin America has been the notion of "nation-building" – the forging of a unified nationality based on a discernible national identity. Nationalist doctrine is malleable, able to coexist, inform and mine other ideologies, and environmental discourses may adopt a nationalist flavour to appeal to latent sentiments of identification (see Evans 1999). Puerto Rico provides an example of how durable nationalism can be, and nationalist sentiments have been expressed in a contemporary form through mobilization on environmental issues (see Box 6.7).

Environmentalism has the potential for coinciding with nationalist ideas that build on a sense of patriotism and the need to defend sovereignty, and in some cases to support claims for autonomy. Nonetheless, this is potentially problematic, as ecological ideas such as the global commons and the transboundary nature of environmental issues challenge traditional notions of state sovereignty (see Smith 2009). With this in mind, some green thinkers such as Eckersley (2004) have argued for the "greening" of notions of sovereignty in order to reinvigorate the state as an instrument of progressive environmental change (see also Barry and Eckersley 2005). Critics of this position suggest that green state sovereignty would merely reinforce varieties of ecological modernization (see below) that reduce politics to a means of attaining an efficient equilibrium between economic and ecological needs (see Smith 2009). However, there are clear limits to the extent to which the goals of certain nationalist positions coincide with those of environmentalism. Hamilton (2002) has argued that civic nationalists who advocate a form of nationality

---

Box 6.7 Puerto Rican nationalism and Vieques

Puerto Rico provides an example of the enduring appeal of nationalism in Latin America and the Caribbean, and how environmental disputes can provide a potent rallying cry. In the 1990s, as Puerto Rico's government reduced its focus on industrialization and moved to tourism development, conflicts emerged over control of land, especially on the coasts (see Baver 2009). The most notable social movement protest unfolded between 1999 and 2003 on the island of Vieques aiming to end the US Navy's use of it as a firing ground. During the 1980s and 1990s, the navy had dropped thousands of tons of bombs and explosives on Vieques. While reasons for the eventual success of the Vieques protests include support from US politicians and an emphasis on human rights and environmental degradation, protesters were also motivated by an undercurrent of nationalist sentiment, which was fuelled by rules that prevented local people cleaning up the site and developing it. As a result of the protests, the live firing area was officially designated a "wilderness preserve" and public access was blocked. However, it remained littered with unexploded ordnance and affected by high levels of contamination from heavy metals and toxic substances. The wildlife designation had, in fact, been a highly political decision that ultimately allowed the authorities to evade responsibility for cleaning up the site. Resentment increased in 2003 when outside developers and speculators began to target the island: the navy's departure had removed an obstacle to development and triggered speculation among property investors, driving up house prices and displacing local residents (see McCaffrey 2009). The US tourism industry even began packaging the island as an eco-tourism destination, disregarding the facts of the original protests. Activists continued to organize acts of civil disobedience demanding that the federal government clean up the area and return it to Vieques residents. McCaffrey (2009) argues that the struggle over Vieques was at root about unequal power relations between the US and Puerto Rico and the island's lack of sovereignty. The struggle for accountability and environmental remediation was part of a broader aspiration for self-determination (see also Carruthers 2008b).

---

based on citizenship as opposed to ethnicity are more likely to find their values compatible with those of contemporary ecologism. Ethnic nationalism – which is associated with ethno-racial accounts of group membership – is generally incompatible with green ideas. Leftwing leaders who have come to power in Latin America since 1998 have often combined the notion of anti-imperialism or the defence of sovereignty with the desire to assert greater control over the economy through policies such as the nationalization of strategic sectors like oil and mineral extraction, sometimes called resource nationalism (see Albro 2005). This defence of sovereignty allows them to associate environmental degradation with foreign investment.

Religious identities. Political ideas are often shaped by religious and cultural traditions, and there is broad recognition of the important role these play in influencing attitudes to the environment and supporting the notion of sustainable development or deterring consumerism (see Assadourian 2010). Poll data suggests that people believe religion can play an active role in encouraging engagement with environmental issues (see Gardner 2010). Sacred texts often contain references to the natural world and advance a vision of man's relationship with it (see Gardner 2010). Religious traditions also contain economic prohibitions, against the overuse of resources or circumscribing the pursuit of wealth, thereby advancing critiques of consumption and advocating notions of the common good. Rituals play a key role in protecting the natural environment in many religious traditions and can be a powerful way of communicating ideas about conservation. Religious taboos concerning gender relations, fertility, childbirth and the optimal size of families are also environmental regulators (see Engelman 2010). Carr (2007) found in a study of a lobster-fishing village in Quintana Roo, Mexico that cultural attitudes about childbearing had changed as the lobster resource declined: villagers tied their family size intentions to the importance of preserving fishing stocks for their children.

The Roman Catholic Church and other religious organizations have played a key role helping organize popular groups and in supporting their activities. In Ecuador, for example, Salesian missionaries organized the first modern indigenous organization in Latin America, the Shuar Federation. The concept of sustainable development has also enabled environmental organizations in Latin America to forge alliances with religious bodies and charities. Catholic Relief Services, one of the largest NGOs in the world, maintains environmental programmes to increase rural income in eight Latin American countries that support community forestry and soil conservation. Religious development organizations such as Cafod are active with sustainable development projects in countries such as Bolivia. Secular charities such as CARE also see reforestation, soil conservation and aquaculture as fundamental to their mission to foster economic development (Price 1994).

In Latin America, religion has often been at the forefront of disputes over resources, and priests have been active in organizing environmental protests throughout the region. In northern Mexico, for example, Catholic bishops have been critical of the unsustainable practices of logging companies (see Simms and Reid 2006). In Honduras, Andres Tamayo, a Catholic priest and the director of the Movimiento Ambientalista de Olancho (MAO, Environmental Movement of Olancho), mobilized local people against illegal logging and the consequences of the Central American-Dominican Republic Free Trade Agreement (DR-CAFTA), which threaten to increase deforestation rates (see Simms and Reid 2006). In 2005, a Brazilian Catholic bishop, Luiz Flavio Cappio, stalled a huge $2 bn irrigation project aiming to divert water from the São Francisco River by staging a hunger strike. Latin America has also been the focus of considerable attention by the World Council of Churches (WCC) Climate Change initiative. The protection of the Amazon has been a prominent focus of the Religion, Science and the Environment (RSE) organization founded in 1995 by the Orthodox ecumenical patriarch of Constantinople, Bartholomew.

Prohibitions against environmental degradation in sacred texts offer an important example of the potential role played by an "ecological ethic" (see Box 6.8). Spiritual leaders have also been at the forefront of criticisms of cultural activities such as consumerism. Christians have organized "carbon fasts" at Lent, and the Anglican church and global organizations such as the International Interfaith Investment Group encourage ethical and sustainable investments.

Recent Latin American theological tradition also provides an important precedent for the development of more radical positions on environmental degradation and sustainable development through "liberation theology". This was an attempt to marry revolutionary socialist principles of egalitarianism and the struggle against oppression with the commitment of many priests to social justice in highly unequal societies. The marriage of liberation theology with

> **Box 6.8** Religion and ecological ethics
>
> Brulle (2002) suggests that the consequences of civilization have confronted all nations, races and cultures with a common ethical problem, making the development of an ecologically sustainable society a necessity. Gardner (2010) argues that the prospects for institutionalizing ecological ethics may be growing as humanity recognizes its dependence on the environment. Ecological ethics attempt to incorporate the natural world in ethical discourse and are "ecocentric", seeking to protect all of nature, as opposed to anthropocentric, restricting ethical importance solely to humanity. Ecological ethics depart from the notion of green citizenship (see above) and imply an appreciation of principles emerging from "traditional ecological knowledge", which may be based on the local spiritual values and ritual practices sustained by indigenous or ancient peoples. They argue that this knowledge needs to be protected or revived in ways that restore human relationships with the natural world. Some interpretations of bioregionalism – the notion that political, cultural and ecological systems yield beliefs based on areas defined by their physical and environmental features – advance an ethic along these lines (see Sale 2000). Developing an ecological ethic will need to employ established spiritual and religious traditions, which already shape the morality of much of humanity and challenge consumerism in many ways. Binding ecological morals in a pluralist, postmodern world, however, need to accommodate cultural diversity and confront conflicting notions of what is sacred and profane (Cooper 1996). According to some scholars, critical theory and the work of Jürgen Habermas (1984, 1987) can potentially make a contribution to this endeavour by offering the basis of a social science that unites theory with practice (see Brulle 2002; Dobson 1996; Eckersley 1990).

ecological arguments has sometimes been called "liberation ecology". A progenitor of this discourse of resistance to poverty and oppression was the Peruvian Catholic theologian Gustavo Gutiérrez (1973; see also Martin 2003). Thinkers such as Gutiérrez argued that the developed world saw the developing world merely as a source of cheap labour and natural resources (see Martin 2003). In recent years, Gutiérrez and other liberation theologians have directed considerable attention to sustainable development (see below) in an effort to promote greater justice and equity (see Boff 1995; Gardner 2006; Ter Haar 2011). Priests and religious organizations inspired by liberation theology have played a prominent role in social struggles in Latin America and the Caribbean, often becoming identified with the protests of rural communities over control of land and natural resources. Priests played a key role in the Sandinista revolution in Nicaragua in 1979, and figures such as Father Ernesto Cardenal were active in developing the revolutionary government's environmental policies. In Ecuador, a Catholic NGO inspired by liberation theology, the Fondo Ecuatoriano Popularum Progressio (FEPP, Ecuadorian Fund for Popular Progress), was instrumental in helping indigenous communities obtain legal recognition for communal lands. The Catholic bishop Samuel Ruíz, a key interlocutor on behalf of the Zapatista guerrillas who rose up in the Mexican state of Chiapas in 1994, was also influenced by liberation theology. In Brazil, the Centro de Estatísticas Religiosas e Investigação Social (CERIS, Centre for Religious Statistics and Social Research), an organization linked to the National Conference of Brazilian Bishops founded in the 1960s as part of the liberation theology movement, supports many local development projects such as agricultural co-operatives and forestry initiatives. Liberationists along with Marxists, anarchists and anti-globalization activists often seek to implement their ideas through charities and NGOs instead of state institutions, adhering to the notion of "postmodern public administration" which aims to respond to the needs of the poor without developing explicitly political strategies (see Martin 2003). Key thinkers who have considered the merits of such a decentred approach include the Spanish liberation theologian Xabier Gorostiaga (1993), who served in the Sandinista revolutionary government in Nicaragua, and the Brazilian theologian Leonardo Boff (1995). In Chile, Brazil, El Salvador and Nicaragua, Christian base communities – grassroots church lay organizations that take on community respon- sibilities – have championed sustainability (Martin 2003). They have often joined struggles for environmental justice either through direct action, such as resisting landowners or promoting agrarian reform, or working through charities and NGOs.

Ethnicity and race. Ethnic and racial themes have been prominent in Latin American thought since Conquest, and many of the great debates of the twentieth century have related to agrarian issues and, by extension, to the indigenous question. Until the 1970s, for example, throughout much of Latin America indigenous people were seen both by elites and by those advancing their interests as powerless neocolonial subjects lacking citizenship rights, and hence off the political radar. This made definitions important elements of struggles between indigenous peoples and states (see Lucero 2003). In Mexico, for example, the Zapatista leader Marcos has used a language to convey his message that challenges established ideas about indigenous people (see Harvey 1998; Stea et al. 2011). The effectiveness of mobilization can depend on the degree to which organizations can build a collective consciousness. An emphasis on identity alone can often be highly localized, making it difficult for diverse groups to interact, while connecting identity to broader struggles is also a challenge because groups may have little in common (see Stahler-Sholk, Vanden and Kuecker 2007). The relationship between race and the environment has grown in prominence as a theme in Latin American social movements. Some scholars such as Sundberg (2008) have even argued that the environment has been fundamental to the formation of systems of racial classification. A resurgence of indigenous mobilization since the 1970s gained momentum with democratization in the 1980s and 1990s and indigenous intellectuals such as Mario Juruna and David Yanomami in Brazil and Rigoberta Menchú in Guatemala gained international prominence (see Chapter 5). New, indigenous perspectives on history and development have emerged in countries such as Ecuador, Guatemala and Bolivia (see, for example, Gustafson 2009; Stephenson 2002). The presidencies of Morales in Bolivia and Alejandro Toledo and Ollanta Humala in Peru have given authority to perspectives that revalue indigenous society, and this has strengthened the association between indigenous peoples and the environment in Latin America and put them at the forefront of debates about ecological management and sustainable development. In Bolivia, indigenous rights became a standard feature of environmental discourse after 1990, when Amazonian indigenous groups began to mobilize (see Steinberg 2003). Conscious of growing awareness of environmentalism, indigenous leaders in Bolivia began to portray their cause in terms of ecological protection and to forge alliances with environmental groups (see Chapter 5). Yet, explanations for the emergence of indigenous movements in Latin America have not focused primarily on their ecological beliefs or commitment to

---

Box 6.9 Afro-Latinos and the environment

Demands for greater pluralism in Latin American and Caribbean politics have been supported by black organizations throughout the region who are increasingly expressing pride in their own history and culture and creating political movements to confront inequality and discrimination. People of African descent have been present in Latin America since Conquest and an important reassessment of their role in history is underway (see Reid Andrews 2004). Black organizations have become influential in Brazil and Colombia, and have also been formed in Peru, Mexico and Ecuador, although accusations of racial discrimination persist. In countries such as Honduras, issues of race and resource use are closely intertwined and identity politics is an important factor in land claims. Mollett (2006) has examined the relationship between race and natural resource conflicts in Honduras involving a struggle between the indigenous Miskito people and the Garifuna, an Afro-indigenous people living on the Caribbean coast. She analyses the role played by racial identifications in disputes originating in the 1950s that revived in 2003 over Lasa Pulan, an area of forest and farmland between the Garifuna village of Plaplaya and the Miskito village of Ibans. She argues that the case demonstrates how natural resource struggles are often also racial struggles, and the heated conflict over Lasa Pulan often employed racialized rhetoric in defence of territorial claims.

---

sustainable development (see above). Nor have conflicts over land and territorial control been primarily about ecological stewardship. However, ethnic themes often become prominent in disputes over territory and resources (see Box 6.9). Hale (2002) has suggested that the rise of indigenous politics suggests collusion between neoliberal and multicultural agendas, since many Latin American states now promote ethnic recognition backed by the global institutions that have promoted neoliberal development. Nonetheless, many of the issues on which indigenous groups campaign coincide naturally with those of ecology movements and parties, and there is often overlap on issues such as sustainable development.

The region-wide transition to democracy in Latin America and the Caribbean opened up space for indigenous organizations to mobilize and NGOs became interested in their concerns and helped them expand (see Chapter 5; Brysk 2000; Keck and Sikkink 1998). Two key themes have since become prominent in discourse about the indigenous relationship with the environment: sustainability and traditional cultural knowledge.

Indigenous peoples' livelihoods depend on access to land and natural resources and maintaining control over these is crucial to them. These communities have often managed to survive in ecologically fragile areas and have developed a deep understanding of their environments and ways to manage resources sustainably (Deruyttere 1997). However, because of their relative isolation, the territories inhabited by indigenous peoples frequently offer development opportunities as sources of water, timber, forest products and medicinal plants, energy, biodiversity, minerals and tourism (IFAD 2003a). As a result, indigenous communities often suffer encroachment by powerful commercial interests (see Amazon Watch 2011). Moreover, there is growing recognition that indigenous people, while having contributed very little to global warming, are among the most heavily at risk from it by virtue of their marginalization and lifestyles. For many indigenous peoples, climate change is already a reality as erratic rainfalls reduce productivity of fields and pastures, storms and floods destroy crops and homes, and desertification and soil erosion remove topsoils. While their diverse livelihoods have enabled them to survive in often harsh environments, the speed of climate change is testing their ability to adapt (see IWGIA et al. 2009; Kronik and Verner 2010; Macchi 2008). Nonetheless, the continuing potency of the "pristine myth" – the notion that at the time of Conquest the Americas were a sparsely populated wilderness, largely undisturbed by humans, where nature reigned and human societies lived in a harmonious equilibrium with their environment (Denevan 1992; see also Volume 1) – and the overlap between indigenous ideas and ecologism tend to nurture a strand of Latin American environmental thought that stresses the sustainability of indigenous production systems, and the unsustainability of non-indigenous ones (see Dore 1996b). Since the Earth Summit in 1992 the value placed on sustainable development (see below) has enhanced the potential of indigenous peoples as "stewards" of natural resources and biodiversity. The World Summit on Sustainable Development in Johannesburg in 2002, for instance, affirmed "the vital role of indigenous peoples in sustainable development" (WSSD 2002; IFAD 2003a).

A defining aspect of indigenous resource management is the role of traditional knowledge and spiritual beliefs, often communicated by elders, which have long shaped norms about resource use in their communities. It has become common for development discourses to accept that indigenous knowledge should be respected and incorporated in planning and decision-making (see Pichón, Uquillas, and Frechione (1999). However, there has been less attention to the potential contribution traditional knowledge and indigenous practices can make in the search for solutions to problems caused by climate change (IWGIA et al. 2009). The International Fund for Agricultural Development (IFAD) has recognized that sensitivity to indigenous cultures and languages and respect for their knowledge systems are crucial to sustainability initiatives (IFAD 2003a). Customary management of resources based on such knowledge may exist alongside secular state management and either complement or contradict it. In Bolivia, the re-establishment of traditional community governance has been an important aspect of the doctrine of influential Aymara figures (see Box 5.8). In some Peruvian highland communities, for example, mechanisms for allocating water to individually cultivated household plots and common land exist in the form of highly ritualized procedures based on established customs but also in the monetized secular state model of allocation administered by a professional water engineer (see Gelles 2000).

Indigenous spirituality, customs, beliefs and institutions reflect a relationship with nature distinct to that of modern, capitalist society that aim at cultural survival through a responsibility for future generations, and indigenous lore is often based on seasonality and a complex understanding of the reciprocal roles played by components of an ecosystem (Clarkson, Morrissette and Régallet 1992). Beliefs and knowledge are often complex and resilient (see Brotherson 1992). In Mexico and the Andes, for example, indigenous and peasant cultures reflect an agrarian tradition and ties to the land that neither marginalization nor industrial agriculture has extinguished (Carruthers 1996). Indigenous belief has also sometimes been appropriated for purely political reasons. Traditional knowledge and beliefs may play an equally important role in non-indigenous peasant communities with the meanings they attribute to different ecosystems such as forests playing a similar role in mediating resources use (see Florescano 1994; Anderson 1994).

In the 1980s, the international community began to acknowledge the role of traditional ecological knowledge (TEK) – the body of knowledge embedded in indigenous societies that governs their relationships with nature – and this was referred to in the Brundtland Report, which suggested that industrialized nations could learn much about sustainable development by drawing on indigenous tradition (see Carruthers 1996; Brundtland et al. 1987). The science of agro-ecology, for example, has been heavily informed by the rescue of traditional practices (see Carruthers 1996, 2008b; Vargas Hernández and Reza Noruzi 2010; IFAD 2003b; Altieri 1995; NACLA 2002).

Recent efforts to address the needs of indigenous peoples reflect a shift in thinking among multilateral agencies about the important role culture can play in development. Experience from development projects suggest that strengthening cultural identity and promoting sustainable development are mutually reinforcing (see Deruyttere 1997). During the Johannesburg summit indigenous represent-atives agreed the "Kimberly Declaration" that sought protection for traditional knowledge systems as collective intellectual property. Indigenous groups have struggled against patent infringement, especially by agricultural and pharmaceutical corporations that seek to profit from their knowledge, and the issue of intellectual property rights became an important theme of indigenous participation in multilateral initiatives. Legal struggles over intellectual property rights and TEK are now important aspects of the international indigenous rights agenda. Kawell (2002) has sketched how over time knowledge about biological resources has come to be seen as a form of property, a process in which Latin America and the Caribbean has played a key role. The 1970s represented a turning point, when the development of new gene technologies and efforts to map genomes created a new "biotech" industry that spawned today's conflicts over the ownership of biological knowledge. At root, the preservation of species diversity is intrinsic to sustainable development, but a number of key principles of sustainable forms of modern agricultural production and agro-ecology associated with indigenous land use have emerged such as organic farming, perennial polycultures, permaculture, no- or low-till techniques and agro-forestry innovations (see Bates and Hemenway 2010; Zimmerer 1997):

Sustainable development

At the heart of green politics in Latin America and the Caribbean lies the tension between environmental protection and economic development. The concept of sustainable development suggests that it is possible to enjoy growth development while also protecting the environment. As a reformist doctrine, it is attractive to policy-makers and has become the dominant "official" discourse promoted by multilateral agencies despite ambiguity that can make it hard to translate into practical policies (see Carter 2007; World Bank 2001). It is premised on the well-established notion that environmental goods and services – such as the Earth's oceans and atmosphere – are global "commons", public goods whose consumption or use by one individual does not or should not reduce availability of that good to another or their right to use it. In 1980, by stressing the interdependence of conservation and development the World Conservation Strategy produced by three international agencies laid the groundwork for the establishment of this concept as a dominant theme (IUCN/UNEP/WWF 1980). In 1983, the UN system established the World Commission on Environment and Development (WCED) and its 1987 report then popularized the notion of sustainable development (Brundtland et al. 1987). The Brundtland Report described sustainable development as "development that meets the needs of the present without compromising the ability of future generations to meet their own needs" (Brundtland et al. 1987). The notion of sustainable development underpinned the first UN Conference on Environment and Development (UNCED) – the Rio Earth Summit in 1992 – which adopted the "Agenda 21" action plan that obliged states to adopt sustainable models. In 1993, the UN Commission on Sustainable Development was established and, in 2002, the World Summit on Sustainable Development was convened in Johannesburg (see WSSD 2002). Since 2002, governments throughout Latin America and the Caribbean have established their own national sustainable development strategies and sub-national authorities have launched their own Agenda 21 initiatives. A UN conference to mark the twentieth anniversary of the Rio Earth summit (Rio+20) was held in Brazil in 2012 in an effort to renew the political commitment to sustainable development and focused heavily on the idea of the "green economy" and the institutional framework required to achieve it (see UNCSD 2011b, 2011a; Stoddart 2011). As a result of this process, sustainable development has become an established aspect of international governance. UNEP (2010) has developed environmental and socioeconomic scenarios to assess how circumstances in Latin America and the Caribbean until 2050 may evolve in order to provide a decision-making tool for governments. This considers the implications for the region of four combinations of social and economic factors – and the policies needed to address them in order to achieve sustainability – in the periods 2000–25 and 2025–50. Its assessment of these "alternative futures" suggests that an unremitting inclusion of sustainability in policy and practice is required if the region is to reduce emissions meaningfully. An important role played by the concept of sustainable development has been ideological, by broadening the popular appeal of environmentalism. The Rio Declaration of 1992 outlined 27 principles for the achievement of sustainable development (see Stoddart 2011). Key principles that inform global governance for sustainable development are as follows:

- *Equity*. The overarching concept of sustainable development established by the Brundtland Commission was equity: intra-generational equity (fairness to living people) and inter-generational equity (fairness to future generations). These oblige the international community to reduce inequality between and within countries and to ensure future generations have sufficient natural resources to sustain themselves (Martin 2003). Equity is a core concern of environmental policy because any measure to prevent or alleviate environmental degradation has distributional implications. The notion of inter-generational equity raises questions about how societies can deliver development that is equal for both present and future generations. Green thinkers have debated this hotly, with some arguing that the burdens of contemporary climate change policies may not be compatible with the need for intra- and inter-generational justice (see Page 2008; Schuppert 2011; Meyer and Roser 2006; Moellendorf 2009; Hyams 2009; Caney 2005). The Brundtland Report also drew attention to a key feature of poverty: environmental damage affects the poorest countries most severely, and poverty, in turn, places huge pressure on natural resources. Within debates about equality, the notion of sustainable consumption has gained importance. This advocates patterns of consumption that respond to basic needs and improve quality of life while minimizing the use of natural resources in order not to jeopardize what is available for future generations. According to the 1998 Human Development

Report (UNDP 1998), consumption must: be shared; strengthen human capabilities; be socially responsible; be sustainable. Organizations such as the Worldwatch Institute, which operates a "Transforming Cultures" project, emphasize the need to change today's consumer cultures towards cultures of sustainability (see websites below).

- *Precaution*. The precautionary principle was enshrined in the Rio Declaration in 1992 and emphasizes that officials need to take a cautious approach in environmental management in order to prevent harmful activities: developers who wish to undertake a specific action must prove that their activities will not harm the environment. This principle is crucial by providing a means of overcoming the scientific disagreements inherent in environmental policymaking because it implies that a lack of certainty should never be used as a reason for postponing measures to stop the environment being damaged. Yet there remains no universally accepted definition of the precautionary principle and efforts to exercise it encounter strong commercial resistance and developmental pressures (see Martin 2003; Stoddart 2011).

- *Democracy and participation*. Sustainable development emphasizes the importance of democracy and participation in solving environmental problems: its requirement for equity means that as the poor shoulder a disproportionate share of the costs of environmental degradation they should have access to the political process in order to address this (see Carter 2007). In Latin America and the Caribbean, the notion of democratic, popular control of resources through sustainable development strategies has been embraced on the left and by social movements. Sometimes this has been put into practice through postmodern public administration (see above) by which sustainable development policies are implemented by NGOs and charities instead of state institutions (Martin 2003). However, public access to environmental information and redress through the justice system are often inadequate in the region (see Chapter 1). One effort to implement this principle was the 1998 UNECE Aarhus Convention. The World Resources Institute and the Access Initiative made the case at Rio+20 in 2012 for regional conventions on environmental access rights (see Stoddart 2011).

- *"Polluter pays"*. This principle makes those who cause environmental pollution responsible for paying the costs of rectifying the damage and was first articulated in 1972 by the OECD. Principle 16 of the Rio Declaration obliges states to ensure environmental costs are "internalized" by polluters. The principle has important implications for the responsibilities of states and for funding solutions to environmental problems. It provides a basis for levying national-level taxes or charges on environmentally damaging activities, making the true costs of these activities realistic. The considerations of externalities in the valuation of ecosystem services – whereby the value of services provided by ecosystems are factored into the true cost of using a natural resource – has risen up the international agenda in recent years.

- **Common but differentiated responsibilities**. This notion was broadly accepted at the 1972 Stockholm Conference but became established at Rio and refers to the need for each state to play its role in achieving sustainable development at a global level, but also establishes that this role is different for each country according to their economic and technical capacity and past contribution to environmental degradation. It was incorporated in the UN Framework Convention on Climate Change (UNFCCC) and was a core principle of the Kyoto Protocol agreed in 1997 (see Stoddart 2011).

Key issues of contestation

The promise of sustainable development in Latin America and the Caribbean is that it offers a way of addressing the tension between economic development and environmental protection. Nonetheless, a key issue is how this concept is interpreted, and differing interpretations may threaten political and administrative conflicts between different levels of government (see Baker 1997). The concept of sustainable development is heavily contested and there have been many different definitions of it (see Seghezzo 2009). Its ambiguity has also led to both confusion and scepticism that it can yield practical policy measures (see Baker 1997). Different interpretations of sustainable development disagree over how much emphasis should be placed on such issues as eliminating poverty, pursuing global equity and moving away from consumerism or on what emphasis should be placed on economic growth (see Carter 2007). Critics of the focus on sustainability also argue that it has shifted attention towards the need for more efficient, cleaner production systems but away from the values underpinning consumer society (see Conca 2001).

Debates have also been influenced by differences within the environmental movement between anthropocentric and non-anthropocentric positions (Pepper 1996; Seghezzo 2009; Norton 2005). A contemporary anthropocentric position is called ecological modernization (see below), which suggests that technical and managerial approaches can solve the environmental crisis and there is no need to change development patterns radically (see Baker 2005). Non-anthropocentric positions are driven by ethical considerations and reject the idea that nature has value only insofar as it serves human interests (see Mason 1999; McShane 2007; Seghezzo 2009).

Growing use of the term "sustainability" in the development discourses of a wide range of actors with conflicting interests means the concept is now being employed in a wide range of circumstances (see Horton 2007). In Central America, for example, multilateral agencies promote sustainable development in order to ensure environmental protection yet advocate a globalized neoliberal economic model, while alternative discourses interpret sustainability in terms of social, political and environmental justice. These different interpretations explain why the experience of sustainable development initiatives has varied considerably across Latin America and the Caribbean. Horton (2007) examines sustainable development projects in Miraflores, Nicaragua, focusing on the establishment of shrimp farming, and at Osa, Costa Rica, focusing on eco-tourism. Both provide examples of non-traditional sustainable development projects linked to the global market and have been praised by multilateral agencies (see Horton 2007). However, the positive assessment of these projects has been contested by members of the communities themselves, who point out that the main beneficiary has invariably been multinational capital.

An idea of the different emphases within interpretations of sustainable development can be gained from examining how different countries in Latin America and the Caribbean have shaped their own national strategies (see ECLAC 2000). In Brazil, the emphasis of sustainable development strategy has been to reinforce an existing focus on poverty reduction (see IISD/Stratos 2004b). The country's Agenda 21 strategy was signed in 2002 by President Fernando Henrique Cardoso (1995–2002) and, among other things, recognizes Brazil's fiscal constraints and even warns against stressing the implementation of sustainable development policies to the detriment of public finances. In Costa Rica, sustainable development has been central to the policy agenda and President José María Figueres (1994–98) made it the theme of his administration. Mexico has sought to integrate sustainable development planning within public administration since 2000 in a more legalistic way and its policy approach has been regional and participative (see IISD/Stratos 2004a). Between 1996 and 2000 the then environment ministry SEMARNAP pioneered the regional Programa de Desarrollo Regional Sustentable (PRODERS, Regional Sustainable Development Programme), which encouraged collaboration in planning and implementation between local and regional actors from civil society organizations (CSOs), non-governmental organizations (NGOs) and government.

A variant of sustainable development, ecological modernization, aims to address barriers to more sustainable growth posed by capitalism by concentrating on making production more environmentally friendly (see Carter 2007). This perspective is associated with business perspectives on "clean technology" that have emerged in Europe (see Milanez and Bührs 2008). It reflects the promise of clean technology and is championed by those who see the possibility for a "natural capitalism" and a new "green industrial revolution" (see White 2002; Von Weizsäcker, Lovins and Lovins 1998; Hawken, Lovins and Lovins 1999). Logically, ecological modernization should have natural traction in the rapidly growing economies of countries such as Brazil and Mexico. Moreover, the greening of political discourse in the region has gone hand in hand with the consolidation of market economics across Latin America and the Caribbean. However, in emerging economies such as Brazil, enthusiasm for clean tech has been driven by foreign actors and this helps to explain why this perspective has gained little influence among businesses (see Milanez and Bührs 2008). The potential risks associated with this form of internationally oriented ecological modernization are a heavy reliance on foreign technology and a disregard for local environmental priorities.

Toke (2011) argues that the role played by some social movements in technological change challenges ecological modernization theory by undermining the idea that industry itself will respond to economic incentives to go green. Social movements played a crucial role in the early development of renewable energy technologies such as wind power, for example, because large energy utilities were initially unwilling or unable to develop such technologies. Technology social movements played a transformative role by seeking to maximize the transfer of knowledge and lobbying for renewables.

In Latin America and the Caribbean, significant emphasis is now being placed on the theme of sustainable consumption and production (see UN/ECLAC 2010). At the World Summit on Sustainable Development in Johannesburg in 2002, governments set as a key goal changing unsustainable patterns of production and consumption, and the Marrakesh Process that began in 2003 designed a 10-year plan to establish policies for creating a "green economy". Latin American and the Caribbean governments have taken a series of steps aimed at strengthening a regional strategy towards these ends. A Council of Government Experts on Sustainable Consumption and Production was established in 2003 under the auspices of UNEP to follow up on the issue and extend participation to the private sector, academia and civil society. Based on its recommendations, the region's environment ministers decided in 2008 to make sustainable consumption and production a priority of the Latin American and Caribbean Initiative for Sustainable Development (ILAC) and agreed programmes aimed at government, enterprises and citizens. These included efforts to promote better public procurement policies and education about sustainable consumption in schools. Some leaders such as Morales of Bolivia and José Mujica of Uruguay have even led by example, eschewing the lavish and high-profile lifestyle of politicians the world over to make a statement about property and consumption. After gaining the presidency in 2012, Mujica continued to live on a ramshackle farm and to give away 90 per cent of his salary to charity (see Hernández 2012).

Commercial efforts to change household consumption patterns have also proliferated in Latin America and the Caribbean, and such ideas as "ethical shopping" and "green consumerism" can now be found throughout the region. Overviews of how countries are responding to the call for sustainable consumption and production suggest progress has been made (UNEP/CEGESTI 2009). By 2012, at least 11 countries in the region had developed or were developing sustainable production and consumption policy frameworks (see UNEP 2012b). Latin American countries have approached this theme in different ways. Argentina, for example, established the Producción Limpia y Consumo Sustentable (DPLyCS, Clean Production and Sustainable Consumption) department within its Secretaria de Ambiente y Desarrollo Sustentable (SAyDS, Secretariat for the Environment and Sustainable Development). In Colombia, a national sustainable consumption and production policy was drafted with the support of UNEP. Mexico made sustainable public procurement a priority and in Brazil, the environment ministry established a Comitê Gestor Nacional de Produção e Consumo Sustentável (CGPCS, Committee for Sustainable Consumption and Production) to draft a national plan to cut energy consumption.

Conclusion

Modern political evolution in Latin America and the Caribbean has been shaped by the contest between leftwing and rightwing ideas based on the underlying motif of class and fashioned by struggles over development strategy. These ideas, in turn, have been informed by the politics of identity in a region of considerable diversity, where the emphasis has been upon nationhood, religion or ethnicity and race. In most cases, established political ideas have had as their strategic focus the merits or otherwise of an existing or preferred development model, making them central to political struggle in the region. Since the end of the Cold War and with democratization, competitive parties have increasingly developed a centrist politics that challenges the rigidity of the former left–right spectrum. Coherent modern ideologies that have ecology as their main focus remain, relatively speaking, newcomers to the region's ideological landscape. Environmentalism has, moreover, had to evolve and coexist with the dominant themes of class and identity that, in many instances, continue to sideline it. However, growing attention to environmental problems globally through recognition of issues such as climate change have in circumstances of democratization created opportunities for champions of environmentalism to influence public opinion. One indication of the success they have had has been the way in which multilateral agencies and governments have embraced the agenda of sustainable development, which has become something of an orthodoxy in governance at every level. In Latin America and the Caribbean, sustainable development – if considered to be a coherent basis for development strategy at all – can be viewed as yet another ideological import akin to other ideas that originated in north Atlantic societies. However, the region's unique social and political legacies and how these are now shaping the development of environmental ideas locally in unique ways increasingly test this position. The growing influence both of the unique fusion of social and environmental ideas reflected through the notion of "socio-environmentalism" and of the reappraisal of indigenous tradition suggest that a new chapter is now being written in the history of ecologism.

Recommended reading

Benton, Lisa and John R Short. 1999. *Environmental Discourse and Practice*. Blackwell: Oxford.

Dobson, Andrew and Derek Bell (eds). 2006. *Environmental Citizenship*. Cambridge, MA: MIT Press.

Irwin, Alan. 2002. *Sociology and the Environment: A Critical Introduction to Society, Nature and Knowledge*. Cambridge: Polity Press.

Peet, Richard and Michael Watts (eds). 1996. *Liberation Ecologies: Environment, Development, Social movements*. London: Routledge.

Useful websites

Amigransa environmental organization: www.amigransa.blogia.com

Climate and capitalism online ecosocialist journal: http://climateand capitalism.com/

Ecosocialist International Network: www.ecosocialistnetwork.org/

Foundation for Deep Ecology: www.deepecology.org/movement.htm

Indigenous Knowledge and Peoples (IKAP): www.ikap-mmsea.org/index. html

International Institute for Sustainable Development (IISD), Latin America and Caribbean Regional Coverage: http://larc.iisd.org/

International Work Group for Indigenous Affairs (IWGIA): www.iwgia. org/environment-and-development/sustainable-development

Rio+20 Institutional Framework for Sustainable Development: www. earthsummit2012.org/conference/themes/institutional-frame work-for-sd

UN Commission on Sustainable Development (CSD): www.un.org/esa/ dsd/index.shtml.

United Nations Conference on Sustainable Development (UNCSD) 2012 (Rio+20): www.uncsd2012.org/rio20/index.php?menu=17

UN Department for Economic and Social Affairs, Division for Sustainable Development: www.un.org/esa/dsd/

World Business Council for Sustainable Development, Latin America Regional Network: www.wbcsd.org/templates/TemplateWBCSD5/ layout.asp?type=p&MenuId=NjM&doOpen=1&ClickMenu=LeftMenu

Worldwatch Transforming cultures blog: http://blogs.worldwatch.org/ transformingcultures/

References

Aagesen, David. 2000. "Rights to Land and Resources in Argentina's Alerces National Park", *Bulletin of Latin American Research*, Vol. 19, No. 4 (October), pp. 547–69.

Acuña, Guillermo. 1999. *Marcos regulatorios e institucionales de América Latina y el Caribe: 1980–1990*. Santiago: Economic Commission for Latin America and the Caribbean. Available online at www.eclac.org/publicaciones/xml/0/4350/lcl1311e.pdf [accessed September 2012].

Adamson, Joni, Mei Mei Evans and Rachel Stein (eds). 2002. *The Environmental Justice Reader*. Tucson: University of Arizona Press.

Agüero, Felipe. 1998. "Conflicting Assessments of Democratization: Exploring the Fault Lines", in Felipe Agüero and Jeffrey Stark (eds), *Fault Lines of Democracy in Post-Transition Latin America*. Coral Gables, FL: North-South Center Press.

Aguilar Rojas, Grethel and Alejandro Iza (eds). 2009. *Derecho Ambiental en Centroamérica*, Vols. 1–2. UICN Serie de Política y Derecho Ambiental No. 66. Gland, Bonn and San José, Costa Rica: IUCN Environmental Law Centre and Oficina Regional de Mesoamérica. Available online at http://data.iucn.org/dbtw-wpd/edocs/EPLP-066-1.pdf [accessed September 2012].

Agyeman, Julian, Robert Bullard and Bob Evans (eds). 2003. *Just Sustainabilities: Development in an Unequal World*. Cambridge, MA: MIT Press.

Akinwumi, Akinbola E. 2006. "Review: The Latin American Social Movement Paradigm: Challenging the Neoliberal (Dis)Order", *Latin American Perspectives*, Vol. 33, No. 6, *Migration, the Global Economy, and Latin American Cities* (November), pp. 182–88.

Albro, Robert. 2005. "The Indigenous in the Plural in Bolivian Oppositional Politics", *Bulletin of Latin American Research*, Vol. 24, No. 4 (October), pp. 433–53.

Alcock, Frank. 2008. "Conflicts and Coalitions Within and Across the ENGO Community", *Global Environmental Politics*, Vol. 8, No. 4 (November), pp. 66–91.

Altieri, Miguel A. 1995. *Agroecology: The Science of Sustainable Agriculture*. Boulder, CO: Westview Press.

Altieri, Miguel A and Víctor Manuel Toledo. 2011. "The Agroecological Revolution in Latin America: Rescuing Nature, Ensuring Food Sovereignty and Empowering Peasants", *Journal of Peasant Studies*, Vol. 38, No. 3 (July), pp. 587–612.

Alvarez, Sonia E, Evelina Dagnino and Arturo Escobar. 1998. "Introduction: The Cultural and the Political in Latin American Social Movements", in Sonia E Alvarez et al. (eds), *Cultures of Politics. Politics of Cultures: Re-Visioning Latin American Social Movements*. Boulder, CO: Westview Press.

Amazon Watch. 2011. "New Maple Energy Oil Spill in the Peruvian Amazon", 13 July 2011. Available online at http://amazonwatch. org/news/2011/0713-new-maple-energy-oil-spill-in-the-peruvian-amazon [accessed June 2012].

Amorim Neto, Octoberavio. 2002a. "Presidential Cabinets, Electoral Cycles, and Coalition Discipline in Brazil", in Scott Morgenstern and Benito Nacif (eds), *Legislative Politics in Latin America*. Cambridge: Cambridge University Press.

——. 2002b. "Critical Debates: The Puzzle of Party Discipline in Brazil", review article, *Latin American Politics and Society*, Vol. 44, No. 1 (April), pp. 127–44.

Anderson, Leslie E. 1994. *The Political Ecology of the Modem Peasant*. Baltimore, MD: Johns Hopkins University Press.

Andersson, Kristen, Gustavo Gordillo de Anda and Frank van Laerhoven. 2009. *Local Governments and Rural Development: Comparing Lessons from Brazil, Chile, Mexico, and Peru*. Tucson: University of Arizona Press.

Andrée, Peter. 2007. *Genetically Modified Diplomacy: The Global Politics of Agricultural Biotechnology and the Environment*. Vancouver: UBC Press.

Andrews, Cecile and Wanda Urbanska. 2010. "Inspiring People to See that Less is More", in Linda Starke and Lisa Mastny (eds), *2010 State of the World: Transforming Cultures: From Consumerism to Sustainability*. Washington, DC: Worldwatch Institute.

Angus, Ian (ed.). 2009. *The Global Fight for Climate Justice: Anticapitalist Responses to Global Warming and Environmental Destruction*. Winnipeg: Fernwood Publishing.

Annis, Sheldon (ed.). 1992. *Poverty, Natural Resources, and Public Policy in Central America*. New Brunswick, NJ: Transaction Publishers/Overseas Development Council.

Antal, Edit, Lauren Baker and Gerard Verschoor. 2007. *Maize and Biosecurity in Mexico: Debate and Practice*. Amsterdam: Centre for Latin American Studies and Documentation. Available online at www.cedla. uva.nl/50_publications/pdf/cuadernos/cuad22.pdf [accessed September 2012].

Arceneaux, Craig L. 2001. *Bounded Missions: Military Regimes and Democratization in the Southern Cone and Brazil*. University Park: Pennsylvania State University Press.

Arthur, Charles. 1996. "Confronting Haiti's Environmental Crisis", in Helen Collinson (ed.), *Green Guerrillas: Environmental Conflicts and Initiatives in Latin America and the Caribbean. A Reader*. London: Latin America Bureau.

Assadourian, Erik. 2010. "Introduction, Traditions Old and New", in Linda Starke and Lisa Mastny (eds), *2010 State of the World. Transforming Cultures: From Consumerism to Sustainability*. Washington, DC: Worldwatch Institute.

Assies, Willem, Gemma van der Haar and André Hoekema (eds). 2000. *The Challenge of Diversity: Indigenous Peoples and Reform of the State in Latin America*. West Lafayette, IN: Purdue University Press.

Athanasiou, Tom and Paul Baer. 2002. *Dead Heat: Global Justice and Global Warming*. New York: Seven Stories Press.

Avina. 2011. "Latin America's Environmental Prosecutors Network Produces a Manual in Peru", *Avina Foundation Annual Report*. Available online at www.avina.net/eng/nota/red-de-fiscales-ambientales [accessed September 2012].

Ayres, Wendy, Kathleen Anderson and David Hanrahan. 1998. "Setting Priorities for Environmental Management: An Application to the Mining Sector in Bolivia", World Bank Technical Paper 398. Washington, DC: World Bank.

Bäckstrand, Karin and Eva Lövbrand. 2007. "Climate Governance Beyond 2012: Competing Discourses of Green Governmentality", in Mary E Pettenger (ed.), *The Social Construction of Climate Change: Power, Knowledge, Norms, Discourses*. Aldershot: Ashgate.

Baiocchi, Gianpaolo. 2001. "Participation, Activism, and Politics: The Porto Alegre Experiment and Deliberative Democratic Theory", *Politics and Society*, Vol. 29, No. 1 (March), pp. 43–72.

Baker, Susan. 1997. *The Politics of Sustainable Development*. Oxford: Routledge.

——. 2005. *Sustainable Development*. Oxford: Routledge.

Ballve, Marcelo. 2003. "Brazil's New Eye on the Amazon", *NACLA Report on the Americas*, Vol. 36, No. 6 (May/June), p. 32.

Barcena, Alicia, et al. 2002. *Financing for Sustainable Development in Latin America and the Caribbean: From Monterrey to Johannesburg*. Santiago: Economic Commission for Latin America and the Caribbean/ United Nations Development Programme.

——. 2011. "Sustainable Development in Latin America and the Caribbean 20 Years on from the Earth Summit: Progress, Gaps and Strategic Guidelines", LC/L 3346, August 2011, 2011-457. New York: United Nations. Available online at www.eclac.org/rio20/noticias/paginas/9/43799/REV.Rio+20-Sustainable_development.pdf [[accessed April 2012].

Barkdull, John and Paul G Harris. 2002. "Environmental Change and Foreign Policy: A Survey of Theory", *Global Environmental Politics*, Vol. 2, No. 2 (May), pp. 63–91.

Barlow, Maude. 2004. "The Struggle for Latin America's Water", *NACLA Report on the Americas*, Vol. 38, No. 1 (July/August), p. 15.

Barmeyer, Niels. 2003. "The Guerrilla Movement as a Project: An Assessment of Community Involvement in the EZLN", *Latin American Perspectives*, Vol. 30, No. 1 (January), *Indigenous Transformational Movements in Contemporary Latin America*, pp. 122–38.

Barreira, Ana, Paula Ocampo and Eugenia Recio. 2007. *Medio Ambiente y Derecho Internacional: Una Guía Práctica*. Madrid: Instituto Internacional de Derecho y Medio Ambiente/Caja Madrid Obra Social.

Barrios, Salvador, Holger Görg and Eric Strobl. 2003. "Multinational Enterprises and New Trade Theory: Evidence for the Convergence Hypothesis", *Open Economies Review*, Vol. 14, No. 4 (October), pp. 397–418.

Barry, John and Robyn Eckersely (eds). 2005. *The State and the Global Ecological Crisis*. Cambridge, MA: MIT Press.

Bates, Albert and Toby Hemenway. 2010. "From Agriculture to Permaculture", in Linda Starke and Lisa Mastny (eds), *2010 State of the World. Transforming Cultures: From Consumerism to Sustainability*. Washington, DC: Worldwatch Institute.

Baud, Michiel, Fabio de Castro and Barbara Hogenboom. 2011. "Environmental Governance in Latin America: Towards an Integrative Research Agenda", *European Review of Latin American and Caribbean Studies*, 90 (April), pp. 79–88.

Baumgartner, Frank and Bryan D Jones. 1993. *Agendas and Instability in American Politics*. Chicago, IL: University of Chicago Press.

Barkdull, John and Paul G Harris. 2002. "Environmental Change and Foreign Policy: A Survey of Theory", *Global Environmental Politics*, Vol. 2, No. 2 (May), pp. 63–91.

Baver, Sherrie. 2009. "Environmental Politics in Paradise: Resistance to the Selling of Vieques", *NACLA*, blogs, 21 August 2009. Available online at https://nacla.org/node/6074 [accessed June 2012].

bbc.co.uk. 2004. "México: crece escándalo verde", bbc.co.uk, 26 February 2004. Available online at http://news.bbc.co.uk/hi/spanish/latin_america/newsid_3490000/3490452.stm [accessed December 2011].

——. 2006. "UN in Guatemala 'racism' warning", bbc.co.uk, 15 March 2006.

Available online at http://news.bbc.co.uk/2/hi/americas/4810566.stm [accessed February 2010].

Becker, Marc. 2008. *Indians and Leftists in the Making of Ecuador's Modern Indigenous Movements*. London: Duke University Press.

Beckman, Ludvig. 2008. "Do Global Climate Change and the Interest of Future Generations Have Implications for Democracy?", *Environmental Politics*, Vol. 17, No. 4 (August), pp. 610–24.

Beckman, Ludvig and Edward A Page.2008. "Perspectives on Justice, Democracy and Global Climate Change", *Environmental Politics*, Vol. 17, No. 4 (August), pp. 527–35.

Beder, Sharon. 2001. "Research Note: Neoliberal Think Tanks and Free Market Environmentalism", *Environmental Politics*, Vol. 10, No. 2 (summer), pp. 128–33.

Behre, C. 2003. "Mexican Environmental Law: Enforcement and Public Participation Since the Signing of NAFTA's Environmental Co-operation Agreement", *Journal of Transnational Law and Policy*, Vol. 12, No. 2 (spring), pp. 327–43. Available online at www.law.fsu.edu/journals/transnational/vol12_2/behre.pdf [accessed May 2012].

Belejack, Barbara. 2002. "Bio 'Gold' Rush in Chiapas on Hold", *NACLA Report on the Americas*, Vol. 35, No. 5 (March/April), pp. 23–28.

Bellon, Mauricio R. 2010. "Review of Edit Antal, Lauren Baker and Gerard Verschoor, *Maize and Biosecurity in Mexico: Debate and Practice* (2007)", *Bulletin of Latin American Research*, Vol. 29, No. 3 (July), pp. 388–90.

Bennett, Colin J. 1988. "Regulating the Computer: Comparing Policy Instruments in Europe and the US", *European Journal of Political Research*, Vol. 16, No. 5 (September), pp. 437–66.

Benton, Lisa and John R Short. 1999. *Environmental Discourse and Practice*. Blackwell: Oxford.

Betsill, Michele M. 2006. "Transnational Actors in International Environmental Politics", in Michele Betsill et al. (eds), *International Environmental Politics*. New York: Palgrave Macmillan.

Betsill, Michele M and Elisabeth Corell. 2001. "NGO Influence in International Environmental Negotiations: A Framework for Analysis", *Global Environmental Politics*, Vol. 1, No. 4 (November), pp. 65–85.

Biermann, Frank and Klaus Dingwerth. 2004. "Global Environmental Change and the Nation State", *Global Environmental Politics*, Vol. 4, No. 1 (February), pp. 1–22.

Biermann, Frank, et al. (eds). 2011. *Transforming Governance and Institutions for a Planet under Pressure: Revitalizing the Institutional Framework for Global Sustainability: Key Insights from Social Science Research*. Rio+20 Policy Brief #3. Conference, "Planet Under Pressure:

New Knowledge Towards Solutions". Available online at www.icsu.org/rio20/policy-briefs/InstFrameLowRes.pdf.

Birdsall, Nancy and David Wheeler. 1993. "Trade Policy and Industrial Pollution in Latin America: Where are the Pollution Havens?", *Journal of Environment and Development*, Vol. 2, No. 1 (January), pp. 137–49.

Birnir, Jóhanna Kristín. 2008. "Party Regulation in Central and Eastern Europe and Latin America: The Effect on Minority Representation and the Propensity for Conflict", in Benjamin Reilly and Per Nordlund (eds), *Political Parties in Conflict-Prone Societies*. New York: UN University Press.

Black, Richard. 2012. "Whales to gain Panama Canal traffic protection", bbc.co.uk, 6 July 2012. Available online at www.bbc.co.uk/news/science-environment-18720380 [accessed August 2012].

Blackman, Allen, Richard Morgenstern and Elizabeth Topping. 2006. *Institutional Analysis of Colombia's Autonomous Regional Corporations (CARs)*. Washington, DC: Resources for the Future. Available online at www.rff.org/rff/documents/rff-rpt-colombiacars.pdf [accessed January 2012].

Blackman, Allen, Sandra Hoffman, Richard Morgenstern and Elizabeth Topping. 2005. *Assessment of Colombia's National Environmental System (SINA)*. Washington, DC: Resources for the Future.

Blokland, Kees. 1995. "Peasant Alliances and 'Concertation' with Society", *Bulletin of Latin American Research*, Vol. 14, No. 2 (May), pp. 159–70.

Bloomberg New Energy Finance/UNEP. 2011. *Global Trends in Renewable Energy Investment 2011*. Analysis of Trends and Issues in the Financing of Renewable Energy. Frankfurt: United Nations Environment Programme, Bloomberg New Energy Finance and Frankfurt School of Finance & Management.

Blum, Nicole. 2008. "Environmental Education in Costa Rica: Building a Framework for Sustainable Development?", *International Journal of Educational Development*, Vol. 28, No. 3, pp. 348–58.

Boff, Leonardo. 1995. *Ecology and Liberation: A New Paradigm*. Maryknoll, NY: Orbis Books.

Bookchin, Murray. 1982. *The Ecology of Freedom: The Emergence and Dissolution of Hierarchy*. Palo Alto, CA: Cheshire Books.

——. 1986. *Toward an Ecological Society*. Montreal: Black Rose Books.

——. 1990. *The Philosophy of Social Ecology: Essays on Dialectical Naturalism*. Montreal: Black Rose Books.

Boza, Mario A. 1993. "Conservation in Action: Past, Present, and Future of the National Park System of Costa Rica", *Conservation Biology*, Vol. 7, No. 2 (June), pp. 239–47.

Bradley, Ruth. 2006. "Chile's Environmental NGOs", *Business Chile Magazine* (online), 1 May 2006. Available online at www.businesschile. cl/en/news/reportaje-principal/chile%E2%80%99s-environmental-ngos [accessed June 2012].

Branford, Sue and Jan Rocha. 2002. *Cutting the Wire: The Story of the Landless Movement in Brazil*. London: Latin American Bureau.

Breen, Sheryl D. 2001. "Ecocentrism, Weighted Interests, and Property Theory", *Environmental Politics*, Vol. 10, No. 1 (January), pp. 36–51.

Bright, Christopher. 1999. "Invasive Species: Pathogens of Globalization", *Foreign Policy* 116 (fall), pp. 50–63.

Brotherson, Gordon. 1992. *The Book of the Fourth World: Reading the Native Americas through their Literature*. Cambridge: Cambridge University Press.

Broughton, Alan. 2011. "Venezuela: Land Reform, Food Sovereignty and Agroecology", *Synthesis/Regeneration* 55 (spring). Available online at www.greens.org/s-r/55/55-14.html [accessed October 2011].

Brown, David S, Christopher Brown and Scott W Desposato. 2007. "Promoting and Preventing Political Change through Internationally Funded NGO Activity", *Latin American Research Review*, Vol. 42, No. 1, pp. 126–38.

Brown, Donald A. 2002. *American Heat: Ethical Problems with the United States' Response to Global Warming*. Lanham, MD: Rowman & Littlefield.

Bruckerhoff, Joshua J. 2008. "Giving Nature Constitutional Protection: A Less Anthropocentric Interpretation of Environmental Rights", *Texas Law Review*, February 2008. Available online at www.allbusiness.com/legal/constitutional-law/8894685-1.html [accessed August 2011].

Brulle, Robert J. 2002. "Habermas and Green Political Thought: Two Roads Converging", *Environmental Politics*, Vol. 11, No. 4 (winter), pp. 1–20.

Brundtland, Gro Harlem, et al. 1987. "Report of the World Commission on Environment and Development: Our Common Future", Annex to General Assembly document A/42/427, Development and International Co-operation: Environment. Available online at www.un-documents. net/wced-ocf.htm [accesed September 2012].

Brysk, Alison. 2000. *From Tribal Village to Global Village: Indian Rights and International Relations in Latin America*. Stanford, CA: Stanford University Press.

Building Bridges Collective. 2010. *Space For Movement? Reflections from Bolivia on Climate Justice, Social Movements and the State*. Leeds: Building Bridges Collective. Available online at http://spaceformovement. files.wordpress.com/2010/08/space_for_movement2.pdf [accessed February 2014].

Busch, Per-Olof, Helge Jörgens and Kerstin Tews. 2005. "The Global Diffusion of Regulatory Instruments: The Making of a New International Environmental Regime", *Annals of the American Academy of Political and Social Science*, Vol. 598, No. 1 (March), pp. 146–67.

Caldwell, Lynton. 1990. *Between Two Worlds: Science, the Environmental Movement and Policy Choice.* Cambridge: Cambridge University Press.

Calvache, Alejandro, Silvia Benitez and Aurelio Ramos. 2011. *Fondos de Agua, Conservando la Infraestructura. Verde. Guía de Diseño, Creación y Operación.* Bogotá: Alianza Latinoamericana de Fondos de Agua/ The Nature Conservancy/Fundacion Femsa/Banco Interamericano de Desarrollo.

Caney, Simon. 2005. "Cosmopolitan Justice, Responsibility, and Global Climate Change", *Leiden Journal of International Law*, Vol. 18, No. 4 (December), pp. 747–75.

——. 2008. "Human Rights, Climate Change, and Discounting", *Environmental Politics*, Vol. 17, No. 4 (August), pp. 536–55.

Cardona Castillo, Hugo. 2008. "Decentralization and Environmentally Sound Decision Making: Policy Implications", LACEEP Working Paper No. 3, April 2008. Cartago: Latin American and Caribbean Environmental Economics Program. Available online at www.laceep.org/ media/docs/working_papers/cardona.pdf [accessed February 2014].

Carey, John M. 1997. "Institutional Design and Party Systems", in Larry Diamond, Marc F. Plattner, Yun-han Chu and Hung-mao Tien (eds), *Consolidating the Third Wave Democracies: Themes and Perspectives.* Baltimore, MD: Johns Hopkins University Press.

Carroll, Rory. 2011. "Drugs barons accused of destroying Guatemala's rainforest", guardian.co.uk, 13 June 2011. Available online at www.theguardian.com/world/2011/jun/13/guatemala-rainforest-destroyed-drug-traffickers.

Carruthers, David V. 1996. "Indigenous Ecology and the Politics of Linkage in Mexican Social Movements", *Third World Quarterly*, Vol. 17, No. 5 (December), pp. 1007–28.

——. 2001. "Environmental Politics in Chile: Legacies of Dictatorship and Democracy", *Third World Quarterly*, Vol. 22, No. 3 (June), pp. 343–58.

——. 2007. "Environmental Justice and the Politics of Energy on the US–Mexico Border", *Environmental Politics*, Vol. 16, No. 3 (June), pp. 394–413.

—— (ed.). 2008a. *Environmental Justice in Latin America: Problems, Promise and Practice.* London: MIT Press.

——. 2008b. "Introduction: Popular Environmentalism and Social Justice in Latin America", in David V Carruthers (ed.), *Environmental Justice in Latin America: Problems, Promise and Practice.* London: MIT Press.

Carter, Miguel. 2010. "The Landless Rural Workers Movement and Democracy in Brazil", *Latin American Research Review*, Vol. 45, special issue, pp. 186–217.

Carter, Neil. 2007. *The Politics of the Environment: Ideas, Activism, Policy.* Cambridge: Cambridge University Press.

——. 2010. "The Greens in the 2009 European Parliament Election", *Environmental Politics*, Vol. 19, No. 2 (March), pp. 295–302.

Carvalho, Georgia O. 2000. "The Politics of Indigenous Land Rights in Brazil", *Bulletin of Latin American Research*, Vol. 19, No. 4 (October), pp. 461–78.

Castiglioni, Rossana. 2012. "Social Policy Reform and Continuity under the Bachelet Administration", in Jordi Díez and Susan Francheschet (eds), *Comparative Public Policy in Latin America*. London: University of Toronto Press.

Catón, Matthias and Fernando Tuesta Soldevilla. 2008. "Political Parties in Conflict-Prone Societies in Latin America", in Benjamin Reilly and Per Nordlund (eds), *Political Parties in Conflict-Prone Societies*. Tokyo: UN University Press.

CELAC (Comunidad de Estados Latinoamericanos y Caribeños). 2011. *Plan de Acción de Caracas 2012: Cumbre de la Comunidad de Estados Latinoamericanos y Caribeños*, 2–3 December 2011, Caracas. Caracas: Comunidad de Estados Latinoamericanos y Caribeños.

Chalmers, Douglas, Scott Martin and Kerianne Piester. 1997. "Conclusion. Associative Networks: New Structures of Representation for the Popular Sectors?", in Douglas Chalmers et al. (eds), *The New Politics of Inequality in Latin America: Rethinking Participation and Representation*. Oxford: Oxford University Press.

Chambers, W Bradnee and Jessica F Green (eds). 2005. *Reforming International Environmental Governance: From Institutional Limits to Innovative Reforms*. Tokyo: UN University Press.

Chasek, Pamela S, David L Downie and Janet Welsh Brown. 2006. *Global Environmental Politics*, 4th edn. Boulder, CO: Westview Press.

Chernela, Janet M. 2011. "Barriers Natural and Unnatural: Islamiento as a Central Metaphor in Kuna Ecotourism", *Bulletin of Latin American Research*, Vol. 30, No. 1 (January), pp. 35–49.

Christoff, Peter. 1996. "Ecological Citizens and Ecologically Guided Democracy", in Brian Doherty and Marius de Geus (eds), *Democracy and Green Political Thought: Sustainability, Rights and Citizenship*. London: Routledge.

Clapp, Jennifer. 2003. "Transnational Corporate Interests and Global Environmental Governance: Negotiating Rules for Agricultural Biotechnology and Chemicals", *Environmental Politics*, Vol. 12, No. 4 (winter), pp. 1–23.

Clapp, Jennifer and Peter Dauvergne. 2005. *Paths to a Green World: The Political Economy of the Global Environment.* Cambridge, MA: MIT Press.

Clarkson, Linda, Vern Morrissette and Gabriel Régallet. 1992. *Our Responsibility to the Seventh Generation: Indigenous Peoples and Sustainable Development.* Winnipeg: International Institute for Sustainable Development.

Clemons, Karlie Shea. 2009. "Hydroelectric Dams: Transboundary Environmental Effects and International Law", *Florida State University Law Review*, Vol. 36, pp. 487–536.

Cobb, Roger W and Charles Elder. 1983. *Participation in American Politics: The Dynamics of Agenda-Building.* Baltimore, MD: Johns Hopkins Universtiy Press.

ComAmbiental. 2011. "El ambiente en la política porteña", *ComAmbiental* online, Buenos Aires, 11 May 2011. Available online at www.comambiental.com.ar/2011/05/el-ambiente-en-la-politica-portena.html [accessed May 2012].

Compston, Hugh. 2009a. "Introduction: Political Strategies for Climate Policy", *Environmental Politics*, Vol. 18, No. 5 (September), pp. 659–69.

——. 2009b. "Networks, Resources, Political Strategy and Climate Policy", *Environmental Politics*, Vol. 18, No. 5 (September), pp. 727–46.

Conca, Ken. 2001. "Consumption and Environment in a Global Economy", *Global Environmental Politics*, Vol. 1, No. 3 (summer), pp. 53–71.

Conca, Ken and Geoffrey D Dabelko (eds). 2002. *Environmental Peacemaking.* Washington, DC: Woodrow Wilson Center Press.

Cook, Paul. 2011. "Extracting the truth about Colombia's mining industry", www.guardian.co.uk, 26 October 2011. Available online at http://www.theguardian.com/global-development/poverty-matters/2011/oct/26/extracting-truth-colombia-mining-industry [accessed September 2012].

Cooper, Marilyn M. 1996. "Environmental Rhetoric in the Age of Hegemonic Politics: Earth First! and the Nature Conservancy", in Carl Herndl and Stuart Brown (eds), *Green Culture.* Madison: University of Wisconsin Press.

Cox, Gary W and Matthew D McCubbins. 2001. "The Institutional Determinants of Economic Policy Outcomes", in Stephen Haggard and Matthew D McCubbins (eds), *Presidents, Parliaments and Policy.* Cambridge: Cambridge University Press.

Cox, Gary W and Scott Morgenstern. 2002. "Epilogue: Latin America's Reactive Assemblies and Proactive Presidents", in Scott Morgenstern and Benito Nacif (eds), *Legislative Politics in Latin America.* Cambridge: Cambridge University Press.

CSIS (Center for Strategic and International Studies), et al. 2003.

US–Mexico Transboundary Water Management: Recommendations for Policymakers for the Medium and Long Term. A Report of the US–Mexico Binational Council. Washington, DC: Center for Strategic and International Studies /Instituto Tecnológico Autónomo de México/University of Texas at Austin.

Dalton, Russell J. 1994. *The Green Rainbow: Environmental Groups in Western Europe.* New Haven, CT: Yale University Press.

——. 2005. "The Greening of the Globe? Crossnational Levels of Environmental Group Membership", *Environmental Politics*, Vol. 14, No. 4 (August), pp. 441–59.

Dalton, Russell J, Scott C Flanagan and Paul Allen Beck (eds). 1984. *Electoral Change in Advanced Industrial Democracies: Realignment or Dealignment?* Princeton, NJ: Princeton University Press.

Dalton, Russell J, Steve Recchia and Robert Rohrschneider. 2003. "The Environmental Movement and the Modes of Political Action", *Comparative Political Studies*, Vol. 36, No. 7 (September), pp. 743–71.

Dangl, Benjamin. 2010. *Dancing With Dynamite: Social Movements and States in Latin America.* Oakland, CA: AK Press.

Dawson, Jonathan. 2010. "Ecovillages and the Transformation of Values", in Linda Starke and Lisa Mastny (eds), *2010 State of the World. Transforming Cultures: From Consumerism to Sustainability.* Washington, DC: Worldwatch Institute.

De Almeida, Lucio Flavio and Felix Ruiz Sanchez (translated by Laurence Hallewell). 2000. "The Landless Workers' Movement and Social Struggles against Neoliberalism", *Latin American Perspectives*, Vol. 27, No. 5, *Radical Left Response to Global Impoverishment* (September), pp. 11–32.

de Graaf, John. 2010. "Reducing Work Time as a Path to Sustainability", in Linda Starke and Lisa Mastny (eds), *2010 State of the World. Transforming Cultures: From Consumerism to Sustainability.* Washington, DC: Worldwatch Institute.

De la Torre, Augusto, Pablo Fajnzylber and John Nash. 2009. *Low Carbon, High Growth: Latin American Responses to Climate Change.* Washington, DC: World Bank.

Deere, Carmen Diana and Frederick S Royce (eds). 2009. *Rural Social Movements in Latin America: Organizing for Sustainable Livelihoods.* Gainsville: University of Florida Press.

Deere, Carmen Diana and Magdalena León. 2001. "Institutional Reform of Agriculture under Neoliberalism: The Impact of the Women's and Indigenous Movements", *Latin American Research Review*, Vol. 36, No. 2, pp. 31–63.

Denevan, William M. 1992. "The Pristine Myth: The Landscape of the

Americas in 1492", *Annals of the American Association of Geographers*, Vol. 82, No. 3 (September), pp. 369–85.

Deruyttere, Anne. 1997. *Indigenous Peoples and Sustainable Development: The Role of the Inter-American Development Bank*. IDB Forum of the Americas, 8 April, 1997. Washington, DC: IDB.

Desmarais, Annette Aurélie. 2009a. "Voices From Maputo: La Vía Campesina's Fifth International Conference", *NACLA Report on the Americas*, Vol. 42, No. 3 (May/June), pp. 22–26.

——. 2009b. "Building a Transnational Peasant Movement", *NACLA Report on the Americas*, Vol. 42, No. 3 (May/June), pp. 24–25.

Dessler, Andrew E and Edward A Parson. 2006. *The Science and Politics of Global Climate Change: A Guide to the Debate*. Cambridge: Cambridge University Press.

Di John, Jonathan. 2009. *From Windfall to Curse? Oil and Industrialization in Venezuela, 1920 to the Present*. University Park: Pennsylvania State University Press.

Di Paola, Maria Eugenia. 2004. *Pilot Project on Environmental Compliance and Enforcement Indicators in Latin America: The Case of Argentina*. Buenos Aires: Fundación Ambiente y Recursos Naturales. Available online at www.inece.org/conference/7/vol1/34_Di%20Paola.pdf [accessed May 2012].

Diamond, Larry. 1999. *Developing Democracy: Toward Consolidation*. Baltimore, MD: Johns Hopkins University Press.

Diamond, Larry, Jonathan Hartlyn, Juan Linz and Seymour Martin Lipset (eds). 1999. *Democracy in Developing Countries: Latin America*, 2nd edn. Boulder, CO: Lynne Rienner.

Diamond, Sara. 2010. "Brazil's Native Peoples and the Belo Monte Dam: A Case Study", *NACLA Report on the Americas*, Vol. 43, No. 5 (September/October), pp. 25–31.

Diani, Mario and Elisa Rambaldo. 2007. "Still the Time of Environmental Movements? A Local Perspective", *Environmental Politics*, Vol. 16, No. 5 (November), pp. 765–84.

Díaz-Briquets, Sergio and Jorge Pérez-López. 2000. *Conquering Nature: The Environmental Legacy of Socialism in Cuba*. Pittsburgh: University of Pittsburgh Press.

Díez, Jordi. 2008. "The Rise and Fall of Mexico's Green Movement", *European Review of Latin American and Caribbean Studies*, 85 (October), pp. 81–99.

——. 2012. "Presidentialism and Policy-making in Latin America: The Case of Mexico", in Jordi Díez and Susan Francheschet (eds), *Comparative Public Policy in Latin America*. London: University of Toronto Press.

Díez, Jordi and Reyes Rodriguez. 2008. "Environmental Justice in

Mexico: The Peñoles Case", in David V Carruthers (ed.), *Environmental Justice in Latin America: Problems, Promise, and Practice*. London: MIT Press.

Díez, Jordi and Susan Francheschet (eds). 2012. *Comparative Public Policy in Latin America*. London: University of Toronto Press.

Dobson, Andrew. 1996. "Democratizing Green Theory: Preconditions and Principles", in Brian Doherty and Marius de Geus (eds), *Democracy and Green Political Thought: Sustainability, Rights and Citizenship*. London: Routledge.

Dobson, Andrew and Derek Bell (eds). 2006. *Environmental Citizenship*. Cambridge, MA: MIT Press.

Domínguez, Francisco, Geraldine Lievesley and Steve Ludlam. 2011. *Right-wing Politics in the New Latin America: Reaction and Revolt*. London: Zed Books.

Domínguez, Jorge. 2000. *The Future of Inter-American Relations*. New York: Routledge.

Dore, Elizabeth. 1996a. "Capitalism and Ecological Crisis: Legacy of the 1980s", in Helen Collinson (ed.), *Green Guerrillas: Environmental Conflicts and Initiatives in Latin America and the Caribbean. A Reader*. London: Latin America Bureau.

——. 1996b. "How Sustainable were Pre-Columbian Civilizations?", in Helen Collinson (ed.), *Green Guerrillas: Environmental Conflicts and Initiatives in Latin America and the Caribbean. A Reader*. London: Latin America Bureau.

Downs, Anthony. 1972. "Up and Down with Ecology: The 'Issue-Attention' Cycle", *Public Interest*, 28 (summer), pp. 38–50.

Dryzek, John S. 1987. *Rational Ecology: Environment and Political Economy*. Oxford: Blackwell.

Eagleton, Terry. 2012. *Why Marx Was Right*. London: Yale University Press.

Eckersley, Robyn. 1990. "Habermas and Green Political Theory: Two Roads Diverging", *Theory and Society*, Vol. 19, No. 6, pp. 739–76.

——. 2004. *The Green State: Rethinking Democracy and Sovereignty*. Cambridge, MA: MIT Press.

Eckstein, Susan Eva and Timothy P. Wickham-Crowley (eds). 2003. *What Justice? Whose Justice? Fighting for Fairness in Latin America*. Berkeley: University of California Press.

ECLAC (Economic Commission for Latin America and the Caribbean). 2000. *Sustainable Development: Latin American and Caribbean Perspectives*. Based on the Regional Consultative Meeting on Sustainable Development, 19–21 January 2000, Santiago, Chile. Santiago: Economic Commission for Latin American and the Caribbean.

ECLAC, OLADE (Organización Latinoamericana de Energía) and GTZ (German Technical Co-operation Agency). 2009. *Situación y perspectiva de la eficiencia energética en América Latina y El Caribe.* Available at: www.iadb.org/intal/intalcdi/PE/2009/04314.pdf.

Edelman, Marc. 2008. "Transnational Organizing in Agrarian Central America: Histories, Challenges, Prospects", in Saturnino Borras et al. (eds), *Transnational Agrarian Movements: Confronting Globalization.* Chichester: Wiley-Blackwell.

EIA (Environmental Investigation Agency). 2005. *The Illegal Logging Crisis in Honduras: How US and EU Imports of Illegal Honduran Wood Increase Poverty, Fuel Corruption and Devastate Forests and Communities.* Washington, DC: Environmental Investigation Agency/Center for International Policy. Available online at http://www.eia-international.org/wp-content/uploads/Honduras-Report-English-low-res.pdf [accessed February 2014].

Eltz, Melanie, Urvashi Narain, Alessandro Orfie and Robert Schneider. 2010. *Strengthening Environmental Institutions and Governance: What Should be the Role of the World Bank Group?* The World Bank Group 2010 Environment Strategy Analytical Background Papers. Washington, DC: World Bank.

Engelman, Robert. 2010. "Environmentally Sustainable Childbearing", in Linda Starke and Lisa Mastny (eds), *2010 State of the World. Transforming Cultures: From Consumerism to Sustainability.* Washington, DC: Worldwatch Institute.

EREC (Economic Commission for Latin America and the Caribbean)/ Greenpeace. 2007. *Energy Revolution: A Sustainable Latin America Energy Outlook.* Amsterdam and Brussels: European Renewable Energy Council/Greenpeace.

EU-LAC (European Union–Latin America and Caribbean Foundation). 2008. "Lima Declaration", Fifth Latin America and Caribbean– European Union Summit, Lima, 16 May 2008. Available online at www.eeas.europa.eu/lac/docs/declaration_en.pdf [accessed December 2011].

Evans, Sterling. 1999. *The Green Republic: A Conservation History of Costa Rica.* Austin: University of Texas Press.

Evenson, Fredric. 1998. "A Deeper Shade of Green: The Evolution of Cuban Environmental Law and Policy", *Golden Gate University Law Review,* Vol. 28, No. 3. Available online at http://digitalcommons.law.ggu.edu/ggulrev/vol28/iss3/8 [accessed September 2012].

Faber, Daniel. 1991. "A Sea of Posion", *The Conquest of Nature 1492–1992,* special edn., *NACLA Report on the Americas,* Vol. 25, No. 2 (September), pp. 31–36.

——. 1993. *Environment Under Fire: Imperialism and the Ecological Crisis in Central America*. New York: Monthly Review.

——. 2002. "A Revolution in Environmental Justice and Sustainable Development: The Political Ecology of Nicaragua", in John Byrne, Leigh Glover and Cecilia Martinez (eds), *Environmental Justice: International Discourses in Political Economy, Energy and Environmental Policy*. London: Transaction.

Fabra, Adriana and Eva Arnal. 2002. "Review of Jurisprudence on Human Rights and the Environment in Latin America", Background Paper No. 6, Joint United Nations Environment Programme–Office of the United Nations High Commissioner for Human Rights, Expert Seminar on Human Rights and the Environment, 14–16 January 2002, Geneva.

Falkner, Robert. 2004. "The First Meeting of the Parties to the Cartagena Protocol on Biosafety", *Environmental Politics*, Vol. 13, No. 3 (autumn), pp. 635–41.

Farthing, Linda. 2009. "Bolivia's Dilemma: Development Confronts the Legacy of Extraction", *NACLA Report on the Americas*, Vol. 42, No. 5 (September/October), pp. 25–29.

Fearnside, Philip M. 2000. "Deforestation Impacts, Environmental Services and the International Community", in Anthony Hall (ed.), *Amazonia at the Crossroads: The Challenge of Sustainable Development*. London: Institute of Latin American Studies.

FIDA (Foro Interamericano de Derecho Ambiental). 2008. Draft Background Note, National Focal Points' Meeting, Inter-American Forum on Environmental Law (FIDA), Supreme Court of Justice Brasilia, 7, 8 and 9 May 2008.

Figueres, Christiana (ed.). 2002. *Establishing National Authorities for the CDM: A Guide for Developing Countries*. Washington, DC: International Institute for Sustainable Development/Center for Sustainable Development in the Americas.

Fischhendler, Itay. 2008. "When Ambiguity in Treaty Design Becomes Destructive: A Study of Transboundary Water", *Global Environmental Politics*, Vol. 8, No. 1 (February), pp. 111–36.

Fitz, Don. 1998. "The 1997 Elections in Mexico and the Rise of the Greens", *Synthesis/Regeneration*, 15 (winter). Available online at www.greens.org/s-r/15/15-04.html [accessed October 2011].

Florescano, Enrique. 1994. *Memory, Myth, and Time in Mexico: From the Aztecs to Independence* (translated by Albert G Bork and Kathryn R Bork). Austin: University of Texas Press.

Forero, Oscar A and Michael R Redclift. 2006. "The Role of the Mexican State in the Development of Chicle Extraction in Yucatán, and the

Continuing Importance of Coyotaje", *Journal of Latin American Studies*, Vol. 38, No. 1 (February), pp. 65–93.

Foweraker, Joe. 1998. "Institutional Design, Party Systems and Governability – Differentiating the Presidential Regimes of Latin America", *British Journal of Political Science*, Vol. 28, No. 4 (October), pp. 651–76.

——. 2001. "Grassroots Movements and Political Activism in Latin America: A Critical Comparison of Chile and Brazil", *Journal of Latin American Studies*, Vol. 33, No. 4 (November), pp. 839–65.

Foweraker, Joe, Todd Landman and Neil Harvey. 2003. *Governing Latin America*. Cambridge: Polity Press.

Francheschet, Susan and Jordi Díez. 2012. "Introduction", in Jordi Díez and Susan Francheschet (eds), *Comparative Public Policy in Latin America*. London: University of Toronto Press.

Francia, Néstor. 2007. Participación en el Foro "Ecosocialismo del Siglo XXI". Cited in María Pilar García-Guadilla, 2009, "Ecosocialismo del siglo XXI y modelo de desarrollo bolivariano: los mitos de la sustentabilidad ambiental y de la democracia participativa en Venezuela", *Revista Venezolana de Economía y Ciencias Sociales*, Vol. 15, No. 1 (January–April), pp. 187–223.

Franko, Patrice. 1999. *The Puzzle of Latin American Economic Development*. Lanham, MD: Rowman & Littlefield.

Fraser, Barbara J. 2003. "Joining Forces for Peru's Rainforest", *NACLA Report on the Americas*, Vol. 36, No. 6 (May/June), p. 13.

Gámez, Rodrigo, et al. 1993. "Costa Rica's Conservation Program and National Biodiversity Institute (INBio)", in Walter Reid et al. (eds), *Biodiversity Prospecting: Using Genetic Resources for Sustainable Development*. Washington, DC: World Resources Institute.

Garcia-Acevedo, Maria Rosa. 2004. "Conflict in the Borderlands", *NACLA Report on the Americas*, Vol. 38, No. 1 (July/August), p. 19.

García-Guadilla, María Pilar. 2005. "Environmental Movements, Politics and Agenda 21 in Latin America", Civil Society and Social Movements Programme Paper No. 16, October 2005, United Nations Research Institute for Social Development. Geneva: UNRISD.

——. 2009. "Ecosocialismo del siglo XXI y modelo de desarrollo bolivariano: los mitos de la sustentabilidad ambiental y de la democracia participativa en Venezuela", *Revista Venezolana de Economía y Ciencias Sociales*, Vol. 15, No. 1 (January–April), pp. 187–223. Available online at www.scielo.org.ve/scielo.php?script=sci_arttext&pid=S1315-64112009000100010&lng=pt&nrm=iso&tlng=pt [accessed September 2012].

Gardner, Gary. 2006. *Inspiring Progress: Religions' Contributions to Sustainable Development*. New York: W.W. Norton.

——. 2010. "Engaging Religions to Shape Worldviews", in Linda Starke and Lisa Mastny (eds), *2010 State of the World. Transforming Cultures: From Consumerism to Sustainability*. Washington, DC: Worldwatch Institute.

Gaventa, John and Camilo Valderrama. 1999. *Participation, Citizenship and Local Governance*. Background note prepared for workshop "Strengthening Participation in Local Governance". Institute of Development Studies, Brighton. Available online at www.uv.es/~fernandm/Gaventa,%20 Valderrama.pdf [accessed September 2012].

Gedicks, Al. 2001 *Resource Rebels: Native Challenges to Mining and Oil*. Cambridge, MA: South End Press.

GEF (Global Environment Facility)/UNDP (United Nations Development Programme)/SGP (Small Grants Programme). 2010. *El reino de los ecologistas eternos: historias de vida detrás del SGP en el Perú*. Lima: Global Environment Facility/United Nations Development Programme/Small Grants Programme.

Gelles, Paul H. 2000. *Water and Power in Highland Peru: The Cultural Politics of Irrigation and Development*. New Brunswick, NJ: Rutgers University Press.

Gilly, Adolfo. 2008. "Racism, Domination and Bolivia", *Counterpunch Magazine* online, 1 October 2008.

González Martínez, Alfonso. 1992. "Socio-Ecological Struggles in Mexico: The Prospects", *International Journal of Sociology and Social Policy*, Vol. 12, Nos. 4–7, pp. 113–28.

Gorostiaga, Xabier. 1993. "Latin America in the New World Order", in Jeremy Brecher, John Brown Childs and Jill Cutler (eds), *Global Visions: Beyond the New World Order*. Boston, MA: South End Press.

Goulet, Denis. 2005. "Global Governance, Dam Conflicts and Participation", *Human Rights Quarterly*, Vol. 27, No. 3, pp. 881–907.

Gramsci, Antonio. 1971. *Selections from Prison Notebooks*. London: Lawrence & Wishart.

Grant, Wyn. 2000. *Pressure Groups in British Politics*. Basingstoke: Macmillan.

Greene, Shane. 2006. "Getting over the Andes: The Geo-Eco-Politics of Indigenous Movements in Peru's Twenty-First Century Inca Empire", *Journal of Latin American Studies*, Vol. 38, No. 2 (May), pp. 327–54.

Griner, Steven and Daniel Zovatto (eds). 2005. *Funding of Political Parties and Election Campaigns in the Americas*. San José, Cost Rica: Organization of American States/International Institute for Democracy and Electoral Assistance. Available online at www.idea.int/publications/ fopp_america/upload/Libro_completo.pdf [accessed February 2012].

Grisaffi, Thomas. 2010. "We Are Originarios ...'We Just Aren't from Here':

Coca Leaf and Identity Politics in the Chapare, Bolivia", *Bulletin of Latin American Research*, Vol. 29, No. 4 (October), pp. 425–39.

Guillén, M., 2001. "Is Globalization Civilizing, Destructive of Feeble? A Critique of Five Key Debates in the Social Science Literature", *Annual Review of Sociology*, Vol. 27, pp. 235–60.

Gulbrandsen, Lars. 2003. "The Evolving Forest Regime and Domestic Actors: Strategic or Normative Adaptation?", *Environmental Politics*, Vol. 12, No. 2 (summer), pp. 95–114.

Gupta, Aarti and Robert Falkner. 2006. "The Influence of the Cartagena Protocol on Biosafety: Comparing Mexico, China and South Africa", *Global Environmental Politics*, Vol. 6, No. 4 (November), pp. 23–55.

Gupta, Joyeeta. 2001. *Our Simmering Planet: What to do about Global Warming?* London: Zed Books.

Gupte, Manjusha and Robert V Bartlett. 2007. "Necessary Preconditions for Deliberative Environmental Democracy? Challenging the Modernity Basis of Current Theory", *Global Environmental Politics*, Vol. 7, No. 3 (August), pp. 94–106.

Gustafson, Bret. 2009. *New Languages of the State: Indigenous Resurgence and the Politics of Knowledge in Bolivia*. Durham, NC: Duke University Press.

Gutiérrez, Gustavo. 1973. *A Theology of Liberation*. New York: Orbis.

GWEC (Global Wind Energy Council). 2011. "Latin America: New Wind Capacity in Five Countries". Brussels: Global Wind Energy Council, archived page. Available online at http://dev6.semaforce.be/index.php?id=19 [accessed September 2012].

Haas, Peter. 1992. "Epistemic Communities and International Policy Coordination", *International Organization*, Vol. 46, No. 1, pp. 201–20.

Habermas, Jürgen. 1984. *The Theory of Communicative Action*, Vol. 1, *Reason and the Rationalization of Society*. Boston, MA: Beacon Press.

——. 1987. *The Theory of Communicative Action*, Vol. 2, *Lifeworld and System: A Critique of Functionalist Reason*. Boston, MA: Beacon Press.

Haight, Brown & Bonesteel LLP, George R. Gonzalez and Maria Elia Gastelum. 1999. *Overview of the Environmental Laws of Mexico*. Tucson, AZ: National Law Center for Inter-American Free Trade.

Hale, Charles. 2002. "Does Multiculturalism Menace?: Governance, Cultural Rights and the Politics of Identity in Guatemala", *Journal of Latin American Studies*, Vol. 34, No. 3 (August), pp. 485–524.

Hale, Stephen. 2010. "The New Politics of Climate Change: Why We are Failing and How We will Succeed", *Environmental Politics*, Vol. 19, No. 2 (March), pp. 255–75.

Hall, Anthony (ed.). 2000. *Amazonia at the Crossroads: The Challenge of Sustainable Development*. London: Institute of Latin American Studies.

Hall, Gillette and Harry Anthony Patrinos. 2005. *Indigenous Peoples, Poverty and Human Development in Latin America, 1994–2004*. Washington, DC: World Bank. Available online at http://siteresources. worldbank.org/INTLAC/Resources/FinalExecutiveSummary_Eng_ May05.pdf [accessed June 2012].

Hall, Peter and Rosemary Taylor. 1996. "Political Science and the Three New Institutionalisms", *Political Studies*, Vol. 44, No. 5, pp. 936–57.

Hamilton, Paul. 2002. "The Greening of Nationalism: Nationalising Nature in Europe", *Environmental Politics*, Vol. 11, No. 2 (summer), pp. 27–48.

Hardt, Michael and Antonio Negri. 2000. *Empire*. London: Harvard University Press.

Harvey, Neil. 1998. *The Chiapas Rebellion: The Struggle for Land and Democracy*. Durham, NC: Duke University Press.

Hawken, Paul, Amory Lovins and L Hunter Lovins. 1999. *Natural Capitalism: The Next Industrial Revolution*. London: Earthscan.

Heller, Patrick. 2001. "Moving the State : The Politics of Democratic Decentralization in Kerala, South Africa, and Porto Alegre", *Politics and Society*, Vol. 29, No. 1 (March), pp. 131–63.

Helmke, Gretchen and Steven Levitsky. 2005. "Informal Institutions and Comparative Politics: A Research Agenda", *Perspectives on Politics*, Vol. 2, No. 4, pp. 725–40.

Hernández Castillo, Rosalva Aída and Victoria J Furio. 2006. "The Indigenous Movement in Mexico: Between Electoral Politics and Local Resistance", *Latin American Perspectives*, Vol. 33, No. 2 (March), pp. 115–31.

Hernández, Vladimir. 2012. "José Mujica: The world's 'poorest' president", bbc.co.uk, 15 November 2012. Available online at www.bbc.co.uk/ news/magazine-20243493 [accessed November 2012].

Hilgartner, Stephen and Charles L Bosk. 1988. "The Rise and Fall of Social Problems: A Public Arenas Model", *American Journal of Sociology*, Vol. 94, No. 1 (July), pp. 53–78.

Hill, Barry E, Steve Wolfson and Nicholas Targ. 2004. "Human Rights and the Environment: A Synopsis and Some Predictions", *Georgetown International Environmental Law Review*, Vol. 16, No. 3 (spring), pp. 359–403.

Hobson, Kersty. 2009. "On the Modern and the Nonmodern in Deliberative Environmental Democracy", *Global Environmental Politics*, Vol. 9, No. 4 (November), pp. 64–80.

Hochstetler, Kathryn. 1997. "The Evolution of the Brazilian Environmental Movement and its Political Roles", in Douglas Chalmers et al. (eds), *The New Politics of Inequality in Latin America: Rethinking Participation and Representation*. Oxford: Oxford University Press.

——. 2002. "After the Boomerang: Environmental Movements and Politics in the La Plata River Basin", *Global Environmental Politics*, Vol. 2, No. 4 (November), pp. 35–57.

——. 2003. "Fading Green? Environmental Politics in the Mercosur Free Trade Agreement", *Latin American Politics and Society*, Vol. 45, No. 4 (winter), pp. 1–32.

Hochstetler, Kathryn and Margaret E Keck. 2007. *Greening Brazil: Environmental Activism in State and Society*. Durham, NC: Duke University Press.

Holzinger, Katharina, Christoph Knill and Thomas Sommerer. 2011. "Is There Convergence of National Environmental Policies? An Analysis of Policy Outputs in 24 OECD Countries", *Environmental Politics*, Vol. 20, No. 1 (February), pp. 20–41.

Horton, Lynn R. 2006. "Contesting State Multiculturalisms: Indigenous Land Struggles in Eastern Panama", *Journal of Latin American Studies*, Vol. 38, No. 4 (November), pp. 829–58.

——. 2007. *Grassroots Struggles for Sustainability in Central America*, Boulder, CO: University Press of Colorado.

Houck, Oliver A. 2000. "Environmental Law in Cuba", *Journal of Land Use and Environmental Law*, Vol. 16, No. 1 (fall), pp. 1–81.

Howard, Sarah M. 1998. "Land Conflict and Mayangna Territorial Rights in Nicaragua's Bosawfis Reserve", *Bulletin of Latin American Research*, Vol. 17, No. 1 (January), pp. 17–34.

Humphreys, David. 2004. "Redefining the Issues: NGO Influence on International Forest Negotiations", *Global Environmental Politics*, Vol. 4, No. 2 (May), pp. 51–74.

——. 2006. *Logjam: Deforestation and the Crisis of Global Governance*. London: Earthscan.

Hurwitz, Zachary. 2012. "Dirty Business in Brazil: Rousseff Backslides on the Environment", *NACLA Report on the Americas*, Vol. 45. No 1 (spring), pp. 17–22.

Hyams, Keith. 2009. "A Just Response to Climate Change: Personal Carbon Allowances and the Normal-Functioning Approach", *Journal of Social Philosophy*, Vol. 40, No. 2 (summer), pp. 237–56.

IBWC (International Boundary and Water Commission). 2007. "Mexico Delivers Water to the United States to Fulfill Treaty Obligations", press release, International Boundary and Water Commission, United States section, 12 October.

ICHRP (International Council on Human Rights Policy). 2008. *Climate Change and Human Rights: A Rough Guide*. Versoix: International Council on Human Rights Policy. Available online at www.ichrp.org/files/reports/45/136_report.pdf [accessed March 2012].

IFAD (International Fund for Agricultural Development). 2003a. *Indigenous Peoples and Sustainable Development*, Roundtable Discussion Paper for the Twenty-Fifth Anniversary Session of IFAD's Governing Council. Rome: International Fund for Agricultural Development.

———. 2003b. *The Adoption of Organic Agriculture among Small Farmers in Latin America and the Caribbean: Thematic Evaluation*. Rome: International Fund for Agricultural Development.

Ignatow, Gabriel. 2005. "From Science to Multiculturalism: Postmodern Trends in Environmental Organizations", *Global Environmental Politics*, Vol. 5, No. 2 (May), pp. 88–113.

IISD (International Institute for Sustainable Development)/Stratos. 2004a. "Mexico Case Study", Analysis of National Strategies for Sustainable Development. Available online at Winnipeg: International Institute for Sustainable Development/Stratos. www.iisd.org/pdf/2004/measure_sdsip_mexico.pdf [accessed September 2012].

———. 2004b. "Brazil Case Study", Analysis of National Strategies for Sustainable Development. Available online at Winnipeg: International Institute for Sustainable Development/Stratos. www.iisd.org/pdf/2004/measure_sdsip_brazil.pdf [accessed September 2012].

Inglehart, Ronald. 1995. "Public Support for Environmental Protection: Objective Problems and Subjective Values in 43 Societies", *PS: Political Science and Politics*, Vol. 28, No. 1 (March), pp. 57–72.

Irwin, Alan. 2001. *Sociology and the Environment: A Critical Introduction to Society, Nature and Knowledge*. Cambridge: Polity Press.

IUCN (International Union for Conservation of Nature and Natural Resources)/UNEP (United Nations Environment Programme)/WWF (World Wildlife Fund). 1980. *World Conservation Strategy: Living Resource Conservation for Sustainable Development*. Gland: United Nations Environment Programme/World Wildlife Fund. Available online at http://data.iucn.org/dbtw-wpd/edocs/WCS-004.pdf [accessed September 2012].

Ivanova, Maria. 2010. "UNEP in Global Environmental Governance: Design, Leadership, Location", *Global Environmental Politics*, Vol. 10, No. 1 (February), pp. 30–59.

IWGIA (International Work Group for Indigenous Affairs) et al. 2009. Indigenous People and Climate Change. Briefing paper, UNFCCC Intersessional Meeting, Bangkok. Bangkok: International Work Group for Indigenous Affairs/Asia Indigenous Peoples Pact Foundation/Indigenous Knowledge and Peoples Network.

Jacques, Peter J, Riley E Dunlap and Mark Freeman. 2008. "The Organisation of Denial: Conservative Think Tanks and Environmental Scepticism", *Environmental Politics*, Vol. 17, No. 3 (June), pp. 349–85.

Jakobeit, Cord. 1996. "Nonstate Actors Leading the Way: Debt-for-Nature Swaps", in Robert O Keohane and Marc A Levy (eds), *Institutions for Environmental Aid: Pitfalls and Promise*. Cambridge, MA: MIT Press.

James, Clive. 2006. "Global Status of Commercialized Biotech/GM Crops", ISAAA Briefs No. 35. Ithaca, NY: International Service for the Acquisition of Agri-Biotech Applications.

Jenkins, Rhys. 2010. "China's Global Expansion and Latin America", *Journal of Latin American Studies*, Vol. 42, No. 4 (November), pp. 809–37.

Jiménez, Carolina, Pilar Huante and Emmanuel Rincón. 2006. *Restauración de minas superficiales en México*. Mexico: Secretaría de Medio Ambiente y Recursos Naturales.

Johnston, Barbara Rose (ed.). 2011a. *Life and Death Matters: Human Rights, Environment, and Social Justice*. Walnut Creek, CA: Left Coast Press.

——. 2011b. "Water and Human Rights", in Barbara Rose Johnston (ed.), *Life and Death Matters: Human Rights, Environment, and Social Justice*. Walnut Creek, CA: Left Coast Press.

Jordan, Grant and William Maloney. 1997. *The Protest Business?: Mobilising Campaign Groups*. Manchester: Manchester University Press.

Jörgens, H. 2001. "Research Note – The Diffusion of Environmental Policy Innovations, Findings from an International Workshop", *Environmental Politics*, Vol. 10, No. 2 (summer), pp. 122–27.

JSWG (Joint Summit Working Group). 2010a. "Collaborating to Implement the Inter-American and Summits Agendas: Promoting Environmental Sustainability". Washington, DC: Joint Summit Working Group, Summits of the Americas.

——. 2010b. "Collaborating to Implement Summit Mandates: Promoting Environmental Sustainability." Washington, DC: Joint Summit Working Group, Summits of the Americas.

Kahler, Miles and David Lake. 2003. *Governance in a Global Economy*. Princeton, NJ: Princeton University Press.

Kaimowitz, David. 1996. "Social Pressure for Environmental Reform in Latin America", in Helen Collinson (ed.), *Green Guerrillas: Environmental Conflicts and Initiatives in Latin America and the Caribbean. A Reader*. London: Latin America Bureau.

Karkkainen, Bradley C. 2004. "Post-Sovereign Environmental Governance", *Global Environmental Politics*, Vol. 4, No. 1 (February), pp. 72–96.

Kaufmann, Mark and Jeff Ditz. 1992. "Green Syndicalism", *Libertarian Labor Review*, Vol. 13 (summer), pp. 41–2.

Kawell, JoAnn. 2002. "Who Owns Knowledge?", *NACLA Report on the Americas*, Vol. 35, No. 5 (March/April), pp. 14–17.

Kay, Cristóbal. 2004. "Rural Livelihoods and Peasant Futures", in Robert N Gwynne and Cristóbal Kay (eds), *Latin America Transformed: Globalization and Modernity*, 2nd edn. London: Arnold.

Keck, Margaret E. 2004. "Running Water: Participatory Management in Brazil", *NACLA Report on the Americas*, Vol. 38, No. 1 (July/August), p. 29.

Keck, Margaret E and Kathryn Sikkink. 1998. *Activists Beyond Borders: Advocacy Networks in International Politics*. Ithaca, NY: Cornell University Press.

Kern, Kristine, Helge Jörgens and Martin Jänicke. 2001. *The Diffusion of Environmental Policy Innovations: A Contribution to the Globalisation of Environmental Policy*, Discussion Paper FS II 01-302, Berlin: Wissenschaftszentrum Berlin für Sozialforschung.

Killeen, Timothy J. 2007. *A Perfect Storm in the Amazon Wilderness: Development and Conservation in the Context of the Initiative for the Integration of the Regional Infrastructure of South America (IIRSA)*. Advances in Applied Biodiversity Science No. 7. Arlington, VA: Center for Applied Biodiversity Science/Conservation International. Available online at www.conservation.org/publications/Documents/AABS.7_Perfect_Storm_English.low.res.pdf [accessed February 2012].

Kincaid, John. 2001. "Economic Policy-Making: Advantages and Disadvantages of the Federal Model", *International Social Science Journal*, Vol. 53, No. 167 (March), pp. 85–92.

Kingdon, John. 1995. *Agendas, Alternatives, and Public Policies*, 2nd edn. New York: Longman.

Kitschelt, Herbert, et al. 2010. *Latin American Party Systems*. Cambridge: Cambridge University Press.

Knill, Christoph. 2001. *The Europeanisation of National Administrations*. Cambridge: Cambridge University Press.

Kronik, Jakob and Dorte Verner. 2010. *Indigenous Peoples and Climate Change in Latin America and the Caribbean*. Washington, DC: World Bank.

Kütting, Gabriela. 2004. "Book Review Essay: Environmental Justice", *Global Environmental Politics*, Vol. 4, No. 1 (February), pp. 115–21.

Lambrou, Yianna. 1997. "The Changing Role of NGOs in Rural Chile After Democracy", *Bulletin of Latin American Research*, Vol. 16, No. 1 (January), pp. 107–16.

Latinobarómetro. 2008. *Informe 2008*. Santiago: Corporación Latinobarómetro. Available online at www.latinobarometro.org/docs/INFORME_LATINOBAROMETRO_2008.pdf [accessed September 2012].

Latta, P Alex. 2007a. "Book Reviews: Dobson, Andrew, and Derek Bell, eds. 2006. *Environmental Citizenship*. Cambridge, MA: The MIT Press", *Global Environmental Politics*, Vol. 7, No. 3 (August), pp. 136–37.

——. 2007b. "Locating Democratic Politics in Ecological Citizenship", *Environmental Politics*, Vol. 16, No. 3, pp. 377–93.

Lemos, Maria Carmen and Arun Agrawal. 2006. "Environmental Governance", *Annual Review of Environment and Resources*, Vol. 31, No. 3 (November), pp. 297–325.

Lemos, Maria Carmen and Johanna W Looye. 2003. "Looking for Sustainability: Environmental Coalitions across the State–Society Divide", *Bulletin of Latin American Research*, Vol. 22, No. 3 (July), pp. 350–70.

Light, Andrew. 2001. "The Urban Blind Spot in Environmental Ethics", *Environmental Politics*, Vol. 10, No. 1, pp. 7–35.

Linkogle, Stephanie. 1998. "Soya, Culture and International Food Aid: The Case of a Nicaraguan Communal Kitchen", *Bulletin of Latin American Research*, Vol. 17, No. 1 (January), pp. 93–103.

Linz, Juan J. 1994. "Presidential or Parliamentary Democracy: Does it Make a Difference?", in Juan. J Linz and Arturo Valenzuela (eds), *The Failure of Presidential Democracy: The Case of Latin America*, Vol. 2. Baltimore, MD: Johns Hopkins University Press.

Linz, Juan J and Alfred Stepan (eds). 1996. *Problems of Democratic Transition and Consolidation: Southern Europe, South America, and Post-Communist Europe*. Baltimore, MD: Johns Hopkins University Press.

Lipsky, Michael. 1968. "Protest as a Political Resource", *American Political Science Review*, Vol. 62, No. 4 (December), pp. 1144–58.

Liverman, Diana and Silvina Vilas. 2006. "Neoliberalism and the Environment in Latin America', *Annual Review of Environment and Resources*, No. 31 (November), pp. 327–63.

Loewenstein, Karl. 1965. *Political Power and the Governmental Process*. Chicago: University of Chicago Press.

——. 1986. *Teoría de la Constitución* (translated by Alfredo Gallego Anabitarte). Barcelona: Ariel.

Lomborg, Bjørn. 2001. *The Skeptical Environmentalist: Measuring the Real State of the World*. Cambridge: University of Cambridge.

Loveman, Brian and Thomas M Davies Jr. (eds). 1997. *The Politics of Antipolitics: The Military in Latin America*. Wilmington, DE: Scholarly Resources.

Lucero, José Antonio. 2003. "Locating the 'Indian Problem': Community, Nationality, and Contradiction in Ecuadorian Indigenous Politics", *Latin American Perspectives*, Vol. 30, No. 1 (January), *Indigenous Transformational Movements in Contemporary Latin America*, pp. 23–48.

Macchi, Mirjam. 2008. *Indigenous and Traditional Peoples and Climate Change*. Issues paper. Gland: International Union for Conservation of Nature.

MacDonald, Gordon J and Daniel L Nielson. 1997. "Conclusion: Latin American Foreign Policy and International Environmental Regimes", in Gordon J MacDonald, Daniel L Nielson and Marc A Stern (eds), *Latin American Environmental Policy in International Perspective*. Boulder, CO: Westview Press.

MacDonald, Gordon J and Marc Stern. 1997. "Environmental Politics and Policy in Latin America", in Gordon J MacDonald, Daniel L Nielson and Marc A Stern (eds), *Latin American Environmental Policy in International Perspective*. Boulder, CO: Westview Press.

MacDonald, Gordon J, Daniel L Nielson and Marc A Stern (eds). 1997. *Latin American Environmental Policy in International Perspective*. Boulder, CO: Westview Press.

MacDonald, Laura. 1997. *Supporting Civil Society: The Political Role of Non-Governmental Organisations in Central America*. Basingstoke: Macmillan.

MacNeish, Richard S. 1992. *The Origins of Agriculture and Settled Life*. London: University of Oklahoma Press.

Mainwaring, Scott. 1993. "Presidentialism, Multipartism, and Democracy: The Difficult Combination", *Comparative Political Studies*, Vol. 26, No. 2 (July), pp. 198–228.

Mainwaring, Scott and Timothy Scully (eds). 1995. *Building Democratic Institutions: Party Systems in Latin America*. Stanford, CA: Stanford University Press.

Mander, Jerry and Victoria Tauli-Corpuz (eds). 2006. *Paradigm Wars: Indigenous Peoples' Resistance to Globalization*. San Francisco, CA: Sierra Club Books.

MARN (Ministerio de Ambiente y Recursos Naturales). 2001. *Primera Comunicación Nacional Sobre Cambio Climático*. Guatemala City: Ministerio de Ambiente y Recursos Naturales. Available at: http://unfccc.int/resource/docs/natc/guanc1.pdf [accessed August 2011].

Marsiaj, Juan. 2012. "Federalism, Advocacy Networks, and Sexual Diversity Politics in Brazil", in Jordi Díez and Susan Francheschet (eds), *Comparative Public Policy in Latin America*. London: University of Toronto Press.

Martin, Edward J. 2003. "Liberation Theology, Sustainable Development, and Postmodern Public Administration", *Latin American Perspectives*, Vol. 30, No. 4, *Struggle and Neoliberal Threats* (July), pp. 69–91.

Martinez-Alier, Joan. 2002. *The Environmentalism of the Poor: A Study of Ecological Conflicts and Valuation*. Cheltenham: Edward Elgar.

Mason, Michael. 1999. *Environmental Democracy: A Contextual Approach.* London: Earthscan.

Mattiace, Shannan L. 2003. *To See With Two Eyes: Peasant Activism and Indian Autonomy in Chiapas, Mexico.* Albuquerque: University of New Mexico Press.

McAdam, Doug, Sidney Tarrow and Charles Tilly. 2001. *Dynamics of Contention.* New York: Cambridge University Press.

McAllister, Lesley K. 2008. *Making Law Matter: Environmental Protection and Legal Institutions in Brazil.* Stanford, CA: Stanford University Press.

McAteer, Emily and Simone Pulver. 2009. "The Corporate Boomerang: Shareholder Transnational Advocacy Networks Targeting Oil Companies in the Ecuadorian Amazon", *Global Environmental Politics,* Vol. 9, No. 1 (February), pp. 1–30.

McCaffrey, Katherine T. 2009. "Fish, Wildlife, and Bombs: The Struggle to Clean Up Vieques", *NACLA Report on the Americas,* Vol. 42, No. 5 (September/October), pp. 35–41.

McCarthy, John D and Mayer N Zald. 1977. "Resource Mobilization and Social Movements", *American Journal of Sociology,* Vol. 82, No. 6 (May), pp. 1212–41. Available online at http://uni-leipzig.de/~sozio/ mitarbeiter/m29/content/dokumente/595/mccarthyzald77.pdf [accessed September 2012].

McCormick, John. 2004. "The Role of Environmental NGOs in International Regimes", in Regina S Axelrod, et al. (eds), *The Global Environment: Institutions, Law and Policy.* Washington, DC: CQ Press.

McCormick, Sabrina. 2007. "The Governance of Hydro-electric Dams in Brazil", *Journal of Latin American Studies,* Vol. 39, No. 2 (May), pp. 227–61.

McShane, Katie. 2007. "Anthropocentrism vs. Nonanthropocentrism: Why Should We Care?", *Environmental Values,* Vol. 16, No. 2, pp. 169–85.

McSweeney, Kendra and Shahna Arps. 2005. "A 'Demographic Turnaround': The Rapid Growth of Indigenous Populations in Lowland Latin America", *Latin American Research Review,* Vol. 40, No. 1, pp. 3–29.

Meadows, Donella H, et al. (eds). 1972. *The Limits to Growth: A Report for Club of Rome's Project.* New York: Universe Books.

Mendis, Chinthaka. 2007. *Sovereignty vs. Trans-Boundary Environmental Harm: The Evolving International Law Obligations and the Sethusamuduram Ship Channel Project.* New York: United Nations/Nippon Foundation of Japan Fellowship Programme "Human Resources Development and Advancement of the Legal Order of the World's Oceans".

Messenger, Stephen. 2011. "Brazil Approves Clearing Forest for Belo Monte Dam", www.treehugger.com, 27 January 2011. Available online at www.treehugger.com/corporate-responsibility/

brazil-approves-clearing-forest-for-belo-monte-dam.html [accessed January 2012].

Meyer, David. 2004. "Protest and Political Opportunities", *Annual Review of Sociology*, Vol. 30, pp. 125–45.

Meyer, John, et al. 1997. "World Society and the Nation State", *American Journal of Sociology*, Vol. 103, No. 1 (July), pp. 144–81.

Meyer, Lukas H and Dominic Roser. 2006. "Distributive Justice and Climate Change: The Allocation of Emission Rights", *Analyse & Kritik*, Vol. 28, No. 2, pp. 223–49.

Meyn, Marianne. 1996. "Puerto Rico's Energy Fix", in Helen Collinson (ed.), *Green Guerrillas: Environmental Conflicts and Initiatives in Latin America and the Caribbean. A Reader*. London: Latin America Bureau.

MIF (Multilateral Investment Fund)/Bloomberg. 2012. *Climatescope 2012*. Preview. Assessing the Climate for Climate Investing in Latin America and the Caribbean. Montevideo: MIF/Bloomberg New Energy Finance.

Migdal, Joel S. 1988. *Strong Societies and Weak States: State–Society Relations and State Capabilities in the Third World*. Chichester: Princeton University Press.

Milanez, Bruno and Ton Bührs. 2008. "Ecological Modernisation beyond Western Europe: The Case of Brazil", *Environmental Politics*, Vol. 17, No. 5 (November), pp. 784–803.

Miller, Shawn William. 2007. *An Environmental History of Latin America*. Cambridge: Cambridge University Press.

Moellendorf, Darrel. 2009. "Justice and the Assignment of the Intergenerational Costs of Climate Change", *Journal of Social Philosophy*, Vol. 40, No. 2 (summer), pp. 204–24.

Mol, Arthur P. 2000. "The Environmental Movement in an Era of Ecological Modernisation", *Geoforum*, Vol. 31, No. 1 (February), pp. 45–56.

Mollett, Sharlene. 2006. "Race and Natural Resource Conflicts in Honduras: The Miskito and Garifuna Struggle for Lasa Pulan", *Latin American Research Review*, Vol. 41, No. 1, pp. 76–101.

Montgomery, Shannon. 2009. "Mexico shuts down Canadian mine", *thestar.com*, 9 December 2009. Available online at www.thestar.com/news/world/article/736372--mexico-shuts-down-canadian-mine [accessed September 2012].

Moreno-Sánchez, Rocío del Pilar and Jorge Higinio Maldonado. 2008. *Can Co-Management Improve Governance of a Common-Pool Resource? Lessons from a Framed Field Experiment in a Marine Protected Area in the Colombian Caribbean*, LACEEP Working Paper No. 5, April 2008. Cartago: Latin American and Caribbean Environmental Economics

Program. Available online at www.laceep.org/index.php?option=com_content&task=view&id=28&Itemid=48 [accessed September 2012].

Morgenstern, Scott. 2002. "Explaining Legislative Politics in Latin America', in Scott Morgenstern and Benito Nacif (eds), *Legislative Politics in Latin America*. Cambridge: Cambridge University Press.

Morris, Brian. 1996. *Ecology and Anarchism*. Malvern: Images Publishing.

MOVEV (Movimiento Ecológico de Venezuela). 2011. "Valores del Movimiento Ecológico de Venezuela", Movimiento Ecológico de Venezuela. Available online at http://eccologia.blogspot.co.uk/2011/11/el-movimiento-ecologico-de-venezuela.html [accessed February 2014].

Mueller, Bernardo. 2009. "The Fiscal Imperative and the Role of Public Prosecutors in Brazilian Environmental Policy", *Law & Policy*, Vol. 32, No. 1 (January), pp. 104–26.

Müller-Rommel, Ferdinand. 2002. "The Lifespan and the Political Performance of Green Parties in Western Europe", *Environmental Politics*, Vol. 11, No. 1 (spring), pp. 1–16.

Mumme, Stephen P and Edward Korzetz. 1997. "Democratization, Politics, and Environmental Reform in Latin America", in Gordon J MacDonald et al. (eds), *Latin American Environmental Policy in International Perspective*. Boulder, CO: Westview Press.

Muñoz, Heraldo. 1997. "Free Trade and Environmental Policies: Chile, Mexico, and Venezuela", in Gordon J MacDonald, Daniel L Nielson and Marc A Stern (eds), *Latin American Environmental Policy in International Perspective*. Boulder, CO: Westview Press.

Murillo, Mario A. 2010. "Colombia's Minga Under Pressure", *NACLA Report on the Americas*, Vol. 43, No. 5 (September/October), pp. 13–19.

Murphy, Edward. 2004. "Developing Sustainable Peripheries: The Limits of Citizenship in Guatemala City", *Latin American Perspectives*, Vol. 31, No. 6, *The Struggle Continues: Consciousness, Social Movement, and Class Action* (November), pp. 48–68.

NACLA (North American Congress on Latin America). 2002. "For an Agriculture that Doesn't Get Rid of Farmers", *NACLA Report on the Americas*, Vol. 35, No. 5 (March/April), pp. 29–34.

——. 2009. "Introduction Political Environments: Development, Dissent, and the New Extraction", *NACLA Report on the Americas*, Vol. 42, No. 5 (September/October), p. 11.

——. 2010. "Introduction after Recognition: Indigenous Peoples Confront Capitalism", in *NACLA Report on the Americas*, Vol. 43, No. 5 (September/October), pp. 11–13.

Newell, Peter. 2009. "Bio-Hegemony: The Political Economy of Agricultural Biotechnology in Argentina", *Journal of Latin American Studies*, Vol. 41, No. 1 (February), pp. 27–57.

Nielson, Daniel L and Marc A Stern. 1997. "Endowing the Environment: Multilateral Development Banks and Environmental Lending in Latin America", in Gordon J MacDonald, Daniel L. Nielson and Marc A Stern (eds), *Latin American Environmental Policy in International Perspective*. Boulder, CO: Westview Press.

Noboa, Eduardo. 2011. *Iniciativa para la Transformación y Fortalecimiento del Mercado de Energía Solar Térmica para el Calentamiento de Agua en AL&C*. Quito: Organización Latinoamericana de Energía. Available online at www.solarthermalworld.org/files/Eduardo%20Noboa.pdf?download [accessed May 2012].

Norton, Bryan G. 2005. *Sustainability: A Philosophy of Adaptive Ecosystem Management*. London: University of Chicago Press.

Norton, Paul. 2003. "A Critique of Generative Class Theories of Environmentalism and of the Labour–Environmentalist Relationship", *Environmental Politics*, Vol. 12, No. 4 (winter), pp. 96–119.

O'Brien, Karen L. 1998. *Sacrificing the Forest: Environmental and Social Struggles in Chiapas*. Boulder, CO: Westview Press.

O'Donnell, Guillermo. 1996. "Illusions about Consolidation", *Journal of Democracy*, Vol. 7, No. 2, pp. 34–51.

O'Donnell, Guillermo, Joseph S Tulchin and Augusto Varas (eds) with Adam Stubits. 2008. *New Voices in the Study of Democracy in Latin America*. Washington, DC: Woodrow Wilson International Center for Scholars.

O'Neill, Marie S, et al. 2008. "Air Pollution and Mortality in Latin America: The Role of Education", *Epidemiology*, Vol. 19, No. 6 (November), pp. 810–19.

Oates, Wallace and Robert Schwab. 1988. "Economic Competition among Jurisdictions: Efficiency Enhancing or Distortion Inducing?", *Journal of Public Economics*, Vol. 35, No. 3 (April), pp. 333–54.

OECD (Organization for Economic Co-operation and Development). 2012. "Development: Aid to Developing Countries Falls because of Global Recession", OECD news release, 4 April. Paris: Organization for Economic Co-operation and Development. Available online at www.oecd.org/document/3/0,3746,en_21571361_44315115_50058883_1_1_1_1,00.html [accessed May 2012].

Offen, Karl H. 2004. "The Geographical Imagination, Resource Economies and Nicaraguan Incoproration of the Mosquitia, 1838–1909", in Christian Brannstrom (ed.), *Territories, Commodities and Knowledges: Latin American Environmental Histories in the Nineteenth and Twentieth Centuries*. London: Institute for the Study of the Americas.

OHCHR (Office of the United Nations High Commissioner for Human Rights). 2009. *Annual Report of the United Nations High Commissioner* for Human Rights and Reports of the Office of the High Commissioner and the Secretary-General. *Report of the Office of the United Nations High Commissioner for Human Rights on the Relationship between Climate Change and Human Rights* (A/HRC/10/61). Geneva: Office of the High Commissioner for Human Rights.

Olivares Gallardo, Alberto. 2010. "El Nuevo Marco Institucional Ambiental En Chile", *Revista Catalana De Dret Ambiental*, Vol. 1, No. 1, pp. 1–23.

Orlove, Ben. 2002. *Lines in the Water: Nature and Culture at Lake Titicaca*. Berkeley: University of California Press.

Osa, Maryjane and Cristina Corduneanu-Huci. 2003. "Running Uphill: Political Opportunity in Non-Democracies", *Comparative Sociology*, Vol. 2, No. 4, pp. 605–29.

Pacheco, Margarita. 1996 "Colombia's Independent Recyclers' Union: A Model for Urban Waste Management", in Helen Collinson (ed.), *Green Guerrillas: Environmental Conflicts and Initiatives in Latin America and the Caribbean. A Reader*. London: Latin America Bureau.

Page, Edward A. 2008. "Distributing the Burdens of Climate Change", *Environmental Politics*, Vol. 17, No. 4 (August), pp. 556–75.

Painter, Michael and William Durham (eds). 1995. *The Social Causes of Environmental Destruction in Latin America*. Ann Arbor: University of Michigan Press.

Partido del Sol Costa Rica. 2011. "Nuestros Valores". Available online at www.partidodelsol.com/index.php?option=com_contact&view=conta ct&id=1&Itemid=68 [accessed December 2011].

Partido Ecologista del Perú. 2011. "Propuesta", Partido Ecologista del Perú. Available online at www.partidoecologista.com/propuesta.html [accessed December 2011].

Partido Ecologista Verde Chile. 2011. "Principios", Partido Ecologista Verde. Available online at www.ecologistaverde.cl/ [accessed December 2011].

Partido Verde Argentina. 2011. "Propuesta Verde", platform, Partido Verde. Available online at www.partidoverde.org.ar/ [accessed December 2011].

Partido Verde Brazil. 2011. "Programa", Partido Verde, Convenção Nacional, Brasília/DF, 2005. Available online at http://pv.org.br/ [accessed December 2011].

Partido Verde Colombia. 2011a. "Principios", Partido Verde de Colombia. Available online at www.partidoverde.org.co/ [accesed December 2011].

——. 2011b. "Prioridades Programáticas", Partido Verde de Colombia. Available online at www.partidoverde.org.co/ [accesed December 2011].

——. 2011c. "Estatutos", Partido Verde de Colombia. Available online at www.partidoverde.org.co/ [accesed December 2011].

Partido Verde de Bolivia. 2011. "Capítulo Primero: Sobre nuestra Identidad", Partido Verde de Bolivia. Available online at www.partido-verdebolivia.org/ [accessed December 2011].

Partido Verde Ecologista Costa Rica. 2011. "Principles", Partido Verde Ecologista de Costa Rica. Available online at www.partidoverdeecol-ogista.webs.com/ [accessed December 2011].

Partners for Democratic Change. 2009. "Trends and Best Practices in Environmental Dispute Resolution in Latin America", conference, 3 June, Woodrow Wilson Center, Washington, DC. Summary online at www.partnersglobal.org/news/trends-and-best-practicies-in-environ-mental-dispute-resolution-in-latin-america [accessed October 2011].

Peet, Richard and Michael Watts (eds). 1996. *Liberation Ecologies: Environment, Development, Social Movements*. London: Routledge.

Pepper, David. 1993. *Eco-Socialism: From Deep Ecology to Social Justice*. London: Routledge.

——. 1996. *Modern Environmentalism: An Introduction*. London: Routledge.

Perreault, Thomas. 2003. "Making Space: Community Organization, Agrarian Change, and the Politics of Scale in the Ecuadorian Amazon", *Latin American Perspectives*, Vol. 30, No. 1 (January), *Indigenous Transformational Movements in Contemporary Latin America*, pp. 96–121.

——. 2008. "Popular Protest and Unpopular Policies: State Restructuring, Resource Conflict, and Social Justice in Bolivia", in David V Carruthers (ed.), *Environmental Justice in Latin America: Problems, Promise, and Practice*. London: MIT Press.

Petras, James and Henry Veltmeyer. 2005. *Social Movements and State Power: Argentina, Brazil, Bolivia, Ecuador*. London: Pluto Press.

Phillips, James. 2011. "Resource Access, Environmental Struggles, and Human Rights in Honduras", in Barbara Rose Johnston (ed.), *Life and Death Matters: Human Rights, Environment, and Social Justice*. Walnut Creek, CA: Left Coast Press.

Phillips, Tom and Mattia Cabitza. 2011. "Bolivian road protest threatens to flatten Evo Morales's popularity", guardian.co.uk, 10 October 2011. Available online at www.theguardian.com/world/2011/oct/10/bolivian-road-protest-evo-morales [accessed December 2011].

Pichón, Francisco, Jorje Uquillas and John Frechione (eds). 1999. *Traditional and Modern Natural Resource Management in Latin America*. Pittsburgh: University of Pittsburgh Press.

Pierson, Paul and Theda Skocpol. 2002. "Historical Institutionalism in Contemporary Political Science", in Ira Katznelson and Helen Milner (eds), *Political Science: State of the Discipline*. New York: W.W. Norton.

Pi-Sunyer, Oriol and R Brooke Thomas. 2011. "Mass Tourism on the Mexican Caribbean: Pervasive Changes, Profound Consequences", in

Barbara Rose Johnston (ed.), *Life and Death Matters: Human Rights, Environment, and Social Justice*. Walnut Creek, CA: Left Coast Press.

Poguntke, Thomas. 2002. *Green Parties in National Governments: From Protest to Acquiescence?* Keele European Parties Research Unit Working paper 9. Keele: University of Keele School of Politics, International Relations and the Environment (SPIRE).

Portillo, Mabel. 1998. "Ecologists in Uruguay: People Who Act", *Synthesis/Regeneration*, 15 (winter). Available online at www.greens. org/s-r/15/15-05.html [accessed May 2012].

Price, Marie. 1994. "Ecopolitics and Environmental Nongovernmental Organizations in Latin America", *Geographical Review*, Vol. 84, No. 1 (January), pp. 42–58.

Przeworski, Adam. 1991. *Democracy and the Market: Political and Economic Reforms in Eastern Europe and Latin America*. Cambridge: Cambridge University Press.

Puertorriqueños por Puerto Rico. 2011. Programme, Puertorriqueños por Puerto Rico. Available online at www.porpuertorico.com/ [accessed December 2011].

Pulver, Simone. 2004. "Power in the Public Sphere: The Battles between Oil Companies and Environmental Groups in the UN Climate Change Negotiations, 1991–2003". Ph.D. dissertation. University of California, Berkeley.

——. 2007. "Climate Politics in Mexico in a North American Perspective", Encyclopedia of Earth. Washington, DC: Environmental Information Coalition, National Council for Science and the Environment. Available online at www.eoearth.org/article/Climate_politics_in_Mexico_in_a_North_American_perspective [accessed May 2012].

Purchase, Graham. 1994. *Anarchism and Environmental Survival*, Tucson, AZ: See Sharp Press.

——. 1997. *Anarchism and Ecology*, Montreal: Black Rose Books.

PVEM (Partido Verde Ecologista de México). 2011. "Transparencia, X. Informes de ingresos, gastos, situación patrimonial, inmuebles y donantes, Informes anuales de actividades ordinarias, I. Ingresos and II Egresos", PVEM website, Mexico City, 2011. Available online at www.partidoverde.org.mx/transparencia/X/INFORMEANUAL_PVEM_2009_1.pdf [accessed October 2011].

Rabelo, Carla. 1998. "The Brazilian Green Party: An Historical Summary", *Synthesis/Regeneration*, 15 (winter). Available online at www.greens. org/s-r/15/15-03.html [accessed October 2011].

Radcliffe, Sarah A. 2004. "Civil Society, Grassroots Politics and Livelihoods", in Robert N Gwynne and Cristóbal Kay (eds), *Latin America Transformed: Globalization and Modernity*. London: Hodder.

Randall, Vicky and Lars Svåsand. 2002. "Party Institutionalisation in New Democracies", *Party Politics*, Vol. 8, No. 1 (January), pp. 5–29.

Rankin, Aidan. 1996. "'The Land of our Ancestor's Bones': Wichi People's Struggle in the Argentine Chaco", in Helen Collinson (ed.), *Green Guerrillas: Environmental Conflicts and Initiatives in Latin America and the Caribbean. A Reader*. London: Latin America Bureau.

Reid Andrews, George. 2004. *Afro-Latin America, 1800–2000*. Oxford: Oxford University Press.

Reuters. 2010. "Marina Silva diz querer ser primeira mulher negra a ser presidente", Abril.com/Reuters, 10/06/2010.

Richards, JP and J Heard. 2005. "European Environmental NGOs: Issues, Resources and Strategies in Marine Campaigns", *Environmental Politics*, Vol. 14, No. 1 (February), pp. 23–41.

Riker, W. 1964. *Federalism: Origin, Operation, Significance*. Boston, MA: Little, Brown.

Rivarola Puntigliano, Andrés. 2008: "Suspicious Minds: Recent Books on US–Latin American Relations", *Latin American Politics and Society*, Vol. 50, No. 4 (winter), pp. 157–72.

Roberts, J Timmons and Nikki Demetria Thanos. 2003. *Trouble in Paradise: Globalization and Environmental Crises in Latin America*. London: Routledge.

Robinson, William I. 2007. "Beyond the Theory of Imperialism: Global Capitalism and the Transnational State", *Societies without Borders*, Vol. 2, pp. 5–26.

Rochon, Thomas. 1998. *Culture Moves: Ideas, Activism, and Changing Values*. Princeton, NJ: Princeton University Press.

Rodrigues, Maria Guadalupe. 2000. "Environmental Protection Issue Networks in Amazonia", *Latin American Research Review*, Vol. 35, No. 3, pp. 125–53.

Rohrschneider, Robert and Russell J Dalton. 2002. "A Global Network? Transnational Co-operation among Environmental Groups", *Journal of Politics*, Vol. 64, No. 2 (May), pp. 510–33.

Roper, J Montgomery. 2003. "Bolivian Legal Reforms and Local Indigenous Organizations: Opportunities and Obstacles in a Lowland Municipality", *Latin American Perspectives*, Vol. 30, No. 1 (January), *Indigenous Transformational Movements in Contemporary Latin America*, pp. 139–61.

Roper, J Montgomery, Thomas Perreault and Patrick C Wilson. 2003. "Introduction", *Latin American Perspectives*, Vol. 30, No. 1 (January), pp. 5–22.

Rosenbaum, Walter A. 2003. *Environmental Politics and Policy*, 5th edn. Washington, DC: CQ Press.

Rosset, Peter. 1996. "The Greening of Cuba", in Helen Collinson (ed.), *Green Guerrillas: Environmental Conflicts and Initiatives in Latin America and the Caribbean. A Reader*. London: Latin America Bureau.

——. 2009. "Food Sovereignty in Latin America: Confronting the 'New' Crisis", *NACLA Report on the Americas*, Vol. 42, No. 3 (May/June), pp. 16–21.

Rubin, Jeffrey W. 2004. "Meanings and Mobilizations: A Cultural Politics Approach to Social Movements and States", *Latin American Research Review*, Vol. 39, No. 3, pp. 106–42.

Ryan, John C. 1991. "The Shrinking Forest", *The Conquest of Nature 1492–1992*, special edn., *NACLA Report on the Americas*, Vol. 25, No. 2 (September), pp. 18–19.

Sabatier, Paul A and Hank C Jenkins-Smith (eds). 1993. *Policy Change and Learning: An Advocacy Coalition Approach*. Boulder, CO: Westview Press.

Saith, A. 1985. "'Primitive Accumulation', Agrarian Reform and the Socialist Transition: An Argument", *Journal of Development Studies*, Vol. 22, No. 1, pp. 1–48.

Sáiz, Angel Valencia. 2005. "Globalisation, Cosmopolitanism and Ecological Citizenship", *Environmental Politics*, Vol. 14, No. 2 (April), pp. 163–78.

Sale, Kirkpatrick. 1980. *Human Scale*, New York: Coward, McCann & Geohegan.

——. 2000. *Dwellers in the Land: The Bioregional Vision*. Athens: University of Georgia Press.

Sánchez-Triana, Ernesto, Kulsum Ahmed and Yewande Awe (eds). 2007. *Environmental Priorities and Poverty Reduction: A Country Environmental Analysis for Colombia*. Washington, DC: World Bank.

Sand, Peter H. 2004. "Sovereignty Bounded: Public Trusteeship for Common Pool Resources?", *Global Environmental Politics*, Vol. 4, No. 1 (February), pp. 47–71.

Sandwith, Trevor, Clare Shine, Lawrence Hamilton and David Sheppard. 2001. *Transboundary Protected Areas for Peace and Co-operation*. World Commission on Protected Areas (WCPA) Best Practice Protected Area Guidelines Series No. 7. Cambridge: World Conservation Union/ Department of City and Regional Planning, Cardiff University.

Sartori, Giovanni. 1976. *Parties and Party Systems: A Framework for Analysis*. New York: Cambridge University Press.

Scartascini, Carlos, Pablo Spiller, Ernesto Stein and Mariano Tommasi (eds). 2011. *El juego político en América Latina: ¿Cómo se deciden las políticas públicas?* Colombia: Inter-American Development Bank.

Schlosberg, David. 2004. "Reconceiving Environmental Justice: Global

Movements and Political Theories", *Environmental Politics*, Vol. 13, No. 3 (autumn), pp. 517–40.

Schneider, Stephen H, Armin Rosencranz and John O Niles (eds). 2002. *Climate Change Policy: A Survey*. Washington, DC: Island Press, 2002.

Schuppert, Fabian. 2011. "Climate Change Mitigation and Intergenerational Justice", *Environmental Politics*, Vol. 20, No. 3 (May), pp. 303–21.

Segall-Corrêa AM, et al. 2007. "Evaluation of Household Food Insecurity in Brazil: Validity Assessment in Diverse Sociocultural Settings", *Concurso redSAN 2007*, Memoria, artículos ganadores. Santiago: Iniciativa América Latina y el Caribe Sin Hambre/Food and Agriculture Organization. Available online at www.fao.org/alc/legacy/iniciativa/pdf/memredsan.pdf [accessed September 2012].

Seghezzo, Lucas. 2009. "The Five Dimensions of Sustainability", *Environmental Politics*, Vol. 18, No. 4 (July), pp. 539–56.

Selwyn, Ben. 2011. "Review of Deere, Carmen D and Royce, Frederick S (eds). 2009. *Rural Social Movements in Latin America: Organizing for Sustainable Livelihoods*, University of Florida Press (Gainsville, FL)", *Bulletin of Latin American Research*, Vol. 30, No. 2 (April), pp. 233–35.

Shantz, Jeffrey A. 2002. "Green Syndicalism: An Alternative Red–green Vision", *Environmental Politics*, Vol. 11, No. 4 (winter), pp. 21–41.

Shantz, Jeffrey A and Barry D Adam. 1999. "Ecology and Class: The Green Syndicalism of IWW/Earth First Local 1", *International Journal of Sociology and Social Policy*, Vol. 19, No. 7/8, pp. 43–72.

Sieder, Rachel (ed.). 2002. *Multiculturalism in Latin America: Indigenous Rights, Diversity and Democracy*. Basingstoke: Palgrave Macmillan.

Sikkink, Kathryn. 1993. "Human Rights, Principled Issue-Networks, and Sovereignty in Latin America", *International Organization*, Vol. 47, No. 3 (summer), pp. 411–41.

Silva, Eduardo. 1996. "Democracy, Market Economics, and Environmental Policy in Chile", *Journal of Interamerican Studies and World Affairs*, Vol. 38, No. 4 (winter), pp. 1–33.

——. 1997. "Conservation, Sustainable Development, and the Politics of Native Forest Policy in Chile", in Gordon J MacDonald et al. (eds), *Latin American Environmental Policy in International Perspective*. Boulder, CO: Westview Press.

——. 1999. "Forests, Livelihood, and Grassroots Polities: Chile and Costa Rica Compared", *Eurapean Review of Latin American and Caribbean Studies*, No. 66 (June), pp. 39–73.

Silva, Eduardo et al. 2002. "Making the Law of the Jungle: The Reform of Forest Legislation in Bolivia, Cameroon, Costa Rica, and Indonesia", *Global Environmental Politics*, Vol. 2, No. 3 (August), pp. 63–97.

Simms, Andrew with Hannah Reid. 2006. *Up in Smoke? Latin America and the Caribbean: The Threat from Climate Change to the Environment and Human Development. The Third Report from the Working Group on Climate Change and Development*. London: New Economics Foundation/ International Institute for Environment and Development /Progressio. Available online at www.foe.co.uk/resource/reports/upinsmoke-latamerica.pdf [accessed September 2012].

Simon, Joel. 1997. *Endangered Mexico – An Environment on the Edge*. London: Latin America Bureau.

Simonian, Lane. 1995. *Defending the Land of the Jaguar: A History of Conservation in Mexico*. Austin: University of Texas Press.

Slater, David (ed.). 1985a. *New Social Movements and the State in Latin America*. Amsterdam: CEDLA.

——. 1985b. "Social Movements and a Recasting of the Political", in David Slater (ed.), *New Social Movements and the State in Latin America*. Amsterdam: CEDLA.

Smith, Graham. 2001. "Taking Deliberation Seriously: Institutional Design and Green Politics", *Environmental Politics*, Vol. 10, No. 3 (autumn), pp. 72–93.

Smith, Mick. 2007. "Wild-life: Anarchy, Ecology, and Ethics", *Environmental Politics*, Vol. 16, No. 3 (June), pp. 470–87.

——. 2009. "Against Ecological Sovereignty: Agamben, Politics and Globalisation", *Environmental Politics*, Vol. 18, No. 1 (February), pp. 99–116.

Spoerer, Matilde. 2013. "The Environmental Decision under Dispute: Citizen Participation, Collective Action and Political Influence in the Barrancones' Case". Paper presented at the International Conference on Public Policy Grenoble, France, June 26, 27 and 28, 2013. Available online at www.icpublicpolicy.org/Policymaking-in-Latin-America [accessed July 2013].

Sponsel, Leslie (ed.). 1995. *Indigenous Peoples and the Future of Amazonia: An Ecological Anthropology of an Endangered World*. Tucson: University of Arizona Press.

——. 2011. "The Master Thief: Gold Mining and Mercury Contamination in the Amazon", in Barbara Rose Johnston (ed.), *Life and Death Matters: Human Rights, Environment, and Social Justice*. Walnut Creek, CA: Left Coast Press.

Srinivas, RK. 2001. "Profile – Demystifying Dams and Development: The World Commission on Dams and Development", *Environmental Politics*, Vol. 10, No. 3 (autumn), pp. 134–38.

Stahler-Sholk, Richard, Harry E Vanden and Glen David Kuecker. 2007. "Introduction; Globalizing Resistance: The New Politics of Social Movements in Latin America", *Latin American Perspectives*, Vol. 34,

No. 2, *Globalizing Resistance: The New Politics of Social Movements in Latin America* (March), pp. 5–16.

Stanley, Denise. 1996. "David vs. Goliath: Fishermen Conflicts with Mariculturalists in Honduras", in Helen Collinson (ed.), *Green Guerrillas: Environmental Conflicts and Initiatives in Latin America and the Caribbean. A Reader.* London: Latin America Bureau.

Starr, Amory. 2000. *Naming the Enemy: Anti-Corporate Movements Confront Globalization.* London: Zed Books.

Stea, David, et al. 2011. "Mexico's Second Institutionalized Revolution: Origins and Impacts of the Chiapas Declarations", in Barbara Rose Johnston (ed.), *Life and Death Matters: Human Rights, Environment, and Social Justice.* Walnut Creek, CA: Left Coast Press.

Stein, Ernesto, Mariano Tommasi, Koldo Echebarría, Eduardo Lora and Mark Payne (eds). 2005. *The Politics of Policies. Economic and Social Progress in Latin America, 2006 Report.* New York: Inter-American Development Bank/David Rockefeller Center for Latin American Studies. Available online at www.iadb.org/en/research-and-data/publication-details,3169. html?pub_id=b-2006 [accessed September 2012].

Steinberg, Paul F. 2003. "Understanding Policy Change in Developing Countries: The Spheres of Influence Framework", *Global Environmental Politics*, Vol. 3, No. 1 (February), pp. 11–32.

Stephenson, Marcia. 2002. "Forging an Indigenous Counterpublic Sphere: The Taller de Historia Oral Andina in Bolivia", *Latin American Research Review*, Vol. 37, No. 2, pp. 99–118.

Stern, Nicholas. 2007. *The Economics of Climate Change: The Stern Review.* Cambridge: Cambridge University Press.

Stoddart, Hannah (ed.). 2011. *A Pocket Guide to Sustainable Development Governance*, 1st edn. London: Stakeholder Forum/Commonwealth Secretariat.

Stoett, Peter J. 2007. "Counter-Bioinvasion: Conceptual and Governance Challenges", *Environmental Politics*, Vol. 16, No. 3 (June), pp. 433–52.

Sundberg, Juanita. 2008. "Tracing Race: Mapping Environmental Formations in Environmetal Justice Research in Latin America", in David V Carruthers (ed.), *Environmental Justice in Latin America: Problems, Promise, and Practice.* London: MIT Press.

Taagepera, Rein and Matthew Soberg Shugart. 1989. *Seats and Votes: The Effects and Determinants of Electoral Systems.* London: Yale University Press.

Tanuro, Daniel. 2010. *L'impossible capitalisme vert.* Paris: Éditions La Découverte.

Tarrow, Sidney. 1994. *Power in Movement: Social Movements, Collective Action, and Politics.* Cambridge: Cambridge University Press.

Tate, C Neal, and Torbjörn Vallinder (eds). 1995. *The Global Expansion of Judicial Power*. New York: NY University Press.

Tecklin, David, Carl Bauer and Manuel Prieto. 2011. "Making Environmental Law for the Market: The Emergence, Character, and Implications of Chile's Environmental Regime", *Environmental Politics*, Vol. 20, No. 6 (November), pp. 879–98.

Teichman, Judith. 2010. "La paradoja de la reforma de mercado exitosa en América Latina: Fortalecer el rol del Estado", *Revista Cultura Económica*, 28 (77–78) (September), pp. 30–45.

——. 2012. "The New Institutionalism and Industrial Policy-making in Chile", in Jordi Díez and Susan Francheschet (eds), *Comparative Public Policy in Latin America*. London: University of Toronto Press.

Ter Haar, Gerrie (ed.). 2011. *Religion and Development: Ways of Transforming the World*. New York: Columbia University Press.

Thomas, Craig W. 2001. "Habitat Conservation Planning: Certainly Empowered Somewhat Deliberative, Questionably Democratic", *Politics and Society*, Vol. 29, No. 1 (March), pp. 105–30.

Tilley, Virginia Q. 2002. "New Help or New Hegemony? The Transnational Indigenous Peoples' Movement and 'Being Indian' in El Salvador", *Journal of Latin American Studies*, Vol. 34, No. 3 (August), pp. 525–54.

Toke, David. 2011. "Ecological Modernisation, Social Movements and Renewable Energy", *Environmental Politics*, Vol. 20, No. 1 (February), pp. 60–77.

Torres Peñaloza, Diego. 1998. "Green Power: An Ecological Alternative in Bolivia", *Synthesis/Regeneration*, 15 (winter). Available online at www.greens.org/s-r/15/15-02.html [accessed October 2011].

Torres, Blanca. 1997. "Transnational Environmental NGOs: Linkages and Impact on Policy", in Gordon J MacDonald, Daniel L Nielson and Marc A Stern (eds), *Latin American Environmental Policy in International Perspective*. Boulder, CO: Westview Press.

Tosun, Jale. 2009. *Environmental Policy in Chile and Mexico: Explaining the Effect of Economic Integration on Regulatory Standards*. Saarbrücken: VDM Verlag Dr. Mueller.

Trittin, Jürgen. 2004. "The Role of the Nation State in International Environmental Policy", *Global Environmental Politics*, Vol. 4, No. 1 (February), pp. 23–28.

Tulchin, Joseph S and Ralph H Espach. 2001. "Latin America in the New International System: A Call for Strategic Thinking", in Joseph S Tulchin and Ralph H Espach (eds), *Latin America in the New International System*. Boulder, CO: Lynne Rienner/Woodrow Wilson International Center for Scholars.

UN (United Nations). 2003. *Monterrey Consensus of the International Conference on Financing for Development*. International Conference on Financing for Development Monterrey, Mexico, 18–22 March 2002. New York: United Nations.

——. 2010. *Millennium Development Goals, Advances in Environmentally Sustainable Development in Latin America and the Caribbean*. United Nations Publication LC/G 2428-P, Santiago de Chile.

UN/ECLAC (Economic Commission for Latin America and the Caribbean). 2010. *Sustainable Development in Latin America and the Caribbean: Trends, Progress, and Challenges in Sustainable Consumption and Production, Mining, Transport, Chemicals and Waste Management*. Report to the 18th Session of the Commission on Sustainable Development of the United Nations. Santiago: UN/Economic Commission for Latin America and the Caribbean.

UNCSD (United Nations Conference on Sustainable Development). 2011a. "Regional, National and Local Level Governance for Sustainable Development", RIO 2012 Issues Briefs No. 10, December 2011. New York: United Nations Conference on Sustainable Development Secretariat. Available online at www.scienzainrete.it/documenti/rs/issues-brief-10 [accessed February 2014].

——. 2011b. *Sustainable Development in Latin America and the Caribbean 20 Years on from the Earth Summit: Progress, Gaps and Strategic Guidelines*. Preliminary version (LC/L 3346). Rio de Janeiro: United Nations Conference on Sustainable Development.

UNDESA (United Nations Department of Economic and Social Affairs)/ UNCSD (United Nations Conference on Sustainable Development). 2011. *Regional, National and Local Level Governance for Sustainable Development*, No. 10, December 2100. New York: United Nations Department of Economic and Social Affairs/United Nations Conference on Sustainable Development Secretariat. Available online at http://sustainabledevelopment.un.org/content/documents/336brief10.pdf [accessed February 2014].

UNDP (United Nations Development Programme). 1998. *Human Development Report 1998*. New York: United Nations Development Programme.

UNEP (United Nations Environment Programme). 2010. *Latin America and the Caribbean: Environment Outlook GEO LAC 3*. Panama City: United Nations Environment Programme. Available online at www. unep.org/publications/contents/pub_details_search.asp?ID=4149 [accessed July 2011].

——. 2012a. *GEO5 Global Environment Outlook: Environment for the Future We Want*. Nairobi: UN Environment Programme (UNEP). Available online at www.unep.org/geo/pdfs/geo5/GEO5_report_full_en.pdf [accessed August 2012].

———. 2012b. *Report of the Council of Government Experts on Sustainable Consumption and Production*, 18th Meeting of the Forum of Ministers of Environment of Latin America and the Caribbean, Quito, Ecuador, 31 January to 3 February 2012. Quito: UNEP Regional Office for Latin America and the Caribbean.

UNEP/CEGESTI (Centro de Gestión Tecnológica). 2009. "Consumo y producción sustentable (CPS). Estado de avances en América Latina y el Caribe". Nairobi: UN Environment Programme /Fundación Centro de Gestión Tecnológica.

UNEP/IISD (International Institute for Sustainable Development). 2005. *Environment and Trade: A Handbook*, 2nd edn. Geneva/Winnipeg: United Nations Environment Programme/International Institute for Sustainable Development.

UNEP/OSA (Oregon State University)/UNA (Universidad Nacional de Costa Rica). 2007. *Hydropolitical Vulnerability and Resilience along International Waters: Latin America and the Caribbean*. Nairobi: United Nations Environment Programme/Oregon State University/ Universidad Nacional de Costa Rica.

UNHRC (United Nations Human Rights Council). 2008. *Promotion and Protection of all Human Rights, Civil, Political, Economic, Social and Cultural Rights, Including the Right to Development*. New York: United Nations Human Rights Council (A/HRC/7/L 21/Rev. 1, 26 March 2008).

University of Manchester. 2009. "Trade Sustainability Impact Assessment (SIA) of the Association Agreement under Negotiation between the European Community and Mercosur, Final Report", revised March 2009. Manchester: University of Manchester, Impact Assessment Research Centre/Institute for Development Policy and Management.

Vaccaro, Ismael, Laura C Zanotti and Jennifer Sepez. 2009. "Commons and Market: Opportunities for Development of Local Sustainability", *Environmental Politics*, Vol. 18, No. 4 (July), pp. 522–38.

Van Cott, Donna Lee. 2005. *From Movements to Parties in Latin America: The Evolution of Ethnic Politics*. Cambridge: Cambridge University Press.

Van den Hombergh, Heleen. 2004. *No Stone Unturned: Building Blocks of Environmentalist Power versus Transnational Industrial Forestry in Costa Rica*. Amsterdam: Dutch University Press.

Van der Heijden, Hein-Anton. 2008. "Green Governmentality, Ecological Modernisation or Civic Environmentalism? Dealing with Global Environmental Problems", *Environmental Politics*, Vol. 17, No. 5 (November), pp. 835–39.

Van Driesche, Jason and Roy Van Driesche. 2000. *Nature Out of Place: Biological Invasions in the Global Age*. Washington, DC: Island Press.

Van Klaveren, Alberto. 2001. "Political Globalisation and Latin America", in Joseph Tulchin and Ralph Espach (eds.), *Latin America in the New International System*. Boulder, CO: Lynne Rienner/Woodrow Wilson International Center for Scholars.

Vargas Hernández, José G and Mohammad Reza Noruzi. 2010. "Historical Social and Indigenous Ecology Approach to Social Movements in Mexico and Latin America", *Asian Culture and History*, Vol. 2, No. 2 (July), pp. 176–88.

Velasco, Francisco Javier. 2007. Participación en el Foro "Ecosocialismo del Siglo XXI". Cited in María Pilar García-Guadilla, 2009, "Ecosocialismo del siglo XXI y modelo de desarrollo bolivariano: los mitos de la sustentabilidad ambiental y de la democracia participativa en Venezuela", *Revista Venezolana de Economía y Ciencias Sociales*, Vol. 15, No. 1 (January–April), pp. 187–223.

Verde Ecologista Nicaragua. 2007. "Hacia el 2017 (Visión, Valores, Misión y Agenda)". Available online at http://fpva.org.mx/event_nicaragua. htm [accessed December 2011].

Vidal, John. 2011. "Bolivia enshrines natural world's rights with equal status for Mother Earth", www.guardian.co.uk, 10 April 2011. Available online at www.guardian.co.uk/environment/2011/apr/10/ bolivia-enshrines-natural-worlds-rights [accessed April 2012].

Viola, Eduardo J. 1997. "The Environmental Movement in Brazil: Institutionalization, Sustainable Development, and Crisis of Governance since 1987", in Gordon J MacDonald et al. (eds), *Latin American Environmental Policy in International Perspective*. Boulder, CO: Westview Press.

Vogel, David. 1995. *Trading Up: Consumer and Environmental Regulation in a Global Economy*. Cambridge, MA: Harvard University Press.

Von Weizsäcker, Ernst U, Amory B Lovins and L Hunter Lovins. 1998. *Factor Four: Doubling Wealth, Halving Resource Use: The New Report to the Club of Rome* London: Earthscan.

Wallace, David R. 1992. *The Quetzal and the Macaw: The Story of Costa Rica's National Parks*. San Francisco: Sierra Club Books.

Wapner, Paul. 2002. "Horizontal Politics: Transnational Environmental Activism and Global Cultural Change", *Global Environmental Politics*, Vol. 2, No. 2 (May), pp. 37–62.

Warren, Kay B and Jean E Jackson (eds). 2002. *Indigenous Movements: Self-Representation, and the State in Latin America*. Austin: University of Texas Press.

Weber, Max. 1947/1997. *The Theory of Social and Economic Organization* (translated by AM Henderson and Talcott Parsons). New York: The Free Press.

Weidner, Helmut and Martin Jänicke (eds). 2010. *Capacity Building in National Environmental Policy: A Comparative Study of 17 Countries*. New York: Springer.

Weinberg, Bill. 2003. "Mexico: Lacandon Selva Conflict Grows", *NACLA Report on the Americas*, Vol. 36, No. 6 (May/June), pp. 26.

——. 2010a. "Beyond Extraction: An Interview With Rafael Quispe", *NACLA Report on the Americas*, Vol. 43, No. 5 (September/October), p. 21.

——. 2010b. "Bolivia's New Water Wars: Climate Change and Indigenous Struggle", *NACLA Report on the Americas*, Vol. 43, No. 5 (September/October), pp. 19–24.

Welsh, Ian. 2007. "In Defence of Civilisation: Terrorism and Environmental Politics in the 21st Century", *Environmental Politics*, Vol. 16, No. 2 (April), pp. 356–75.

Westra, Laura and Bill Lawson (eds). 2001. *Faces of Environmental Racism: Confronting Issues of Global Justice*, 2nd edn. Lanham, MA: Rowman & Littlefield.

WGI (Worldwide Governance Indicators). 2009. Worldwide Governance Indicators, database. Washington, DC: World Bank Institute/World Bank Development Research Group/Brookings Institution.

White, Damian Finbar. 2002. "A Green Industrial Revolution? Sustainable Technological Innovation in a Global Age", *Environmental Politics*, Vol. 11, No. 2 (summer), pp. 1–26.

Wickstrom, Stefanie. 2008. "Cultural Politics and the Essence of Life: Who Controls the Water?", in David V Carruthers (ed.), *Environmental Justice in Latin America: Problems, Promise, and Practice*. London: MIT Press.

Wilkins, Mira. 1998. "An Alternative Approach", in Steven C Topik and Allen Wells (eds), *The Second Conquest of Latin America: Coffee, Henequen, and Oil during the Export Boom, 1850–1930*. Austin: University of Texas Press.

Wilson, Fiona. 2003. "Reconfiguring the Indian Land-Labour Relations in the Postcolonial Andes", *Journal of Latin American Studies*, Vol. 35, No. 2 (May), pp. 221–47.

Wilson, Patrick C. 2003. "Ethnographic Museums and Cultural Commodification: Indigenous Organizations, NGOs, and Culture as a Resource in Amazonian Ecuador", *Latin American Perspectives*, Vol. 30, No. 1 (January), *Indigenous Transformational Movements in Contemporary Latin America*, pp. 162–80.

Winston, Morton. 2002. "NGO Strategies for Promoting Corporate Social Responsibility", *Ethics and International Affairs*, Vol. 16, No. 1 (March), pp. 71–87.

Wöhrnschimmel, Henry, et al. 2008. "The Impact of a Bus Rapid Transit System on Commuters' Exposure to Benzene, CO, PM2.5 and PM10 in Mexico City", *Atmospheric Environment*, Vol. 42, No. 35 (November), pp. 8194–203.

Wolf, Aaron T, Shira B Yoffe and Mark Giordano. 2003. "International Waters: Identifying Basins at Risk", *Water Policy*, Vol. 5, No. 1 (February), pp. 29–60.

Wolf, J, K Brown and D Conway. 2009. "Ecological Citizenship and Climate Change: Perceptions and Practice", *Environmental Politics* Vol. 18 No. 4, pp. 503–21.

Wolff, Jonas. 2007. "(De-)Mobilising the Marginalised: A Comparison of the Argentine Piqueteros and Ecuador's Indigenous Movement", *Journal of Latin American Studies*, Vol. 39, No. 1 (February), pp. 1–29.

Wolford, Wendy. 2008. "Environmental Justice and Agricultural Development in the Brazilian *Cerrado*", in David V Carruthers (ed.), *Environmental Justice in Latin America: Problems, Promise, and Practice*. London: MIT Press.

World Bank. 2001. *Making Sustainable Commitments*. Washington, DC: World Bank.

——. 2003. *World Development Report 2003*. Washington, DC: International Bank for Reconstruction and Development/The World Bank. Available online at www.dynamicsustainabledevelopment.org/showsection.php.

——. 2005. *Indigenous Peoples, Poverty and Human Development in Latin America: 1994–2004*. Washington, DC: World Bank.

——. 2010. *Environmental Dispute Resolution Mechanisms: Concept Note*. World Bank Environment Strategy, Consultations. Washington, DC: World Bank.

——. 2012. *Perfiles indígenas de América Latina. World Bank, Latin America and the Caribbean*. Washington, DC: World Bank. Available online at http://go.worldbank.org/1SW8PE1QZ0 [accessed March 2014].

WSSD (World Summit on Sustainable Development). 2002. *Indigenous Peoples' Plan of Implementation on Sustainable Development*. World Summit on Sustainable Development (WSSD), Johannesburg, South Africa, 2002.

WTO (World Trade Organization). 2004. *Trade and the Environment at the WTO*, background document. Geneva: World Trade Organization.

WTO/UNEP (United Nations Environment Programme). 2009. *Trade and Climate Change: A Report by the United Nations Environment Programme and the World Trade Organization*. Geneva: World Trade Organization/ United Nations Environment Programme.

Yashar, Deborah. 2005. *Contesting Citizenship in Latin America: The Rise of Indigenous Movements and the Postliberal Challenge*. Cambridge: Cambridge University Press.

Yepes, Rodrigo Uprimny. 2007. "Judicialization of Politics in Colombia: Cases, Merits and Risks", *Sur – Revista Internacional de Direitos Humanos* (São Paulo), Vol. 3, Selected edn. Available online at http://socialsciences.scielo.org/scielo.php?script=sci_arttext&pid=S1806-64452007000100003&lng=en&nrm=iso [accessed July 2013].

Young, Zoe. 1999. "NGOs and the Global Environmental Facility: Friendly Foes?", *Environmental Politics*, Vol. 8, No. 1 (January), pp. 246–67.

Zebich-Knos, Michele. 2008. "Ecotourism, Park Systems, and Environmental Justice in Latin America", in David V Carruthers (ed.), *Environmental Justice in Latin America: Problems, Promise, and Practice*. London: MIT Press.

Zimmerer, Karl S. 1997. *Changing Fortune: Biodiversity and Campesino Livelihood in the Peruvian Andes*. London: University of California Press.

Zwart, Ivan. 2003. "A Greener Alternative? Deliberative Democracy Meets Local Government", *Environmental Politics*, Vol. 12, No. 2 (summer), pp. 23–48.

Index